The Economics and Uncertainties of Nuclear Power

Is nuclear power a thing of the past or a technology for the future? Has it become too expensive and dangerous, or is it still competitive and sufficiently safe? Should emerging countries invest in it? Can we trust calculations of the probability of a major nuclear accident? In the face of divergent claims and contradictory facts, this book provides an in-depth and balanced economic analysis of the main controversies surrounding nuclear power. Without taking sides, it helps readers gain a better understanding of the uncertainties surrounding the costs, hazards, regulation and politics of nuclear power. Written several years on from the Fukushima Daiichi nuclear disaster of 2011, this is an important resource for students, researchers, energy professionals and concerned citizens wanting to engage with the continuing debate on the future of nuclear power and its place in international energy policy.

FRANÇOIS LÉVÊQUE is Professor of Economics at Mines ParisTech and a part-time professor at the Robert Schuman Centre for Advanced Studies (European University Institute). He has advised many international bodies on energy policy and the economics of regulation, including the International Energy Agency, the OECD and the European Commission.

The Economics and Uncertainties of Nuclear Power

FRANÇOIS LÉVÊQUE

CAMBRIDGE
UNIVERSITY PRESS

University Printing House, Cambridge CB2 8BS, United Kingdom

One Liberty Plaza, 20th Floor, New York, NY 10006, USA

477 Williamstown Road, Port Melbourne, VIC 3207, Australia

314-321, 3rd Floor, Plot 3, Splendor Forum, Jasola District Centre, New Delhi - 110025, India

103 Penang Road, #05-06/07, Visioncrest Commercial, Singapore 238467

Cambridge University Press is part of the University of Cambridge.

It furthers the University's mission by disseminating knowledge in the pursuit of education, learning and research at the highest international levels of excellence.

www.cambridge.org
Information on this title: www.cambridge.org/9781107455498

First published 2015
First paperback edition 2021

A catalogue record for this publication is available from the British Library

ISBN 978-1-107-08728-6 Hardback
ISBN 978-1-107-45549-8 Paperback

Contents

Abbreviations

ANRE	Agency for Natural Resources and Energy (Japan)
ASN	Autorité de Sûreté Nucléaire
CEA	Commissariat à l'Energie Atomique
EDF	Electricité de France
Ensreg	European Nuclear Safety Regulation Group
EPR	European Pressurized Reactor
GDP	Gross Domestic Product
IAEA	International Atomic Energy Agency
INES	International Nuclear Event Scale
INPO	Institute of Nuclear Power Operations
IRRS	International Regulatory Review Service
IRSN	Institut de Radioprotection et de Sûreté Nucléaire
JNES	Japan Nuclear Energy Safety Organization
MIT	Massachusetts Institute of Technology
NPT	Treaty on the Non-Proliferation of Nuclear Weapons
NRC	Nuclear Regulatory Commission
NSC	Nuclear Safety Commission (Japan)
NSG	Nuclear Suppliers Group
OECD	Organisation for Economic Cooperation and Development
UAE	United Arab Emirates

Introduction

Is nuclear power a thing of the past or a technology for the future? Has it become too expensive and dangerous, or is it still competitive and sufficiently safe? Should emerging countries develop nuclear power or look elsewhere? Can we trust calculations of the risk of a major nuclear accident, given that their results diverge? Is international cooperation on safety and non-proliferation bound to fail or is it in fact gathering strength? The views on all these subjects are contradictory. Often the only common ground between them is their uncompromising, categorical nature. A quick look at the facts certainly fails to yield any obvious answers. The construction projects for new nuclear plants in Europe are behind schedule and well over their original budgets; meanwhile similar projects in China are on target, both for their deadline and budget. Japan, a country renowned for its excellent technology, failed to prevent a major accident at Fukushima Daiichi. The United States, surfing on a shale gas boom, is turning its back on nuclear power. In Europe, the United Kingdom is planning to build several new reactors, whereas Germany is stepping up plans to retire existing plants. Depending on which source you accept, the disaster at Chernobyl caused several hundred fatalities, or several tens of thousands. The number of major accidents observed since the start of nuclear power is greater than the figure forecast by the experts' probabilistic studies. Similarly the perception of nuclear risk is very different from the value calculated by cool-headed scientists. After lengthy debate, the European Union has adopted a common framework for nuclear safety, but the safety authorities are still national agencies and civil liability regimes form a contrasting patchwork. Lastly, with regard to the non-proliferation of nuclear weapons, Iran has signed the international treaty designed to limit the use of civilian nuclear facilities for military ends, but at the same time it has launched a uranium-enrichment programme which bears no relation to its energy requirements.

Faced with so many divergent claims and apparently contradictory facts, we obviously need to take a closer look at what is going on. It is time for in-depth analysis of costs, hazards, risks, safety measures, decisions by specific countries to invest in nuclear power or pull out, and the rules for international governance of the atom. In short, it is time to study and understand the global economics of nuclear power. Such is the purpose of this book.

It is rooted in two convictions.

Firstly, that analysis which does not take sides, for or against nuclear power, can interest readers.

I hope to show that it is possible not to adopt a normative stance on this issue without handing out platitudes. The economic approach adopted here is deliberately positive, the aim being to understand particular situations, explain phenomena and foresee certain developments. In a word, to focus on consequences: the political consequences for a country which decides to invest in nuclear power or retire its existing plants; the effect of a carbon tax on the competitive position of nuclear power; the impact of observed accidents and public opinion's biased perception of risk; the effect of liberalizing electricity markets on nuclear investments; the consequences of industrial nationalism on reactor exports. My aim is to use economics to analyse effects, not to dictate the decisions that public and private-sector policy-makers should make, less still teaching people the *right* way to think and behave.

Secondly, I believe much the best way to throw light on the individual and collective decisions before us is to gain an understanding of the many uncertainties weighing on the cost, risks, regulation and politics of nuclear power. A possible sub-heading for this book might be 'In the Light of Uncertainty'. It is vital to set aside a whole series of categorical claims such as the notion that there is a single *true* cost of nuclear power, be it high or low; that a major nuclear accident will certainly occur somewhere in the world over the next twenty years, or alternatively that a disaster is impossible in Europe; that safety regulation in the US is above reproach, or on the contrary in the hands of the nuclear lobby; that a national nuclear industry is a sure-fire asset for France's future balance of payments, or a complete waste of resources. Such assertions only serve to rubber-stamp decisions that have already been taken. Any attempt to settle the many questions raised by nuclear power must allow for such uncertainties, and to do so they need to be circumscribed. The present work shows how the theory of decision under uncertainty can throw light on nuclear debate, how probabilistic assessment can prompt a reappraisal of beliefs, and how the median voter theorem and the theory of political marketing can explain some public decisions.

The book is in four parts, addressing costs, risks, regulation and politics. Each one provides a wealth of detail on its subject, providing the facts of the matter and their theoretical basis, backed by references to academic literature. I am convinced that a degree of immersion gives the reader proportionately many more insights than a brief summary of ideas and arguments.

Estimating the costs of nuclear power: points of reference, sources of uncertainty

Predictably the first part of a book by an economist is given over entirely to the competitiveness of nuclear power. Does it cost less or more than electricity generated using coal, gas or wind? Does it make financial sense for electricity utilities to invest in nuclear technology? The cost of nuclear power has escalated since the first plants were built. How could it break out of this vicious circle and prevent a further drop in its relative competitive advantage? Financial and economic factors now furnish anti-nuclear campaigners with compelling arguments.

The risk of a major nuclear accident: calculation and perception of probabilities

Measures to enhance safety are among the factors which are making nuclear power increasingly expensive. The second part focuses on the risks of an accident and efforts to limit them. On the one hand, although it is still difficult to assess nuclear risk precisely, it can be analysed dispassionately using a whole series of instruments and methods. As an overall trend, nuclear risk is declining. On the other hand, risk as perceived by the general public, in the wake of major disasters such as Chernobyl or Fukushima Daiichi, is on the rise. So is the public attitude to such hazards irrational? Should government decisions be based on risk as assessed by experts or the general public? Is it possible to narrow the gap between calculated and perceived risk? This part explores in detail the biased perception of probabilities brought to light by experimental psychology, a discipline which now significantly influences economic analysis. It shows how modern probabilistic analysis enables us to reconcile our prior perception of a hazard with input from material knowledge.

Safety regulation: an analysis of the American, French and Japanese cases

The more effective nuclear-safety regulation is, the fewer accidents there will be. How can this technology be expected to inspire confidence among the general public if reactor-safety standards are badly designed by the authorities or improperly applied by operators? But how is effective regulation to be achieved? This is not a simple matter, safety regulation being dogged by imperfections and uncertainty. The third part of the book analyses several examples closely. The Fukushima Daiichi accident has shown that regulation as practised in Japan is an example to be avoided. Regulation operates along very different lines in France and the US, yet both are exemplary on account of the transparency, independence and competence of their respective nuclear safety authorities. If the same criteria were enforced worldwide the risk of an accident would be much lower.

National policies and international governance

The fourth and last part deals with politics, to which decision-making under uncertainty devolves. This process plays a considerable part in nuclear power: witness the diversity of choices made by individual nations. Some countries have embraced the atom for military and economic reasons, whereas others – the majority – have only developed civil nuclear applications. Some countries are now phasing out their nuclear power plants, others are keen to adopt the technology. Why? Over and above national policies, mechanisms of international governance are trying to contain the risk of proliferation, and improve the safety of reactors and their operation, for the good reason that both safety and security have a planetary dimension. But these efforts to institute supranational governance must come to terms with the sovereignty of states. The economic and commercial interests of countries which export nuclear technology are also at stake here. Clearly, political and strategic considerations still weigh heavily on the world market for reactors.

This book aims to adopt a non-partisan stance, neither pro- nor anti-nuclear. But it does not claim to be objective. As in any essay, the choice of issues, facts and perspective reflects the author's personality and situation. I teach at Mines ParisTech, Paris, one of France's top engineering schools. Many of those who have gone on to build and operate France's nuclear industry were educated here.

Many of my former students still work in the industry. Furthermore, the research carried out by my laboratory is funded by EDF, which also numbers among the clients of my consultancy company, alongside other electricity-generating companies elsewhere in the world. This record may prompt some readers to query the independence of the views expressed in the book, perhaps even suspecting the author of having 'sold out' to the international nuclear lobby. Others, familiar with the intellectual freedom which prevails in the academic world and the open minds of energy engineers, will soon set aside such suspicions. Others still will conclude that the author's links with the 'nucleocrats' are after all a guarantee of the validity of the information contained in these pages.

PART I

Estimating the costs of nuclear power

Points of reference, sources of uncertainty

The debate on this topic is fairly confusing. Some present electricity production using nuclear power as an affordable solution, others maintain it is too expensive. These widely divergent views prompt fears among consumers and voters that they are being manipulated: each side is just defending its own interests and the true cost of nuclear power is being concealed.

Companies and non-governmental organizations certainly adopt whatever position suits them best. But at the same time, the notion of just one 'true' cost is misleading. As we shall see in this section there is no such thing as *the* cost of nuclear power: we must reason in terms of costs and draw a distinction between a private cost and a social cost. The private cost is what an operator examines before deciding whether it is opportune to build a new nuclear power plant. This cost varies between different investors, particularly as a function of their attitude to risks. On the other hand the social cost weighs on society, which may take into account the risk of proliferation, or the benefits of avoiding carbon dioxide emissions, among others. The cost of actually building new plant differs from one country to the next. So deciding whether nuclear power is profitable or not, a benefit for society or not, does not involve determining the real cost, but rather compiling data, developing methods and formulating hypotheses. It is not as easy as inundating the general public with contradictory figures, but it is a more effective way of casting light on economic decisions made by industry and government.

Without evaluating the costs it is impossible to establish the cost price, required to compare electricity production using nuclear power and rival technologies. Would it be preferable to build a gas-powered plant, a nuclear reactor or a wind farm? Which technology yields the lowest cost per kWh? Under what conditions – financial terms, regulatory framework, carbon pricing – will private investors see an adequate return on nuclear power? In terms of the general interest, how does taking account of the cost of decommissioning and storing waste affect the competitiveness of nuclear power?

This part answers these questions in three chapters. We shall start in Chapter 1 by taking a close look at the various items of cost associated with nuclear power.[1] We shall look at how sensitive they are to various factors (among others the discount rate and price of fuel) in order to understand the substantial variations they display. Chapter 2 reviews changes in the cost dynamic. From a historical perspective nuclear technology has been characterized by rising costs and it seems most likely that this trend will continue, being largely related to concerns about safety. Finally in Chapter 3 we shall analyse the poor cost-competitiveness of nuclear power, which provides critics of this technology with a compelling argument.

ONE

Adding up costs

Is the cost per MWh generated by existing French nuclear power plants €32 or €49? Does building a next-generation EPR reactor represent an investment of about €2,000 per kW, or twice that amount?

The controversy about the cost price borne by EDF resurfaced when a new law on electricity was passed in 2010,[1] requiring France's largest operator to sell part of the output from its nuclear power plants to downstream competitors. Under this law the sale price is set by the authorities and must reflect the production costs of existing facilities. GDF Suez, EDF's main competitor, put these costs at about €32 per MWh, whereas the operator reckoned its costs were almost €20 higher. How can such a large difference be justified? Is it just a matter of a buyer and a seller tossing numbers in the air, their sole concern being to influence the government in order to obtain the most favourable terms? Or is one of the figures right, the other wrong?

The figures for investments in new nuclear power plants are just as contradictory. Take for example the European Pressurized Reactor, the third-generation reactor built by the French company Areva. It was sold in Finland on the basis of a construction cost of €3 billion, equivalent to about €2,000 per kW of installed capacity. Ultimately the real cost is likely to be twice that amount. At Taishan, in China, where two EPRs are being built, the bill should amount to about €4 billion, or roughly €2,400 per kW of installed capacity. How can the cost of building the same plant vary so much, simply due to a change in its geographical location or timeframe?

The notion of cost

The disparity between these figures upsets the idea, firmly rooted in our minds, that cost corresponds to a single, somehow objective value. Surely if one asks an economist to value a good, he or she will pinpoint its cost like any good land surveyor? Unfortunately it does not work like that. Unlike physical magnitudes, cost is not an objective given. It is not a distance which can be assessed with a certain margin of error due to the poor accuracy of measuring instruments, however sophisticated they may be; nor is it comparable to the invariant and intrinsic mass of a body. Cost is more like weight. Any object, subject to the force of gravity, will weigh less at a certain elevation than at sea level, and more at either Pole than at the Equator. In the same way cost depends on where you stand. It will differ depending on whether you adopt the position of a private investor or a public authority, on whether the operator is subject to local competition or enjoys a monopoly, and so on. Change the frame of reference and the cost will vary.

In economics opportunity plays the same role as gravity in physics. Faced with two mutually exclusive options, an economic agent loses the opportunity to carry out one if he or she chooses the other. If I go to the movies this evening I shall miss a concert or dinner with friends. The cost of forgoing one of the options is known as the opportunity cost. As economic agents must generally cope with non-binary options, the opportunity cost refers more precisely to the value of second-best option forgone. As preferences are variable (Peter would rather see a movie than spend the evening with friends; for John it is the opposite), the opportunity cost depends on which economic agent is being considered. As a result it is eminently variable. Ultimately there may be as many costs as there are consumers or producers. Regarding our present concern, the cost of building nuclear power plants in Russia, which exports gas, will be different from the cost borne by another state. Investing in nuclear plants to generate electricity, rather than combined-cycle gas turbines, enables locally produced gas to be directed to a more profitable outlet. The economic concept of opportunity cost puts an end, once and for all, to any idea that cost might be an objective, invariant magnitude.

Moreover, it should be borne in mind that cost relates, not to a good or service, but to a decision or action. The opportunity cost is not the cost of something, rather the cost of *doing* something. This of course applies to the cost of production, which is defined by economists using an equation, the production function. This function expresses the relation, for a particular technology, between the quantity produced – a kWh for instance – and the minimum production factors required to obtain such output: labour, capital, natural resources. The production function enables us to determine the cost of an additional unit of the good, or the marginal cost, the opportunity of this additional production being measured against the decision not to produce. The production function also allows us to determine the fixed cost of production, this time compared with the alternative option of producing nothing at all. The fixed cost is not zero, because before producing the first unit, it was necessary to invest in buildings and machines. So, even if the infrastructure is not used, it must be paid for.

To assess officially the cost of a good or service, it is advisable to ask an accountant, using the appropriate methods. An accountant will calculate direct costs, in other words the costs directly related to the product (e.g. steel purchases in car manufacturing), and indirect costs (R&D expenditure, overheads, etc.) depending on the prevailing rules on cost allocation. Accountants will distinguish between operating and maintenance costs, and between capital expenditure drawing on shareholders' equity or on borrowing in order to make investments. For 2010 France's Court of Auditors estimated that the accounting cost, not including decommissioning, of electricity production by EDF's nuclear fleet amounted to €32.30 per MWh.[2] This figure corresponds to annual operating and maintenance expenditure of nearly €12 billion, to produce 408 TWh, and €1.3 billion annual capital costs, restricted to provision for depreciation. Obviously the production cost found by an accountant depends on the method used. Using the full cost accounting method for production the Court of Auditors found a total cost of €39.80 per MWh. This figure is higher than the previous one, because the first method, cited above, only includes depreciation in the capital costs, but does not allow for the fact that the fleet would cost more, in constant euros, to build now than it did in the past. With the full-cost accounting method for production, assets not yet depreciated are remunerated and the initial investment is paid back in constant currency.

To conclude, neither an approach based on accountancy nor on economics yields a single cost. For one kWh of nuclear electricity, much as for any other good or action, the idea of a true or intrinsic cost for which accountants or economists can suggest an approximate solution is misleading. On the other hand, as we shall see, their methods do help to understand variations in costs, identify the factors which determine costs, compare such costs for different technologies, and also observe the efficiency of operators. All these data are valuable, indeed necessary, to deciding whether or not to invest in one or other electricity-generating technology.

Social, external and private costs

So cost is not invariant. Moreover, sometimes it is quite simply impossible to put a figure on it. This additional complication concerns the external effects of using nuclear power generation, be they negative – such as the unavoidable production of radioactive waste and damage in the event of accident – or positive: avoiding CO_2 emissions and reducing energy dependency. Such external effects (or 'externalities' in the jargon of economics) explain the disparity between the private cost, borne by producers or consumers, and the social cost, borne by society as a whole.

Economic theory requires us to fill the gap. Because of this disparity, the decisions taken by households and businesses are no longer optimal in terms of the general interest; their decisions no longer maximize wealth for the whole of society. For example, if it costs €10 less per MWh to generate electricity using coal rather than gas, but the cost of the damage caused by emissions from coal is €11 higher, it would be better to replace coal with gas. Otherwise society loses €1 for every MWh generated. But in the absence of a tax or some other instrument charging for carbon emissions, private investors will opt to build coal-fired power plants. Hence the economic concept of internalizing external effects.

How, then, are externalities to be valued in order to determine the social cost of nuclear power? How much does it cost to decommission reactors and store long-term waste? What price should be set for releasing one tonne of carbon into the atmosphere? How can the cost of a major nuclear accident be estimated? What method should be used to calculate the external effects of nuclear power generation on security with respect to energy independence or the risk of proliferation?

We shall see that the answers to these questions raise not so much theoretical or conceptual issues as practical difficulties posed by the lack of data and information. As a result, the positive and negative external effects of nuclear power are only partly internalized. But then the same is true of other sources of energy.

External effects relating to independence and security

We shall start with the trickiest question: putting a figure on the effects of national independence. This is such a complicated task that no one has ever attempted it. Analysis so far has only been qualitative. We often hear that nuclear electricity production contributes to the energy independence of the country developing it. It purportedly yields greater energy security. Many political initiatives are justified by such allegations (see Chapter 10), but the terms of the debate are muddled. Conventionally energy dependence refers to the supply of oil products. The latter weigh down the balance of trade of importing countries and subject them to price shocks and the risk of shortages in the event of international conflict. Nuclear electricity production only replaces oil and its derivatives in a marginal way. Only 5 per cent of the electricity generated worldwide is produced using oil derivatives.

In fact it would make more sense to look at gas, to justify the claim that nuclear power contributes to energy independence and security. In this respect Europe, for example, is dependent on a small number of exporting countries. The European Union imports two-thirds of the gas it requires and the Russian Federation is its main supplier. One may remember the disruption of Russian gas transit through Ukraine in the winter of 2008–9. As a knock-on effect, gas deliveries to Europe were held up for almost three weeks. Millions of Poles, Hungarians and Bulgarians were deprived of heating and hundreds of factories ground to a halt. There is no doubt that Poland's determination sooner or later to start nuclear electricity production is partly due to the need to reduce its dependence on Russia. On the other hand we have heard no mention of calculations putting a figure on the expected benefit: a calculation resulting in acceptance, for instance, of nuclear power costing €5 or €10 per MWh more than that of electricity generated using imported gas. The concepts of energy independence and security are too fuzzy to measure. The best one can do is estimate the cost of the shortfall for the Polish economy per day of disrupted supply. But to calculate the gain in independence, this cost would have to be multiplied by the probability of such disruption. However, in forty-one years Russia has only failed to honour its commitments twice, with one interruption lasting two days, and the other twenty. It would be difficult, on the basis of such a small number of events, to extrapolate a probability for the future.

To take full account of security issues, allowance must be made for the risk of military or terrorist attacks, and the risk of proliferation (see Chapter 13). In this case the externality is negative and could counterbalance nuclear power's advantage in terms of energy independence. A nuclear power plant is vulnerable to hostile action. For example, during the Iran–Iraq war in 1980–88 the nuclear plant being built at Bushehr in Iran was bombed several times by Iraqi forces. All other things being equal, the higher the number of nuclear plants in a country, the larger the number of targets available to enemy action.

The development of civilian applications for the atom may entail the additional risk of facilitating proliferation of nuclear weapons. Nuclear weapons can be manufactured using plutonium or highly enriched uranium. The latter may be obtained by using and stepping up enrichment capacity that already exists for producing fuel for nuclear reactors. Such fuel must contain about 5 per cent of uranium-235, whereas the concentration of this fissile isotope must exceed 80 per cent in order to produce a bomb. Plutonium is obtained from reprocessing spent fuel.

No country has so far used fissile material from commercial reactors to produce weapons (see Chapter 13). Reactors used – purportedly at least – for civilian research have however been used to produce plutonium which can be used in weapons. India and North Korea are two instances of this diversion. Iran's nuclear programme also substantiates the claim that civilian nuclear materials may be diverted toward military purposes.

One way of reducing the risk of proliferation would be to guarantee countries launching programmes to develop nuclear power a supply of fuel for their reactors. In this way they would no longer need their own enrichment capacity. This measure would restrict the spread of enrichment technology, which can be diverted from its original civilian purpose. The United Arab Emirates has, for example, made a commitment not to produce its own fuel. The UAE will have to import it. Similarly the Russians will guarantee a supply of fuel for the nuclear plants they are due to build in Turkey. However, agreements of this sort are contrary to the goal of reducing energy dependence often associated with the decision to resort to nuclear power, there being only a limited number of potential fuel suppliers. It seems likely that in the long run more countries will want to have their own enrichment units, at least once they have a sufficient number of reactors.

There are no firm figures for the external effects of nuclear power on national and international security, any more than there are for energy independence. Any attempt to calculate such figures is hampered by the scope of these concepts, both too broad and too fuzzy. It would probably be wiser to leave it up to the diplomats and military strategists to persuade their governments – using qualitative arguments – to revise, upwards or downwards, the cost of resorting to nuclear power in their country.

The price of carbon

How are we to assess nuclear power's contribution to combating global warming? Stated in these terms the question is too general to allow an economist to provide an accurate answer. There are too many uncertainties regarding the goal being sought and the consequences if no action is taken. How is global warming to be defined? How large a share should be attributed to human activity? Which greenhouse gases should be taken into account? We are back to the previous problem. On the other hand, values may be suggested for the benefit of nuclear power in relation to reducing CO_2 emissions to the atmosphere. To calculate this benefit we need to know the price per (metric) tonne of carbon emissions, which can then be combined with the emissions avoided for each MWh generated.

At first sight this seems straightforward. At a theoretical level, all the textbooks on environmental economics explain how to determine the optimal price of a pollutant. In practical terms trade in CO_2 emissions credits provides an indication of the price of carbon. But in fact, the problem is still a thorny one: we lack the data to apply the theory and the carbon markets produce the wrong price signals.

The theory for determining the optimal price of a pollutant emission is simple enough in principle. The optimal price is found at the point where the curve plotting the marginal cost of pollution abatement intersects the curve for the marginal benefit of the avoided damage. The general idea is that the level of pollution which is economically satisfactory for society is the point beyond which further abatement costs more than the benefit from avoiding additional damage. Or put the other way round, it is the point below which the situation would not serve the public interest, the cost of additional abatement being lower than the benefit it would yield: abatement is consequently worth carrying out. This coincides with a basic economic principle according to which all actions for which the social cost is lower than the social benefit should be carried out. As is the case with any equilibrium, the optimal price corresponds to the optimal amount of pollution. Normative economics does not prescribe zero pollution. The economically optimal amount of waste or effluents is only equal to zero in the rare event of it being less expensive to eliminate pollution, down to the last gram, rather than suffering the damage it entails.

Applying this theory is another matter. The data required to plot curves for CO_2 emissions abatement and avoided damage do not exist. Obviously there are estimates of the cost of various actions such as insulating homes or recycling waste, which in turn limit carbon emissions to the atmosphere. But economists need future costs, not just current costs. The former are unknown, because technological innovation – such as carbon capture and storage – has yet to yield conclusive results. It would also be necessary to know the cost of measures to adapt to global warming. It may be more economical, at least for part of the temperature increase, to adapt to the situation rather than combating it. But it is future generations which will have to adapt. How can we know how much it will cost them? We cannot ask them. The same applies to the damages suffered by our descendants. How could they be calculated without an exact idea of their extent and without questioning those who might be exposed to them? For example the cost of migration to escape changing geographical conditions depends on the individuals concerned, in particular how much value they attach to the loss of their land. The last, but by no means the smallest, obstacle to assessing damages is the lack of a robust formula for converting the concentration of CO_2 in the atmosphere into temperature increase. It is not the amount of carbon which causes the economic loss but the climate change it may bring about. In this situation economists are dependent on the scientific knowledge of climatologists. Unfortunately analysis of the exact consequences for climate change of a rise in the amount of greenhouse gas stored in the atmosphere is still tentative.

But does looking at the markets make it any easier to find the price of carbon? At first sight, yes. Since 2005 Europe has had a market for tradable emissions permits. On this market the price of a tonne of CO_2 fluctuated on either side of €15 in 2009–10 (equivalent to €55 a tonne of carbon, a tonne of CO_2 containing 272 kilograms of this element). Given that generating one MWh using coal releases roughly a tonne of CO_2, the operators of coal-fired plants had to pay an average of €15 per MWh for their emissions in 2009–10. In other words, all other things being equal, if in the course of this period, 1 MWh generated by a coal-fired power plant had been replaced by 1 MWh generated by a nuclear plant, €15 would have been saved. Projecting ourselves into the future and anticipating that the market price of carbon will double, switching electricity production from coal-fired to nuclear power plants would save €30 per MWh.

So far, so good. On the basis of the market price we can obtain the opportunity cost we sought, be it past or future. In addition the private and social costs seem to have been reconciled: private operators are forced to make allowance for the price of carbon emissions when choosing to invest in coal-fired or nuclear plants. Thanks to the market, the external effect has been internalized.

In fact, nothing has been settled. For two reasons. Firstly, the European Emissions Trading Scheme is not a market for polluters and polluted, but an exchange for companies at the source of emissions. It reflects the abatement performance of the various players, but in no way the damage done. Secondly, the market was badly calibrated. The prices it reveals are not sufficient to achieve the targets set by the EU for reducing CO_2 emissions. We shall now take a closer look at these two reasons.

Economic theory explains that externalities occur in the absence of a market, so the answer is to design one. With no market, there is no price, hence no purchasing cost and no accountable expenditure. When manufacturers discharge harmful emissions into the atmosphere, they are using the latter as a huge tip, access to which is free of charge. Some polluters are not against the principle of a toll system, particularly for the sake of their image. Similarly, to improve the market value of their home, some residents would be prepared to pay polluters to restrict their emissions. But there being no marketplace where polluters and polluted can meet, pollution is free; it appears in no accounting system and remains an external cost.

The European market for tradable emissions permits is not a place of exchange between polluters and polluted. On the contrary it brings together companies to which individual CO_2 emissions quotas have been distributed, but for a total amount capped below the level of industry's overall emissions. Let us suppose that, for example, 100,000 permits, each for a tonne of CO_2, are allocated, whereas emissions from polluting companies amount to 120,000 tonnes. In this fictitious case, the companies would have to reduce emissions by 20,000 tonnes. In some companies the cost of cutting CO_2 emissions is low, for others it is higher. The first group will become sellers and carry out more abatement, the second group will buy permits and abate less. At equilibrium, the price will be equal to the marginal cost of eliminating the last tonne required to meet the limit. The advantage of this market is that expenditure by industry on cutting emissions is minimized. Economic theory demonstrates that a tax yields a similar benefit. With a tax on each unit of pollution, companies with low costs for cutting emissions will abate more to reduce their liability for taxation; on the other hand companies with high abatement costs will pay proportionately more tax and do less to cut emissions. The main difference between a permit and a tax is the initial variable selected by the competent authority. In the case of a tax, the price is set in advance and deploying the instrument will show *ex post* the corresponding cut in emissions. For example, a tax pegged at €20 a tonne will lead to a 20,000 tonne drop in emissions. For a permit, the amount is decided first and the market then reveals the price per tonne of emissions avoided. If an upper limit of 100,000 tonnes is set to reduce emissions by 20,000 tonnes the market will balance out at a price of €20 a tonne.

The decision to base the system on price or quantity is closely related to the political consensus underpinning the action. In the first instance agreement was reached on the level of the acceptable surcharge per unit, in particular for consumers and business. Here the unknown factor was the amount of abatement; it might be too low, but in any case the economic conditions were such that a higher surcharge could not be applied. In the second instance agreement was reached on the level of a significant reduction that needed to be achieved, in particular according to scientific experts.

The unknown was the price to be paid for such a reduction, but in any case setting a lower target for pollution abatement would certainly not have achieved the desired environmental effect. This is obviously an oversimplification. In the absence of accurate data on the cost of abatement, orders of magnitude may sometimes be posited. When the initial level of taxation is announced, business and government may be able to estimate how much pollution will be abated within a certain range. In the other case, when the initial abatement target is published, the various players can estimate an approximate price. Once the first variable has been set, the second is not usually completely unpredictable. However, as the European example (see box) shows, the initial calibration may be faulty.

The preceding discussion of the price of carbon is important, as we shall see, for it is one of the determining factors in the competitiveness of nuclear power: without taxes on CO_2 emissions or in the absence of an emissions trading scheme, nuclear power cannot compete with coal or even gas. Furthermore, a consideration of how the cost of carbon is assessed highlights the dual role played by economic analysis. In the world of perfect information posited by economic theory, such analysis would enable us to set the optimal level of abatement, at the intersection between the cost of the damage done by an additional tonne of emissions and the cost of reducing pollution by an additional tonne. The role of government would be simply to plot curves and enforce the resulting target price or quantity. Economic analysis would dictate its prescriptions to policy-makers. In the real world of limited information in which we live, economics occupies a humbler position and the roles are reversed. Political decisions, through voting, debate or consultation lead to the definition of an acceptable level of either damages or expenditure. Economic analysis mainly intervenes to minimize the cost of achieving the degree of damage decided by government or to maximize the quantity produced corresponding to the level of expenditure set by government.

The failures of the EU Emissions Trading Scheme

By mid-2013 the price of CO_2 had dropped to less than €5 a tonne. Five years earlier the European Commission predicted that by this point in time it would be worth €30. The financial crisis and the drop in industrial output obviously explain part of the difference. But in 2006 the price had already fallen below €15 a tonne. The main structural reason behind the persistently low price of CO_2 is the failure to create scarcity, too many permits having been distributed. The resulting downward pressure on prices has been exacerbated by lower than expected emission-abatement costs. The European CO_2 trading system does not fulfil its purpose: it does not send a reliable signal enabling industry to curtail long-term investments, in particular enabling electricity utilities to choose between various generating technologies according to their CO_2 emissions performance.

The case of the United Kingdom is a perfect illustration of this failure. The UK has undertaken to halve CO_2 emissions by 2030. To achieve this target it plans to set a carbon-price floor at €40 a tonne by 2020 and €87 by 2030. The price in the EU Emissions Trading Scheme (ETS) will only exert an influence if it exceeds these price-floors, which is unlikely to happen very often unless the ETS is reformed in the meantime. France offers another example. In 2009 the government was planning to introduce a carbon tax as an incentive to reduce the use of oil products. The rates recommended to achieve a fourfold cut in emissions by 2050 were €32 a tonne in 2010, rising to €100 a tonne in 2030, and twice that amount by mid-century.[3] The ETS price for carbon is far below the value recommended by experts to achieve long-term targets for reducing emissions.

Decommissioning and waste: setting the right discount rate

Nuclear-power companies are responsible for the waste and by-products they produce. In this field, much as elsewhere, the polluter-pays principle applies. This principle is not disputed by the operators of nuclear plants, nor yet by opponents of nuclear power. So the controversy does not centre on the need to internalize the costs of decommissioning reactors and storing waste (spent fuel, decommissioning debris), but on the amount to be set aside now to cover these costs, thus ensuring that these back-end activities can be carried out tomorrow.

Worldwide we have almost no experience of dismantling power plants and burying radioactive waste. Nowhere in the world has anyone built a permanent storage facility for burying long-term waste. In France not a single nuclear power plant has been completely decommissioned. Work decommissioning the Chooz A reactor, in the Ardennes, is only scheduled to end in 2019. The reactor was commissioned in 1967 and shut down twenty-four years later. World-wide less than twenty commercial reactors have been completely dismantled.

The lack of references makes appraisal very uncertain. We cannot rule out the possibility that the technical costs of dismantling and the costs of waste-management may prove very high. However, even if this were the case, it would have little effect on the return on investment from a new nuclear power plant. The return is not very sensitive to this parameter because the costs at the end of a nuclear plant's service life are very remote in time, and a euro tomorrow is worth less than a euro today, and even less the day after tomorrow. Future costs or benefits are wiped out by the rate of exchange used to convert present funds into future funds (or vice versa). For example, at an annual rate of 8%, €1 million would only be worth €455 in a century. This amount drops to €0.20 after two centuries and in

500 years it would have dwindled to almost nothing. Taking the same rate of 8% and supposing that decommissioning would cost 15% of the total cost of a new reactor, this share only represents 0.7% of the total cost if decommissioning is carried out forty years after construction. This rate, known as the discount rate, plays a decisive part in assessing the costs of decommissioning plant and managing waste. To avoid wiping out such costs, a discount rate close to zero would need to be used. Certain environmental conservation groups advocate this position, but there is little support among economists. We shall now look in greater detail at how the discount rate works.

To avoid confusion, we should start by explaining what this rate is not. Firstly, the discount rate bears no relation to inflation. The latter, whether its origin is monetary or results from indexing wages, is a phenomenon which raises prices. Consumers will buy less tomorrow because the same shopping basket will cost more. Secondly, the discount rate does not reflect the risks associated with the investment project being assessed. Such risks cast doubt on income and expenditure and change the way they are estimated, but not due to the discount rate.

To convert current euros into future euros we must start from existing knowledge. Despite the limited experience mentioned above, we do have preliminary orders of magnitude.

In 2012 France's Court of Auditors used the EDF estimate of how much it would cost to decommission its fifty-eight reactors. The cost entered in the company's accounts amounts to €18 billion, equivalent to €300 per kW of installed capacity. In comparison with assessments in other countries, and consequently relating to reactors and conditions which may be very different, this figure is near the lower end of the range. The management consultants Arthur D. Little estimated that the upper value in Germany would be close to €1,000 per kW. In the United States estimates of the cost of decommissioning the Maine Yankee plant, completed in 2005, are in the region of €500 per kW.

As for waste destined to be buried in deep geological repositories, only very preliminary estimates have been made. Work is still focusing on pilot schemes or has barely started. The only site currently operating stores radioactive waste of military origin at Carlsbad, New Mexico. This waste is easier to manage because it does not release any heat. To store the amount of long-term waste produced by a reactor in one year, the order of magnitude currently cited is €20 million. This figure is based on various British, Japanese and French estimates.[4] The amount is likely to change with progress by research and technical know-how. In 2005 France's Nuclear Waste Authority (Andra) estimated that it would cost a little under €20 billion to build and operate a deep geological repository. Five years later the price was adjusted to €36 billion. The second amount makes allowance for additional parameters, integrating return-on-experience from excavating underground galleries, requirements for greater capacity and tougher safety constraints, among others.

The timescales we are dealing with here are very long. Some categories of nuclear waste will go on emitting radiation for several hundred thousand years. For example, plutonium-239 has a half-life – the time required for half the radioactive atoms to disintegrate – of 24,000 years. For technetium-99 it rises to 211,000 years and for iodine-129 it is 15.7 million. Such time spans are stupendous when compared to the scale of human life. Our most distant ancestors, *Australopithecus*, appeared on Earth 4 million years ago and modern humans (*homo sapiens*) only emerged about 200,000 years ago. Of course there are no plans for the storage facilities to operate for such long periods. For example the deep geological repository projected by Andra is expected to last for 120 years, from the start of construction to final closure. If a decision were taken now to invest in a new reactor, the plant would be commissioned in 2020 and operate for sixty years. Only in 2100 would decommissioning be complete, with the last tonnes of waste finally being buried in 2200. These economic deadlines are short compared with the half-life of certain waste products, but nevertheless dizzying. A century is a very long time in the life of an economy, with its multiple crises. Government bonds, the investments with the longest time span, spread over periods of twenty or sometimes thirty years, stretching to fifty in exceptional cases.

With such long timeframes, how can we account for this expenditure now? The reference to government bonds suggests a preliminary approach to the discount rate and its basis. If someone offers to give you €100 today or in twenty years' time, there is no need to think twice. If you take the €100 now you can make a very sound investment in US Treasury bonds. Thanks to the interest you will have more than €100 in twenty years. You will thus be able to consume more than if you had agreed to wait before receiving the funds. The decision, based on a simple trade-off, justifies the use of discounting and the long-term interest rate may be used to find the future value of today's euros. With 4% interest, €100 today will be worth €220 in twenty years or, inversely, €100 from twenty years ahead would be worth only €45.60 at present. However, using this interest rate to discount the value does not solve the problem, if the aim is to determine the value of a euro in a century. As the business weekly *The Economist* amusingly observed,[5] 'At a modest 2% rate [...] a single cent rendered unto Caesar in Jesus' time is equivalent to [...] thirty times the value of the entire world economy today.'

Furthermore, interest rates only partly justify discounting. According to economic theory discounting is necessary for two reasons: people are impatient and future generations will be better off. Economic agents display a pure time preference for the present. Instead of taking an interchangeable value, let us suppose that the choice concerns the possibility of attending the performance of an opera in the course of the coming year, or the same performance in five years' time. Which ticket would you choose? The interest rate argument does not hold because you can neither lend nor resell the ticket. If you do not use it, it will be wasted. It is highly likely that you will opt for the performance in the coming year, rather than waiting five years. This impatience is reflected in a pure time preference for the present, which crushes future consumption to give it less weight.

It is more difficult to illustrate the notion that future generations will be better off. The discount rate depends on the growth rate of the economy and a barbaric term, the elasticity of inter-temporal substitution in consumption. The overall idea is that the richer you are, the less satisfaction an additional euro will yield. If you give €100 to someone with a low income, you will be making them a present worth much more than if you give the same amount to a millionaire. Marginal utility decreases with income. Consequently, if society is €1 billion richer tomorrow, it will respond less to this gain than now. With an ordinary utility function, society ten times better off than at present, and elasticity equal to 1, contemporary society would see its well-being increase ten times more for each marginal unit of consumption (€1 billion) than tomorrow's society. So it would be advisable to limit our efforts to provide benefits for future generations.

Economists thus provide the following key, forged by Frank Ramsey in 1928,[6] for calculating the discount rate: the discount rate (d) is equal to the sum of the pure preference rate for the present (p) and the product of the elasticity of the marginal utility of consumption (e) multiplied by the growth rate of per capita GDP (g), in other words $d = p + eg$ (see box). With the three values often used [2; 2; 2], the discount rate is 6 per cent.

The discount rate cuts both ways, exerting a decisive influence on decisions regarding public and private investment, but it is impaired by numerous unknowns. One recent attempt to reduce this tension has involved using a rate that varies over time – rather than being constant – declining as it advances into the future. The per capita growth rate can be used to illustrate the intuition behind this idea: the more remote the future, the greater the uncertainty regarding economic and technological progress; so, the greater our caution

Interpreting and selecting p, e and g

The pure preference rate for the present may be seen as an equity parameter, its value depending on how fairly we wish to treat future generations. Let us suppose that the output from a new nuclear plant entails a waste-management cost of 100 in a century, but yields a present gain because nuclear technology is cheaper. If we want to treat future generations even-handedly, we should only commit ourselves to the investment if its present benefit for us is greater than 100. In this case we would apply a pure preference rate equal to zero. This position in favour of equality between generations is defended by some economists, including Frank Ramsey. It rejects the idea of discrimination depending on the date of birth and involves treating all generations on the same footing, even if they are more prosperous. If we want to treat our descendants slightly less favourably (if, for example, we are convinced they will find smarter means of storage or recycling), we need to use a slightly positive preference rate. A gain of 14 will then suffice (equal to 100 discounted at 2% over 100 years). If, on the other hand, we are feeling selfish and have no concern for what comes after, the rate will be very high: even if nuclear power only yields a unit gain, it is worth taking, its value exceeding 100 in the future (0.40 today is enough to get 100 in a century with an 8% discount rate). We may also interpret the pure preference rate in terms of our chances of survival. With a one-in-ten chance of mankind not surviving for 100 years (following, for example, collision with a meteorite), the value of the preference rate is 0.1; it rises to 1 if we assume the likelihood of survival is 0.6 (a 4-in-10 chance of the end of the world).

The elasticity of the marginal utility of consumption also measures equity. The greater the difference in utility for a marginal unit of consumption between low- and high-income households, the more justification there is for high levels of transfer, through taxation for instance, from rich to poor. Such transfers raise the utility of the whole of society. In other words, this parameter reflects our attitude to unequal levels of consumption, between different people in the present day, or between them and their descendants. Unlike the previous variable, the difference in treatment is not related to time. The more egalitarian we are, the more we favour redistribution from rich to poor and the higher the value we need to use for elasticity when calculating the discount rate. If we assume that future generations will be richer than today, it is legitimate to limit our efforts to improve their welfare. Looked at another way, elasticity equal to 1 would be unfair. Given a constant population it would justify spending 1% of today's GDP to give future generations the benefit of an additional 1% of GDP, even if they are incomparably more prosperous. Per capita fractions of GDP can therefore be traded between generations on equal terms. The elasticity of marginal utility may also be linked to risk. According to economic theory risk aversion is proportional to elasticity. The higher the elasticity, the more a person is prepared to pay for the certainty of consuming 100, rather than a random outcome (for example, a one-in-two chance of consuming 200, or zero). Taking a higher value for this parameter, which is then multiplied by the growth rate of per capita GDP, is tantamount to assuming that the present generation is averse to risk.

Setting the three values which make up the discount rate is no easy matter; but they will play a decisive role in how we act now. An instance of this point is the controversy prompted by the publication of the Stern Review in 2006.[7] This report caused quite a stir because it concluded that substantial, immediate expenditure (about 1% of GDP) was needed to reduce greenhouse gas emissions. This recommendation contradicted the conclusions of most climate-change economists, who suggested a more gradual

increase in expenditure. The work of the US economist William
D. Nordhaus,[8] for example, recommends a carbon tax of $13 a
tonne over an initial period in order to internalize the damage
done by global warming. Nicholas Stern prescribed $310 a tonne.
Half of this difference is simply due to the discount rate used by
the two parties: 4% for the former, 1.4% for the latter.

In his estimate Stern uses a preference rate for the present
of 0.1 and elasticity of 1. These two values represent the lower
limits of the ranges economists generally accept. His choice is
open to criticism because it raises a logical contradiction. A low
preference rate for the present should go hand-in-hand with high
elasticity or, on the other hand, low elasticity should match a high
preference for the present. It would be mistaken to suppose that
one of these two parameters reflects equity between generations,
the other solidarity within a single generation. A low value for
the elasticity of the marginal utility due to consumption can be
justified on the grounds of reducing inequality between rich and
poor, regardless of when they were born. This choice coincides
with a high preference rate for the present, which endorses the idea
that the present generation should only make limited sacrifices
for future generations (given that the latter will be better off,
as Stern posits with a positive growth rate for per capita GDP).
Using a simplified economic model the Cambridge economist,
Partha Dasgupta,[9] has demonstrated that the parameters used by
Stern would lead to inconceivably high saving ratios. With a
preference rate for the present of 0.1, elasticity of 1, and a world
with neither technological progress nor population growth, we
should be investing 97.5% of our current output in boosting the
standard of living of future generations.

The Stern Review asks whether it makes economic sense to
spend 1% of today's GDP to prevent damage amounting to 5% of
GDP in a century. The three values it uses, [0.1; 1; 1.3], would

lead to a discounted benefit five times *greater* than the cost. But if we use [2; 2; 2] the discounted benefit would be ten times *smaller* than the cost! In other words, with a 1.4% discount rate it is entirely justifiable to spend 1% of GDP on reducing greenhouse gas emissions, whereas with a 6% discount rate it would be quite out of the question.

We have so far set aside the question of the third parameter, the future growth rate of per capita GDP. Its value is just as uncertain as the others, but setting it does not raise equity-related issues. Looking back in time, the annual growth rate of per capita GDP was 1.4% in the UK from 1870 to 2000, and 1.9% in France. However these averages conceal significant variations. In the UK the growth rate was 1% in 1870–1913, 0.9% in 1913–50, 2.4% in 1950–73, and 1.8% from 1973 to 2000. Over a very long period of time – 1500 to 1820 – it is estimated to have been 0.6%. Which of these different rates should we use? The growth rates for the next century or two may be very different. Nor can we rule out a negative growth rate, though it is not very likely. However, global warming in excess of 6°C in 200 years could have precisely that effect.

regarding action that might jeopardize the well-being of future generations, the lower the discount rate should be. Christian Gollier recommends using a 5% annual discount rate for costs borne over the next thirty years, dropping to 2% for subsequent costs.[10] It is also possible to set the discount rate on a downward path, with either several steps or a steady decline. In a report submitted to the British government in 2002,[11] Oxera Consulting Ltd suggested adopting a 3.5% rate from 0 to 30 years, 3% from 31 to 75 years, 2.5% from 76 to 125 years, and so on, with the rate ultimately bottoming out at 1% after 300 years. In France the Lebègue report,[12] on a review of discount rates in public investment, recommended a 4% rate for the first 30 years, then a rate that would steadily decrease to reach 3% after 100 years, tending towards 2% for a time horizon of over 300 years.

A varying rate also seems to represent a compromise between two demands: on the one hand taking account of our preference for the present and our contribution through technical progress to the prosperity of future generations; and on the other hand allowing for the potentially very negative consequences of our action, or inaction, with regard to future generations.[13]

It is obviously up to the relevant authorities to ensure that adequate provision is made for the projected costs of decommissioning and waste management, in accordance with the discount rate they have decided. In both the United States and France the government took such measures long ago. Left to themselves, utilities would stand to gain by underestimating future expenditure on this work and by opting for high discount rates in order to minimize projected costs. In the US and France – but also in many other countries – today's consumers are paying for tomorrow's expenditure. There are no hidden costs for decommissioning and waste which once internalized would make the cost of nuclear electricity production prohibitive (see box).

So back-end activities have no significant impact on the cost competitiveness of existing or new nuclear power. Unless of course one adopts a very low, or even zero, discount rate for very distant time horizons – as is the case in the Stern Review's calculations for climate change (see the last but one box above). In my opinion, this stance – which its advocates justify by the hazardous nature of nuclear waste and its very long life – boils down to using inconsistent economic reasoning to endorse a legitimate argument. In this part we have not allowed for the possibility that such waste might represent a risk for future generations. The only waste-related costs taken into account are the preventive costs built into the quality of repositories and their supervision. These costs vary depending on the safety standards set

Taking into account the costs of decommissioning and waste

In France, regulation is based on special discounted provisions imposed on EDF. They appear on its balance sheet and the utility is required to secure them with specific cover assets. The law sets an upper limit for the discount rate pegged to 30-year government bonds, currently close to 3%. With this rate EDF's provisions for decommissioning and waste amount to €28 billion. They would increase by 21% with a 2% discount rate, adding 0.8% to the overall cost of a MWh. Furthermore, if just the cost of decommissioning were to rise by 50% (amounting to €30 billion as opposed to €20 billion), the cost of electricity would increase by 2.5%.[14] If the cost of deep geological repositories were to double, it would result in a 1% increase. In the US a special fund has been set up to cope with the future expense of deep repositories for spent fuel. Utilities pay a fee into the fund equal to $1 per MWh they generate. The Department of Energy checks at regular intervals that the fee is sufficient. For this purpose it has developed about thirty cash-flow models designed to balance out by 2133.[15] These scenarios depend on a large number of parameters, including the discount rate. The lowest rate considered is 2.24% per year. Two out of the four scenarios based on this rate result in a deficit, whereas the proportion is only one in four for the scenarios using a higher rate. The figures above are valid for existing reactors in the US and France. For new nuclear plants, the time horizon for expenditure would be longer, so decommissioning and waste-management costs would have even less impact on the present value of projects. A Massachusetts Institute of Technology study on the future of nuclear power puts the overnight cost of building a reactor at $4,000 per kW, and the cost of decommissioning it at $700 per kW, or 17.5%.[16] Spreading decommissioning expenditure out between the 41st and 110th year after the reactor is commissioned, and assuming a 6% discount rate, would bring the present value of decommissioning down to $11 per kW. This value would be five times higher ($52) if the rate was almost halved (3.5%). But as before, this cost is negligible compared with construction costs. With the above discount rates, the 17.5% shrinks to 0.2% or 1.3%, respectively.

by government for decommissioning and storage. To take a trivial example, the cost of a repository increases in relation to the length and depth of its tunnels. On the other hand, we have made no allowance for the cost of possible accidents, despite the fact that the risk does exist. Protecting future generations against a disaster of this sort poses the problem of assessing the uncertain damages associated with events with a very low probability and a very high cost. The release of radioactive substances into the atmosphere following the meltdown of a reactor core raises the same question: how is one to estimate the costs without knowing how the risks are distributed? We shall address this key question in the following part. The discount rate is of only limited value for finding an answer. The wrong solution would be to give the matter no further thought and select a very low, or zero, value to allow for the hazards of waste. Making allowance for a possible disaster caused by downstream activities may mean opposing the construction of new nuclear reactors without it being necessary to hide behind a very low or zero discount rate.

Liability in the event of accident

The parts of this book devoted to risks and regulation deal in detail with the cost of major accidents and the legal framework for the civil liability of nuclear power. But we need to mention the matter briefly here, many authors having suggested that estimates of the cost of nuclear power fail to make allowance for the risk of disaster.

The operators of nuclear power plants are liable in the event of accident, but it is true that in most cases an upper limit is placed on such liability. The amount of compensation they must pay in the event of massive radioactive emissions is less than the value of the damage. In France, for instance, the limit is €91.5 million. It will soon be raised to €700 million. Such caps on liability raise the question of whether the costs of major accidents are sufficiently internalized. According to the opponents of nuclear power, limited liability is equivalent to a hidden subsidy. A Swedish study estimated that the Chernobyl disaster cost nearly $400 billion.[17] There is no way of settling the matter without a detailed review of the expected and observed frequencies of accidents and the uncertainty surrounding the level of damage. Here we shall make do with a much simplified examination of the risk involved, in order to determine how much impact it has on the full cost of existing nuclear plants and new reactors.

Risk is classically defined as the result of multiplying the probability of an accident by the severity of the outcome. For the sake of argument, we shall take the highest values cited in the literature for these parameters. We shall suppose that there is one chance in 100,000 that a disaster may occur during one year of a reactor's service life, a probability 100 times higher than the figure cited by Areva for the EPR. We shall then suppose that the massive release of radioactivity causes damage to public health and the environment worth €1 trillion, ten times higher than the provisional estimates for Fukushima. So the risk is equal to $0.00001 \times 1{,}000{,}000{,}000{,}000$, or €10 million a year. Supposing that the reactor's annual production amounts to 10 million MWh, the risk would be equivalent to €1 per MWh, or between 1 and 2 per cent of the estimates of the average cost of new nuclear. This scratch calculation shows that, under much simplified conditions – in particular with no allowance for uncertainty – internalizing the full cost of an accident has only a very slight impact on the cost of nuclear electricity.

We should however point out that, on the basis of these hypothetical data, the upper limits on liability currently in force mean that only a relatively small share of costs is internalized. If we take the case of the €91.5 million limit in France, it only amounts to 0.4 per cent of the full cost of an accident we took as an illustration.[18] Raising the limit to €700 million would still leave 97 per cent unaccounted for. In other words internalization is indeed partial, but internalizing the full cost would only result in a slight increase in the cost of nuclear electricity.

Technical and financial production costs

Here at last we may venture onto more solid ground. Engineers do not base their decisions on externalities which are so difficult to grasp and estimate. On the contrary they work on data relating in particular to the costs of reactors built in the past and current operating costs. They can use proven, widely accepted methods for calculating costs, in particular for project funding. They juggle with concrete, steel, enriched uranium, man-months, assets and deadlines.

To come to grips with the subject we shall start with construction. This involves an overnight cost and a capital cost. The overnight cost refers to a hypothetical construction project completed in an instant, or 'overnight'. Spending on material, machines and wages is entered into the accounts at the prices in force when construction starts. This does not overlook financial costs; they are simply processed separately. It takes from five to ten years to build a power plant, from initial preparation of the site to the moment it is connected to the grid. During this time there is no return on investment. On the contrary, it represents a cost. If the operator borrows half the amount it needs from banks, at a 4 per cent real interest rate (allowing for inflation), and funds the rest out of its own resources at 6 per cent, for instance, the average cost of capital is 5 per cent. This cost must be added to the overnight cost to obtain the cost of investment, or installed cost.

The overnight cost is useful if we want to make an abstraction from the variability of construction lead-times. It makes comparisons easier, because construction times vary depending on the reactor model and size, but also due to non-technical causes, particularly changes in the prevailing regulatory framework or local opposition. In the US, for example, the shortest construction project lasted less than four years, but the longest one took twenty-five years.

Although it overlooks such factors the overnight cost can vary a great deal. Firstly, over time. On a per kW basis the first reactors were much cheaper than at present. We shall examine this dynamic in the following chapter. The overnight cost also varies geographically. In its 2010 study of electricity production costs the OECD noted a difference of one to three between the overnight costs, expressed in $ per MW, for building a reactor in South Korea and Switzerland.[19] The size, model and country (cost of labour, regulatory framework, etc.) are not the same, but such a large difference may nevertheless come as a surprise. However, it is not specific to nuclear power. The OECD observed a similar disparity for gas, with South Korea and Switzerland once again at the two extremes.

The overnight construction cost is one of the three main factors affecting the cost of generating nuclear electricity. The other two are the load factor and the financing cost (see box).

Once construction of the plant is complete, expenditure concerns fuel and other operating and maintenance costs. Roughly speaking fuel costs represent between 5% and 10% of the cost of generating electricity, with the other costs totalling between 20% and 25%. The cost of fuel varies depending on the amount of electricity generated, because it is depleted as the chain reaction proceeds. It is this chain reaction which releases heat, used in turn to generate electricity. The level of production has little impact on the other operating costs, which may be treated as relatively fixed, at least as long as the reactor is in service. When the nuclear plant is finally shut down, most of these costs disappear.

Load factor and cost of financing

Nuclear power plants are characterized by very long construction times and a very high fixed investment cost compared to a variable operating cost, particularly with respect to fuel expenses.

As a result, if a reactor does not operate at full capacity, once it has been built, the fixed cost must be paid off by a smaller amount of electricity production, which in turn makes each MWh more expensive. Over the past decade the load factor of existing nuclear plants was about 95% in South Korea, 90% in the US and 70% in Japan. To illustrate the weight of this factor, we may use an example from the book by Bertel and Naudet:[20] improving the load factor from 75% to 85% boosts output by 13% and cuts the cost of a MWh by 10%.

The financing cost or interest during construction (IDC) depends on how long it takes to build the plant, but also on the choice of discount rate. As the overnight construction cost is spread over several years, expenditure must be discounted. The calculation uses the date on which the plant was commissioned as its baseline and a discount rate decided by the operator. The difference between this discounted expenditure and the overnight cost measures the financing cost. For a private-sector operator the discount rate may range from 5% to 10%. With construction lasting six years, the overnight cost must be multiplied by 1.16 with a 5% discount rate, and by 1.31 with a 10% rate. Obviously the sooner construction is complete, the sooner income will start to flow in, with interim interest reduced accordingly. In the example borrowed from Bertel and Naudet, shortening the construction time to five years reduces the cost of financing by 27%, with a 10% discount rate, and by 13% with a 5% discount.

Adding up the costs: the levelized cost method

The technical and financial costs of building and operating a nuclear power plant, the downstream costs of decommissioning and processing waste, and the external costs (avoided carbon emissions, accidents) must all be added up to obtain the full cost of nuclear power. It will then be possible to monitor variations in this cost over time and to compare it with the cost of electricity generated using other technologies. To do so, we need to convert the euros at different points in time into constant euros and MWs into MWhs. The discount rate is used for the first conversion. The second operation is required in order to add up fixed costs – expressed as value per unit of power, for example in € per MW – and variable costs – expressed as value per unit of energy, for example in € per MWh. By definition, one MWh is the amount of electricity generated by one MW of power in one hour. A 1,000 MW nuclear plant operating at full capacity round the clock will generate 8,760,000 MWh a year. To allocate investment costs we need to know or anticipate the plant's load factor and its projected service life.

The full cost is worth knowing, but what is really important is whether it is greater or less than the revenue, in order to determine whether there is a net gain for the utility or any other company venturing into nuclear power. So far we seem to have disregarded revenue. Nor have we addressed the price of electricity and how it is sold. However, in conceptual terms, there is no difference between a cost and a benefit. One switches back and forth between them just by changing the sign. They are two sides of the same coin: a purchasing cost for a producer is a source of income for its supplier; an avoided carbon emission cost is a benefit for the environment.

Cost–benefit analysis, which compares discounted costs and benefits, is the canonical method used by economists to estimate the private or social merits of a project or decision. However, a variant is used in the field of electricity, the levelized cost. It is used to determine the price of electricity required to balance income and outgoings throughout a power plant's service life. In a way it takes the opposite route to the economic canon: instead of calculating a project's rate of return as a function of assumptions on the future price of electricity, this variant sets a zero profit rate from which to deduce a price for electricity which balances discounted income and outgoings. For example, taking €75 per MWh as the levelized cost of the EPR plant at Flamanville, in western France, means it will break even if the average price recorded reaches this level during the plant's operational service life for the projected number of hours' operation. But bear in mind that zero profit does not mean that there is no return on capital. The outgoings accounted for by this method include the cost of bankers' loans and raising funds from investors.

The levelized cost method goes back to before liberalization of the electricity sector and the creation of wholesale electricity markets. It enabled a regulator to determine the sale price of a monopolistic operator on the basis of the latter's costs. It also allowed the two parties to identify, by comparison, the cheapest generating technology in which to invest in order to meet rising demand. For the economics of today's electricity markets, only the comparison is of any interest. In principle private operators, not government, take decisions on investment. Operators tend to base such decisions on forecasts of future electricity prices and consequently on cost–benefit analysis. On the other hand, to decide whether it is preferable to add coal or gas-fired or nuclear plant to existing capacity, they will use the levelized cost variant, because it makes it easier to compare technologies. In practice, even after liberalization of the electricity market, government has continued to have a say in the choice of generating technology. At the very least it plays a part in some European countries setting long-term targets for decarbonizing electricity generation in line with policy on emissions abatement. In this case the average discounted social cost will be used. Technical and financial costs, including back-end costs (site remediation and waste management), are added to estimates of external effects (such as accidents, pollutant emissions), unless they have already been fully integrated in private costs due to regulatory or legal constraints (liability, carbon tax, safety standards). Applying this method in the general interest also involves discounting future factors differently. The authorities' choice of discount rate is based on notions of equity discussed above, not on bank interest rates and investors' demands regarding the rate of return.

Predictably, the disparities between levelized cost estimates are even greater than those observed between estimates of overnight construction costs, the latter being just one component of the former. According to the OECD the cost of construction varied by a factor of one to three between South Korea and Switzerland. In the case of the levelized cost these two countries still occupy the upper and lower extremities of the range, but with a one-to-five variation in estimates: $29 MWh for South Korea; $136.5 MWh for Switzerland.[21]

The values taken into account for the overnight cost of construction and its duration, the load factor and discount rate explain much of the disparity between the various estimates of nuclear costs. The cost may be multiplied by four if only extreme, yet realistic, values are taken into account. Take for example the base case in the 2009 MIT study,[22] an update of the 2003 MIT study.[23] The estimated cost of $84 per MWh is based on four parameters [$4,000 per kWe; 5 years; 85%; 10%]. Taking the extreme values [$2,000 per kWe; 4 years; 95%; 5%], on the one hand, and [$5,000 per kWe; 6 years; 75%; 12%] on the other, we obtain, respectively, a levelized cost of $34 per MWh and $162 per MWh. The operating costs, including the cost of fuel, weigh less heavily in the balance, whereas decommissioning and waste-management costs weigh more heavily. Of course we are referring here to the cost of next-generation nuclear plants. For ageing reactors nearing the end of their service life, operation accounts for the lion's share of costs. Furthermore, decommissioning expenditure being imminent, it adds substantially to costs unless the operator has already made sufficient provision.

Allowing for external effects does not significantly change the ranking of cost determinants. According to the simplistic estimate discussed earlier, at the most the risk of an accident only adds one euro to the average cost per MWh. This is negligible compared with the cost of a new facility, and low even compared to the cost of operating existing plant. However, it is still only partly internalized, the liability of operators being capped at low levels in the event of an accident. Nuclear power's advantage with regard to CO_2 emissions could certainly be taken into account as a social benefit. It could have a substantial impact on the levelized cost of nuclear power if the price for CO_2 emissions was in the upper range (€50 to €100 per tonne). However, it makes more sense to integrate the price of carbon in the levelized cost of technologies responsible for emissions: indeed, it is integrated through taxes or emissions permits which directly affect these technologies. We shall consequently examine its impact when discussing the relative competitiveness of nuclear power (see Chapter 3).

TWO

The curse of rising costs

It is well known that the cost of a technology drops as it is deployed and becomes more widely used. We have all noticed that we pay less for using a telephone, computer or airplane than our parents did, simply because the cost of these goods has been substantially reduced since the first products rolled off factory production lines. Economic theory cites two causes to explain this phenomenon: the scale effect and the learning effect. The first one is both familiar and intuitive. The bigger the factory, the less each unit costs to produce. In other words, the unit cost of large production runs is lower than for smaller volumes. At the start of a technology cycle the capacity of each production unit is relatively small, in particular because demand is still limited. Subsequently the size of factories gradually increases, stabilizing when diseconomies of scale start to appear (due, for instance, to time spent moving from one workshop to another). The learning effect in manufacturing is linked to the know-how which accumulates over time. The most intuitive example to illustrate this point is the repetition of a single task. You may spend more than ten minutes folding your first paper hen, but barely a minute after making a thousand or so. Manufacturing an airliner, steam turbine or solar panel is much the same. The learning effect is generally measured by the learning rate which corresponds to the reduction in cost when cumulative production doubles. The cost per kWh of wind power, for example, drops by about 10 per cent each time installed capacity doubles.[1]

Nuclear technology displays the opposite trend. The per-kW construction cost of the most recent reactors, in constant (inflation-adjusted) euros or dollars, is higher than that of the first reactors. A technology with rising costs is a very strange beast, which requires closer study, particularly as this feature distinguishes it from several competing technologies, such as wind or solar. If nuclear engineering firms fail to find a solution in the near future, the cost of nuclear power will continue to rise, undermining its competitiveness.

The rising costs of nuclear power

The rising cost of building nuclear reactors is a well-established fact. In particular, it has been studied in depth for installed capacity in the US. The overnight cost of the first reactors, built in the early 1970s, was about $1,000_{2008}$ per kW. It has increased steadily ever since, reaching $5,000_{2008}$ per kW for the most recent reactors, built in the early 1990s. In other words, a one-to-five difference in constant dollars. The increase in the installed cost is even more striking. The average construction time has increased with time, so interim interest has increased too. The time taken to build a nuclear power plant has risen from between five and six years for the first plants to be connected to the grid to more than twice as long for the most recent units. The average total cost per kWh displays the same upward trend. Maintenance and operating costs have dropped and the load factor has improved with time, but these two factors are not enough to counteract the very large increase in the fixed cost of construction.[2]

In France the overnight construction cost reported by EDF for its various plants was made public for the first time in a 2010 report by France's Court of Auditors.[3] It amounted to €860_{2010} per kW for the first four reactors at Fessenheim and Bugey, commissioned in the late 1970s, and €1,440_{2010} per kW for the last four reactors, at Chooz and Civaux, which came online in the early 2000s.[4] Although it is less than twice the initial amount, the increase is nevertheless substantial.

Nuclear power consequently has a record of rising costs. But what is the explanation for this anomaly? A great many factors may have come into play, such as the rising cost of materials and machinery, or the lack of economies of scale. The figures cited above are the result of several forces, invisible to the naked eye, which may conceal causes exerting an opposite force, with varying degrees of influence. To highlight all these factors we need to use a statistical method known as econometrics. This tool enables us to isolate each of the factors determining a phenomenon and to measure their respective influence. As early as 1975 econometrics was used to scrutinize the costs of nuclear power in the US.[5] Other work using the same method has been done since, yielding very interesting results.

Firstly, these studies show the absence of any significant economies of scale. The cost per MW of installed capacity is no lower for the construction of the largest reactors. Why? Because they are not just scaled-up replicas of their predecessors. They are more complex, fitted with more parts and components, often of a different design. Some research even shows diseconomies of scale. For instance, Robin Cantor and James Hewlett, in a paper based on Geoffrey Rothwell's work,[6] calculated that a 1% increase in the size of a reactor resulted in a 0.13% rise in the overnight cost per kW.[7] They demonstrated in a first step that, other things being equal – in other words, maintaining the other factors they examined at a constant level – the construction cost was significantly less with higher reactor power (a 1% increase in capacity cut the cost by 0.65%). However another key factor, construction time, also varied with size. Increasing the size by 1% added 0.6% to construction time, entailing in turn a 0.78% increase in cost. The net effect was therefore 0.78 – 0.65, making a 0.13% increase in cost. Large reactors would have been more economical had they been built as quickly as their smaller counterparts.

Secondly, there were few if any learning effects. This result concerns possible savings for the nuclear vendor. For example, according to Martin Zimmerman,[8] if the experience accumulated by a firm rises from four to eight units, it reduces the overnight cost by 4%. Taking the US nuclear industry as a whole it is difficult to isolate the learning effect specifically. The figures show that the cost increases with the overall volume of installed capacity in the US. However, this correlation is not due to diseconomies of learning but rather, as we shall see below, to regulation, which, with passing time, has increased the construction cost of all reactors. It is important to remember that a correlation does not necessarily mean there is a relation of cause and effect. There is a correlation between sales of ice cream and suntan lotion, but one does not drive the other. The correlation is due to a single hidden variable, the weather, which affects sales of both products.

Thirdly, learning effects appear or are simply greater when utilities act as the prime contractors on projects, rather than simply purchasing a turnkey plant. There is less incentive for engineering firms to cut costs. But diminished economies of learning may also be due to their market power and a better understanding of costs. Firms may take advantage of their experience to boost profits, to the detriment of their customers. This conceals learning effects.

Lastly the rising costs were not the result of the accident in 1979 at Three Mile Island, though it did contribute to the trend.[9] The partial reactor meltdown which occurred there delayed some ongoing construction projects, but the rising costs also concern the overnight cost, which is not directly impacted by the duration of the project. Furthermore, the slowdown in the US nuclear programme started before the accident. In 1977 the volume of capacity ordered but subsequently cancelled exceeded built and commissioned capacity. The two curves crossed over. The already visible rise in costs partly explains the slowdown in the US programme.

One variable is missing yet omnipresent: safety regulation. But this variable is hard to measure, unlike reactor capacity or construction time. The number of texts and their length is not much use as an indicator, making no distinction between major and minor regulations. As a result, safety regulation is rarely taken into account as a variable in econometric equations. In 1979 two authors, Soon Paik and William Schriver,[10] invented an ad hoc index in an attempt to integrate regulation. They listed all the regulations issued by the US Nuclear Regulatory Commission (NRC) and sorted them into four categories, depending on their supposed importance. They were thus able to calculate that between 1967 and 1974 regulation had caused a 70 per cent increase in the investment cost per kW. In most other publications economists have used a temporal milestone (start or end of construction, issue of building permit) as an approximation for regulation. The work of the NRC continued at a steady rate all the way through the period during which nuclear plants were being built in the US; every year it published new standards, rules and measures. The regulation variable may thus be correlated with time. Any simple variable representing the passing of time, such as the year when a nuclear plant is connected to the grid, is just as useful as a complex indicator based on compiling and analysing NRC publications. Using temporal milestones to inform the regulation variable, US economists estimate that it is responsible for a 10% to 25% annual increase in construction costs.

The inflation in safety regulation is by far the largest factor in the escalating costs observed in the US. Stricter regulations require larger numbers of safety devices and systems, thicker containment walls, and completely isolated control rooms. In response to these tougher requirements engineers design increasingly complex facilities and systems. Only at the end of the 1990s did it occur to anyone that a possible solution might be to make things simpler, leading to Westinghouse's AP1000, which is based on a passive safety system. Rather than increasing the number of back-up pumps, for instance, a gravity-fed flow would be maintained if the cooling system failed. In the meantime safety was reflected in higher construction inputs and overall a more cumbersome framework for coordinating the construction of plants. The frequent changes in regulations also had a direct impact on the duration of construction projects. Work on a large number of US power plants had to be stopped in order to make allowance for new rules introduced since the start of work. Longer lead times meant higher financial costs, which of course added to the cost of investment. When new rules required additional inputs, this also impacted indirectly on the overnight cost. And, despite it being based on the assumption that a plant was built in one night, longer lead times pushed up overnight costs in the US.

At first sight, analysis of the escalating costs of nuclear power in the US might suggest that stricter safety requirements imposed by the regulator are to blame. But several factors contradict such a simplistic conclusion. It is not so much the severity of regulation as its defects that cost US nuclear power so dearly. Fluctuating rules and shifting priorities, excessive delays in decision-making and an inadequate understanding of the fundamental technical issues may generate excess costs for utilities, which far outstrip the impact of rising safety requirements. It seems more probable that, up to the end of the 1970s, the regulations did not so much attempt to raise the original safety level as simply to achieve it. It is far from easy to assess the safety level of a nuclear power plant, particularly before the fact, simply on the basis of drawings. Building and operating a plant may ultimately reveal that it does not meet the safety targets set by the regulator, and the operator, at the design stage. So the regulator intervenes to ensure that the original safety targets are fulfilled. This may remedy defective quality but does not raise its level. Some authors, such as Mark Cooper,[11] assert that early US reactors were quite simply defective in safety terms and that regulation imposed a form of making good. Lastly, if we read between the lines of escalating US costs we may detect serious shortcomings in industrial organization. Divided into a large number of utilities, often small and limited in territorial reach, and with a host of engineering firms, the industrial organization failed to achieve sufficient standardization of procedures, reactor models and construction practices. Apart from Bechtel, which built twenty-four reactors, the experience of engineering firms and operators was limited to building just a few nuclear plants. In short, unlike many other fields of technology in which the US led the way, the development of nuclear power on an industrial scale was not a great success.

The picture in France was very different, whatever its critics may have maintained (see box). It has now been firmly established that the escalation in costs was far less spectacular, with overnight costs rising by 1.7 per cent a year, compared with 9.2 per cent in the US.

International comparisons

Econometrics is unfortunately not much help here. On the one hand, only a small amount of work has focused on France's nuclear reactors; on the other, the sample itself is small. In all we only have twenty-nine records of costs. France has a total of fifty-eight reactors, but they were built in pairs and the EDF accounting system did not itemize them separately. With such a small sample, few variables can be tested. With respect to economies of scale, there is no sign of a positive effect, quite the opposite. The nameplate capacity of French reactors increased in three steps, rising from 900 MW for the first reactors, through 1,300 MW for the majority of them, culminating at 1,450 MW for the last four. It is immediately apparent that the cost per kW went up with each *palier*, or step, with a particularly spectacular leap at the end. The overnight cost reached €1,442$_{2010}$ per kW for the last four reactors, compared with an average of €1,242$_{2010}$ per kW for the twenty second-step reactors, or €1,121$_{2010}$ per kW for the first fifty-four overall. Econometric analysis yields no further information on this point; the diseconomies of scale persist. Here again the explanation is to be found in the relation between size and complexity. Not only did the reactors on each step differ

A dizzy rise in costs based on mistaken analysis

In 2010 an academic journal published an article which attracted considerable attention.[12] For the first time the construction costs of French reactors were detailed and tracked over time. But contrary to what everyone imagined, the figures showed that France, despite its assets, had also suffered a steep escalation in costs: the cost of building France's last four reactors was allegedly 4.4 times higher than that of the first four. Worse still, the last reactor to be completed (Civaux 2) purportedly cost 7.5 times more than its cheapest counterpart (Bugey 4). It seemed that through some intrinsic fault nuclear technology was incapable of controlling costs and impervious to learning effects. The large scale of the construction projects, the limited unit count, the need to adapt to different sites, and the task of managing such a complex undertaking all contributed to cancelling out the cost-cutting mechanisms observed elsewhere: standardization, production runs comprising several thousand units and the repetition of almost identical processes.

This diagnosis would have been justified, had it not been founded on a mistaken estimate. In the absence of publicly available data on the construction costs of each French reactor, the author of the article, Arnulf Grubler, extrapolated the cost of plants from EDF's annual report on investments. Work had been carried out on several reactors – often of different sizes – in the course of the same year, so Grubler had broken down annual investment, using a theoretical model of expenditure to estimate the cost of each plant. Unfortunately this extrapolation yielded figures which subsequently proved to be at odds with reality. Far from a more than fourfold increase in the construction cost of reactors, from start to finish, the data later published by the Court of Auditors revealed a slightly less than twofold increase, in no way comparable to what had happened in the US.

in size, they varied in other ways. Each step brought technological advances. For example, the second-step plants were equipped with a completely updated control room and system. The design of the last four was almost completely different. When it comes to learning effects, econometric analysis is more helpful, revealing that the overnight cost of a reactor fell depending on the number of reactors already built on a given *palier*. Each additional reactor brought a 0.5% drop in cost. On the other hand, the effect is no longer visible if we look at the total number of reactors previously built. Apparently the experience gained building one model of reactor did not benefit a different model.

It is essential to grasp the step-related learning effect, because it throws light on a recent controversy. The French nuclear programme offered the best possible conditions for powerful learning effects. The power plants were built by a single operator, EDF, which was able to appropriate all the experience accumulated with each new project. The plants were built in a steady stream over a short period of time. In the space of just thirteen years, from late 1971 to the end of 1984, work started on construction of the first fifty-five reactors. The programme as a whole only slowed down at the end, with work on the last three units starting between late 1985 and mid-1991. The average construction time was consistent, only increasing slightly over time. Unlike what happened in the US, the regulatory framework did not upset construction of nuclear plants. The fleet expanded gradually thanks to cooperation between all the players (EDF, Commissariat à l'Energie Atomique, Framatome, Ministry of Industry), well out of sight of non-specialist outsiders.

So, despite the fact that France enjoyed the most favourable conditions for a gradual drop in the cost of building nuclear power plants, this did not materialize. What went wrong? We may suggest a series of specific explanations: the easiest sites were chosen first; quality assurance was gradually tightened up; the rising price of energy impacted on the price of machinery; project ownership expenses increased.[13]

At a more fundamental level, the French nuclear programme was over-ambitious and nationalist. The standardization and learning effects it made possible were cancelled out by changes in reactor models. The two capacity increases, from 900 MW to 1,300 MW, and then from 1,300 MW to 1,450 MW, coincided with substantial, expensive changes in technology. Some were adopted to make the technology French. In an effort to achieve greater independence and improve its chances of exporting its own reactors, France was determined to break free from the US technology used in the first pressurized-water reactors built there (see Chapter 10). The first stage in this process involved the design of the P'4 variant of the first-step 900 MW reactor. This dispensed with the need to pay licence fees to Westinghouse. The second stage brought the original design of a 1,450 MW reactor, but ultimately only four units were built. This model proved more expensive than its predecessor, due to its greater technological complexity and the exclusive use of components and machinery made in France.[14] In addition, construction times grew longer, reaching an average of 126 months for the last four plants, half as much again as for the plants built during the previous step. The French nuclear programme was nearing its end, indeed rather sooner than expected, because growth in demand for electricity, with a corresponding increase in capacity, had been overestimated. Completion of the last reactors was deliberately spread out in time, to adjust to demand and cope with the gradual winding down of the workforce caused by the end of the construction programme. Things are always clearer with the benefit of hindsight, but it does look as though France could have done without the last four reactors, which would have yielded a substantial saving.

Together the US and France have a total of 162 reactors, equivalent to just under a third of global capacity. What is known about the costs of other reactors? Nothing! There is no public source of data for all the nuclear capacity deployed in the former Soviet Union, Japan, India, South Korea or the People's Republic of China. No figures are available to say whether costs escalated there too, less still at what rate. We can only resort to qualitative reasoning. Apart from South Korea and China, it is hard to imagine costs rising less than in France. South Korea enjoys similar conditions, which should have enabled costs to be contained: swift pace of construction; reasonably similar reactor design and layout; well integrated industry and a single operator; nationalist fervour. In fact it may have done better than France. The picture in China is much more disparate, featuring all types of technology – boiling water, pressurized water, heavy water – and many sources: Canada, Russia, France and even the US. However, less than ten years ago China decided to give priority to building large numbers of its own CPR-1000 reactor, derived from the French 900 MW model. The speed of construction has been stupendous, great efforts have been made to standardize processes and the industry is very well organized. The cost of building this reactor has probably dropped with each new unit.

On the other hand the former Soviet Union and India would be plausible candidates for notching up escalating costs even worse than in the US. In the first case because costs under the socialist system were never a key issue when deciding to invest in infrastructure. Politics had more say than economics in the siting of plants, in the choice of model and the speed of construction. India is well placed too, no country having witnessed such a chaotic civil nuclear programme.

Is there no limit to escalating costs?

Will what happened yesterday hold true tomorrow? We are confronted with a classic case of inductive reasoning. We have seen that the second reactor costs more than the first one, the third one more than the second... and that reactor n costs more than $n - 1$. So can we conclude that the same progression will hold true for $n + 1$ and $n + 2$? The immediate answer is affirmative. If you have only

seen black cats in the past, you will be quite prepared to bet they
are all black. In the past nuclear power has reported rising costs, so
nuclear technology is synonymous with rising costs. It is tempting to
generalize, particularly as new next-generation reactors – the ones
following the nth reactor such as the EPR – are again more expensive
than their predecessors. However, we shall see that it is possible to
upset this progression, even if it is much less likely than the previous
trend continuing. Research would also need to explore new routes,
with industry finding ways of standardizing models and developing
modular machinery. If no spell is found to lift the curse of escalating
costs, nuclear power will be gradually sidelined.

At the beginning of the 2000s costs seemed to stop escalating.
Next-generation reactors were expected to bring improved safety,
but they would also be cheaper than their forebears (see box). On
paper the outlook for nuclear costs was rosy, on both sides of the
Atlantic.

Barely ten years later, the first construction projects soon showed
that the de-escalation everyone hoped to see had not yet started. The
next-generation reactors were even more expensive. Present trends
are after all entirely consistent with those of the past.

In 2009 the MIT published a second report,[15] updating the findings
of the initial study six years earlier. The increase in the overnight
cost was spectacular: expressed in current dollars it doubled, rising
from \$2,000 to \$4,000 per kW.[16] In particular this figure took into
account the estimated costs of eleven projected plants in the US, for
which the relevant utilities had applied to the regulatory bodies for
reactor licensing. Meanwhile, the University of Chicago investigated
applications for construction licences for the Westinghouse AP1000.
On average, the overnight cost quoted in applications was \$4,210$_{2010}$
per kW, multiplied by a factor of 2.3, in constant dollars, compared
with a study seven years earlier.[17]

Unlike what occurred in the US, where next-generation reactors
went no further than the drawing board, construction projects in

Costs at renaissance

After a long, sluggish period in western countries, nuclear power woke up again in the early 2000s. New construction projects were tabled in the US and Europe. Many countries with no previous experience of nuclear power were also eager to enter the technological fray. This, it seemed, marked the so-called renaissance of nuclear power. The International Energy Agency forecast the construction of several hundred new plants by 2030. The outlook on costs was naturally just as upbeat. In 2003 the MIT published a study estimating the cost of building a plant with a next-generation reactor. In its base case it assumed an overnight cost of about \$2,000 per kW, which yielded a levelized cost of \$67 per MWh (with an 11.5% discount rate). To situate the latter cost in relation to the past,[18] let us imagine a scale of 1 to 100 ranking existing US plants by rising cost (calculated in constant dollars, adjusted for inflation and with a uniform 6% interest rate[19]). The MIT's projected plant would be ranked nineteenth, in the top 25% least expensive plants ever built, reaching back to the 1970s. In an even rosier scenario, positing a swifter, more flexible response by administrative bodies for the issue of construction permits, the cost would be lower than any plant previously built in the US. A year later the University of Chicago carried out a similar study, reaching comparable conclusions. On the supply side Westinghouse announced an overnight cost for its AP1000 of \$1,400 per kW and a levelized cost of \$27 per kWh.[20] Predictably, this estimate was more optimistic than the ones produced by university research laboratories.

In France the baseline costs were published by the Ministry of Energy. In 2003 the costs for third-generation nuclear plants were estimated at €1,300 per kW for the overnight cost and €28.4 per MWh for the levelized cost (with an 8% discount rate).[21] With these values the EPR bettered, in terms of cost, the reactors on the last step built in France. Industry was slightly less optimistic, with EDF suggesting an overnight cost of between €1,540 and €1,740 per kW and a levelized cost of €33 per MWh.[22]

Europe got off the ground. Work started on two EPRs, one at Olkiluoto, Finland, the other at Flamanville, France. Here the increase in costs has been even more spectacular. In Finland the initial cost of the project when work started was €3 billion, or €1,850 per kW.[23] It has since been revised upwards on several occasions; delays have accumulated too. The final cost is now estimated at €6.6 billion, or €4,125 per kW. The job was supposed to last four and a half years, with grid connection in mid-2009. In the end, production will not start before 2015, at best: say ten years, to be on the safe side. Work at Flamanville started two years later and took the same unhappy route as its elder sister. The initial cost of €3.3 billion[24] has soared to €8.5 billion[25] and the original construction time of under five years will probably stretch to nine years. In the UK, where EDF is considering construction of two EPRs at Hinkley Point, the reported cost is between €17.2 billion and €19.7 billion.[26] So the first EPRs cost much more than the preceding 1,450 MW reactor model, on which they are based.

The changes in academic studies and industrial quotes are so large that it would be easy to make fun of them, or even to suspect deception. But it would be a mistake. It is only natural that the initial estimates of experts and vendors should be a little optimistic. But for new nuclear neither experience nor facts were available to temper initial optimism. After a long period without any new plant being built, a large share of American and French expertise had vanished. Most of the engineers and senior executives who had taken part in the golden age of nuclear power had either moved to another sector or retired. Furthermore, the first cost estimates were drafted when design of the next-generation reactors was still in its early stages. Millions of man-hours were still needed to finalize detailed plans,[27] which inevitably revealed additional costs. Then it was time to obtain quotes from suppliers and to sign contracts for parts and machinery, a process which took the true understanding of costs one step further. The last set of estimates generally focuses on indexed values, in particular the price of raw materials and building materials. This brought additional price increases, the first decade of the 2000s having seen substantial upward pressure on these commodities. The overnight cost of gas- and coal-fired power plants also increased steeply over this period.[28] The difference with nuclear power was that the initial estimates for the fossil-fuel plants were more accurate. They were based on a building process which had never stopped, nor yet slowed down, all over the world, with hundreds of examples on which to draw.

Optimism may also be dictated by self-interest. Utilities in favour of nuclear power and reactor engineering firms stand to gain by reporting low costs in their initial estimates, by only publishing values at the lower end of their spread estimates. On the other hand, much as any trader selling goods to a small number of buyers, on whose custom the business depends, it is not in the interest of reactor vendors and turnkey plant integrators to announce miraculous figures. Making promises which they know they cannot keep permanently saps their credibility in the eyes of customers, bankers and governments. If there was any deceit regarding costs at the renaissance of nuclear power, it was industry which fooled itself.

To put an end to any notion of across-the-board deceit, it should also be borne in mind that the baseline academic studies did not only work on a set of assumptions favourable to nuclear power. The reason why the first MIT study caused such a stir in 2003 was that it made the iconoclastic choice of a high discount rate, which was unfavourable to nuclear power. The MIT highlighted the high financial risk associated with this investment in liberalized electricity markets. As a result, the assumptions regarding the structure and cost of nuclear capital were less attractive than for gas or coal. Nuclear power involved higher capital outlay, less debt and a 15 per cent return on assets, rather than 12 per cent. Without these assumptions the MIT study would have concluded that the excess cost of nuclear power, compared to gas, was only half as large.[29]

There is no escaping the facts and they are particularly stubborn: nuclear power now is much more expensive than before. For the time being third-generation reactors are still plagued by rising costs, and new reactor models bring additional costs. What does the future hold?

With the same design, costs should certainly drop, but by how much? It is impossible to say whether there will be a slight reduction or a huge one. Take the EPR. Its cost is bound to drop, but how far? First-of-a-kind costs are known to be higher, generally by about 20 to 30 per cent,[30] but it is not known how the excess cost is amortized. Does the full burden fall on the first unit, or is it spread over the first five or ten reactors? For obvious reasons – the first customers do not like teething problems – data of this sort is confidential. Furthermore, there has been a loss of experience on the construction side, following a long period without any new projects. Lastly, the first two EPRs are not being built by the same company.

Seen from abroad, the French nuclear industry may look like a homogeneous block: EDF and Areva, both publicly owned companies, seem barely distinguishable. But in fact they have been keen rivals in recent years. Areva went it alone in Finland, operating as a turnkey plant vendor, rather than just selling a reactor, which is its core business. EDF has long-standing experience as both the prime contractor and project owner of nuclear plants. It sees Areva as an original equipment manufacturer, or even – rather disparagingly – as a boiler manufacturer. So learning effects between Olkiluoto and Flamanville are limited. The two firms have been at loggerheads, rather than confidently pooling their experience. The opposite seems to have happened at Taishan, in China, where two EPR-powered plants are being built. EDF and Areva are working together with the prime owner, the China Guangdong Nuclear Power Group, the utility in Guangdong province. For the time being Taishan-1 is on target for both construction time (five years) and cost (€3 billion). Areva management say this is thanks to the return on experience from the Finnish and French jobs.[31] Certainly, between Olkiluoto and Taishan, the supply deadlines have improved by 65%, engineering man-hours for the nuclear steam-supply system are down by 60% and the time taken to build the main components has been cut by 25% to 40%. So the third reactor seems poised to finish first. Work on Taishan-1 started in 2009, after the other two, but it should be connected to the grid before the end of 2014, several years ahead of Olkiluoto and Flamanville. However, return on experience is not the only reason for the impressive performance in China regarding costs and deadlines. The PRC boasts top-notch civil engineering contractors, can count on a seasoned nuclear industry, is deploying a massive programme (with twenty-eight reactors under construction in 2013), and has the advantage of a cheap, well qualified workforce and a well organized site where work continues round the clock, even at weekends.

The last unknown regarding the scale of the drop in the cost of the EPR relates to the number of units ultimately built worldwide. Four, ten, twenty or more? All other things being equal, the more reactors sold, the lower the cost and vice versa. The serpent eats its tail. Potential buyers are price-sensitive – though we do not know whether this effect is very slight or substantial – and learning effects cut costs, though here again we cannot say by how much.

From a technical point of view the key to lower costs is to be found in standardization and modularity. Standardization requires every unit of a particular reactor model to be identical, which is not always the case, due to specific changes demanded by customers or safety authorities. As mentioned above, standardization allows learning effects; we may add that it also facilitates competition between suppliers, another powerful mechanism pushing costs down. Modularity means construction in modules, in other words component parts which are relatively independent one from another, making it easy to separate them and simply assemble them on-site (structural elements, but also cable ducts, reinforced concrete mats, etc.).[32] A good example of modular building is factory-assembly of the roof timbers of a detached house, rather than erecting them piece by piece on-site. Pre-assembly is advantageous because a factory is a sheltered environment and such operations lend themselves to automation, yielding productivity gains. Pre-assembly also reduces the amount of clutter on a building site, streamlining its organization. So modularity has the potential for substantial gains.

So far, our reasoning has been based on an unchanging technological framework. What happens to the costs entailed by nuclear power if we take into account innovation, and the design and development of new reactors? Past form is far from encouraging. We have seen that in France, where conditions were most favourable, each new model led to an increase in the construction cost per kW of installed capacity. Two insurmountable obstacles seem to be preventing a reduction in the cost of new models. The first relates to the increasingly strict rules on safety. It is hard to imagine the authorities certifying a new model with lower safety performance than its predecessors. As time passes experience gained from building and operating plants reveals defects; progress in science and technology provides solutions to correct them. Furthermore, with time, new political risks may emerge (terrorist hijacking of an aircraft to target a power plant, for instance) and, in general, public opinion is increasingly averse to technological risks. The above is true for countries already equipped with nuclear power. For new players safety requirements may be less stringent and they may not require the latest generation of reactors. But, keen to develop their science and technology, such countries are unlikely to resist the appeal of modernity for long.

So the question is whether it is possible to build reactors which are similar to the current generation, but safer and cheaper. Very probably not, but as it is still too soon to pass judgement on the AP1000, we should allow for a positive outcome. Westinghouse designed this reactor with two aims: to provide a mechanical solution to some of the safety problems; and to simplify the overall design. For example, water tanks are positioned on the roof in order to cool the reactor vessel should the need arise, fed by gravity and the pressure inside the system. This more or less halves the need for pumps, valves and pipework. Four AP1000s are currently under construction in China. It will be interesting to see, in a few years' time, whether they cost substantially less to build than the EPR. If the concept is a success, it could lead to the development of improved versions, using the new design rules, but at even lower cost. Nuclear power may finally cast off the curse of rising costs.

The second, apparently insurmountable obstacle concerns on-site construction and short production runs. Much like other large civil engineering projects – bridges, airports or dams – nuclear power plants are mainly built on-site. Progress may be made towards greater modularity, but there is little hope of a 1,000-MW plant one day being put together like a flat-pack kitchen. Civil nuclear power differs from other electricity-generation technologies in that only a small number of units are built. Whereas hundreds or thousands of wind-farms or coal- or gas-fired plants are ordered worldwide every year, there are just a few dozen new nuclear construction projects. One of the reasons is the trend towards building increasingly large reactors. The scale of fixed costs justifies this option, because they can be recouped on a larger volume of electricity output. But there is nevertheless a downside. All other things being equal, the more powerful the reactor, the smaller the number of identical units built. So production runs are short and only a few similar parts and components are manufactured. The trade-off between economies of scale per unit and manufacturing economies of scale has so far tipped in favour of the former.[33] Giving fresh impetus to small-reactor projects would break with this approach.

The example of small reactors is worth looking at, because it demonstrates the scope for radical innovation, which in my opinion offers the only lasting antidote to the curse of rising costs. People have been developing low-power nuclear reactors for many years. They are used to drive nuclear submarines, drawing on work and trials going back to the 1950s. What is new is the sudden emergence of futurist projects. Take for instance the best-known example, funded by Microsoft founder Bill Gates. The project is being developed by TerraPower, in which Gates is the main shareholder. The initial aim has been to produce a mini-reactor several metres high, running on natural uranium and cooled by liquid sodium. It is based on the travelling-wave principle, with the reaction slowly spreading outwards from the core of a block of uranium. Picture a candle with a flame inside gradually advancing as it consumes the surrounding wax. For the reactor itself, imagine a cylinder less than one metre high, which requires no outside intervention once the reaction has started and which shuts down on its own after several tens of years. We may also cite the project for an underwater nuclear power plant being developed by France's naval defence firm DCNS. In this case the cylinder is 100 metres long and 15 metres in diameter, containing a reactor and remote-controlled electricity generating plant. With several tens of MWs' capacity, it would be located out to sea, several kilometres from the coastline, anchored to the seabed. The cylinders would be modular units, several of which could be placed side by side in the case of higher output requirements. The units would be taken back to a shipyard for maintenance and replaced by other units, much like bottles with a refundable deposit.

These projects, which sound even more fantastic when described so succinctly, will very probably never see the light of day. Either they will founder completely or change so much that the final application bears no resemblance to the initial concept. It matters little to our current concerns. That is how radical innovation works: projects pursuing a large number of original ideas are launched; very few give rise to pilot schemes; an even smaller number lead to commercial projects; and in each case the ongoing redefinition process will shift pilot schemes and commercial goods further and further away from the original idea. Obviously there is no way of knowing in advance whether, out of the hundreds of current and future projects to develop modular small or mini-reactors similar to those discussed above, at least one could reach fruition and enter industrial production. But unless nuclear research moves away from the present model of large, non-modular plants and gigantic construction projects, the costs of nuclear technology will likely continue to rise, which is a serious drawback in the competition between nuclear power and other electricity-generating technologies.

THREE

Nuclear power and its alternatives

We cannot do without oil but we may, on the other hand, stop using the atom. We should never lose sight of the fact that there are several means of generating electricity, using among others coal, gas, oil, biomass, solar radiation and wind. At the scale of a whole country these generating technologies are generally combined to form an energy mix, which may or may not include nuclear power, much as it may or may not include thermal coal or gas, wind or solar.

The various technologies are both competitors and complementary. Conventionally a distinction is made between baseload generating technologies, coal-fired power stations for example, which operate round the clock all year long, and peak generating technologies, such as oil-fired power plants, which only operate at times of peak demand. With a finer mesh, further categories can be distinguished, of semi-baseload and extreme-peak generation. The overall idea is to classify production resources in such a way that the ones with high fixed costs and low variable costs are used for as many hours a year as possible, while on the other hand those with low fixed costs and high variable costs are only used for a few hours a year.

Two categories of baseload technology – coal and nuclear – are in competition, whereas oil-fired technology is complementary. However, in situations where they overlap this ranking may change. For example gas, which tends to be seen as a semi-baseload resource, may play a primary role as a baseload resource; nuclear power may lend itself to load-balancing (as in France, for example) and is con-sequently suitable as a semi-baseload resource.[1] Renewable energy sources also upset the ranking. Hydro-electric power from dams is generally seen as a peaking resource, despite its extremely high fixed cost and variable operating cost close to zero, the explanation being that its variable cost should in fact be treated as a marginal oppor-tunity cost. It is preferable to hold back a cubic metre of water for peak hours with correspondingly high prices, rather than wasting it by generating electricity at times when demand drops and the price is low. Regarding wind and solar, production is intermittent because it depends on the force of the wind or the amount of sunlight, which vary in the course of a day, and from one day to the next, quite beyond our control. Here again variable technical costs are close to zero, but the irregular nature of output makes it impossible to classify these technologies among baseload resources. At the same time, the lack of any way of controlling them means they cannot be treated as peaking resources. If intermittent renewable energy sources play a significant part in the energy mix, back-up capacity must be available – generally gas-fired plants – to take over in the absence of sunlight and wind. Under these circumstances gas and the renewable energy are complementary. However the growth of inter-mittent energy sources pushes the market price of electricity down and baseload and semi-baseload sources operate for shorter periods. This creates competition between nuclear power and gas, on the one hand, and renewable energy sources, on the other.

Lastly, nuclear power and renewables have one characteristic in common: they produce no CO_2 emissions. They may consequently be seen as rivals for achieving the targets set for reducing greenhouse gas emissions, or alternatively, as it seems difficult to rely exclusively on just one of these sources, they may be seen as complementary, with a view to completely carbon-free electricity generation. To simplify matters, any comparison of nuclear electricity should make allowance for two factors: on the one hand its competitive or complementary position in relation to coal or gas, for baseload electricity production; and on the other hand its competitive or complementary position in relation to other carbon-free energy sources.

The relative competitive advantage of nuclear power over gas or coal

The levelized cost enables us to classify the various generating technologies. Which one, out of coal, gas or nuclear power, offers the lowest cost? How do these forms of energy rate in the overall cost ranking? In fact, our obsession with rank prompts us to ask the wrong questions, which only yield contingent answers.

There is no single ranking system because the costs depend on different locations and hypotheses on future outcomes. With regard to nuclear power we have seen that the cost varies from one site to another, from one country to the next, and that it above all depends on the discount rate. The cost of fuel is the key parameter for coal and gas. But the price of energy resources depends on geography. The cost of transporting coal or gas being high, building a fossil-fuel power plant in one place or another yields different results. Furthermore, market prices fluctuate a great deal, particularly for gas, often indexed to the price of oil. The rate of return on an investment in a new fossil-fuel plant depends on assumptions as to how fuel prices will behave over the next ten or twenty years. Consequently it is only possible to use the levelized cost to rank coal, gas or nuclear power on the basis of a very specific set of conditions, valid at the geographical scale of a country and in line with the expectations of specific operators. For example, taking a broad-brush approach to the current position in the US, gas enjoys a comfortable lead, followed by coal, with nuclear power in third place. This ranking may vary between US states depending on the proximity of coal-mining resources and unconventional gas reserves.

We should nevertheless bear in mind a few, almost universal trends and shifts, which also happen to explain to a large extent the current US ranking of baseload generating technologies: before and after climate-change policy; before and after shale gas; before and after deregulation of the electricity market.

In a world with no pollution-abatement measures, coal would lead the pack with the cheapest MWh almost all over the world. But using it to generate electricity causes local pollution (release of dust, soot, sulphur and nitrogen oxides) and CO_2 emissions. The first group is by far the most costly, unless a very high price is set for CO_2 (in excess of \$100 per tonne). In ExternE, the major European study of the externalities of generating electricity, the damage caused by coal, setting aside that linked to CO_2 emissions, was estimated at between \$27$_{2010}$ and \$202$_{2010}$ per MWh. The lower value in this range is about the same as the one reported by William Nordhaus and other authors in a conservative assessment dating from 2011.[2] As for the upper value, it is comparable to that found in a maximalist study by Professor Paul Epstein, at Harvard, published the same year.[3] Taking the values which the experts consider to be the 'best estimates', we may note that the cost of a coal-generated MWh doubles when we include its externalities.

The large divergence between the upper and lower values in the estimates can be partly explained by the different types of plant under consideration and the prevailing environmental standards. In OECD countries the regulatory framework for local emissions from coal is very strict. Part of the externalities is internalized by emissions standards, which raise the overnight cost of coal-fired thermal plants, and consequently the levelized cost of energy for the utility. Similarly, some OECD countries have introduced a carbon price, or are planning to do so. Depending on their level, such taxes and tradable emissions permits internalize, to a greater or lesser extent, a share of CO_2 externalities and add to the variable cost borne by the utility. On the other hand, in most developing or emerging countries, the cost of a coal-generated MWh is still low because neither investors nor utilities pay for any part of the environmental damage entailed, in the absence of both regulations on local pollution and a carbon price. This lack of symmetry explains why it is now almost out of the question to build coal-fired power plants in the US, the UK or Japan, whereas such facilities are springing up in China, Malaysia, Senegal and South Africa. In terms of new electricity-generating capacity being installed, coal is the technology which has enjoyed by far the strongest growth worldwide since 2000. In the long term, the cost of a coal-generated MWh in non-OECD countries is expected to rise, reducing the gap. The localized pollution and damage this technology entails for public health exert pressure which encourages a shift towards other, more expensive technologies which cause less pollution. In OECD countries it is more difficult to predict future developments. The application of R&D work on clean coal, particularly for carbon capture and storage technology, is uncertain. Future trends for the price of CO_2 emissions are equally uncertain.

Gas has a very different environmental profile from coal, with little or no local pollution, and half the volume of CO_2 emissions. This explains its growth in OECD countries, at the expense of coal. The price of gas delivered to the generating plant is generally higher than for coal, but this competitive disadvantage is counterbalanced by incomparably lower environmental costs.[4] There is certainly a before and after unconventional gas here, because this advantage is now being enhanced by lower costs due to new gas-exploitation techniques (horizontal drilling and hydraulic fracturing), and the resulting extension of reserves. In the US, where shale gas was first exploited (alongside Canada), this change means that nuclear power is durably losing its status as a baseload generating technology. Gas is now in first place and is likely to stay there for a long while.

However, it should be borne in mind that unconventional gas currently enjoys a novelty effect, which means its social cost is underestimated. It took decades to estimate the economic externalities of coal, conventional natural gas and nuclear power. They took shape as science advanced in its understanding of the effects of pollution and on-site measurements. The dissemination of scientific advances and the results of metrology, beyond the confines of laboratories and a small number of experts, works on a specific time scale. None of this applies to shale gas, yet. The measurements and studies have barely started, particularly to estimate greenhouse gas emissions and possible damage to aquifers. It is plausible to suppose that what has so far been gained through lower exploitation costs may tomorrow be lost to rising environmental costs. Lastly it is worth noting that the decision by some markets to delink oil and gas prices gives the latter an advantage which is likely to last. Until now, in many countries gas prices were driven up by the rising price of oil. Oil-indexed gas supply contracts were encouraged by various factors: comparable extraction conditions; joint production in some cases; and markets offering imperfect competition, due to the dominant position of monopsonists. In places where the exploitation of conventional gases has developed, this arrangement has been destroyed.

Liberalization of the gas and electricity markets is the third key shift which changes the relative competitiveness of baseload generating technologies. Here too nuclear power has lost ground on the whole. For many years the gas and electricity markets were organized as municipal, regional or national monopolies subject to regulated tariff schemes. Regardless of whether generating companies belonged to the public or private sector, the investments they made were exposed to little risk, being paid back by captive consumers. Dependent on the authorities, these companies often acted as cogs in the implementation of energy policies based on factors related to cost, but also to national independence, scientific prestige, job creation and such.

Instigated by some US states and the UK, privatization and the opening up of the gas and electricity markets to competition upset this model. In its place, or alongside it, another model was established in which the link between production and captive consumption was broken, and in which investment was decided by shareholders and bankers. From being utilities – public service providers – the electricity generating companies became operators at the head of merchant plants, power stations selling electricity to the wholesale market. The risks here were not of the same order. Much like football teams that compete on the same playing field, be it muddy or too hard, one might suppose that liberalization would affect all the electricity generating technologies in the same way. Accordingly the new deal should not alter their competitive positions in relation to one another. In practice this did not prove to be the case for nuclear power, which, as far as the financiers were concerned, involved greater, more serious risks:[5] higher risks of budget overruns and missed deadlines, in the course of construction and during operation (e.g. safety defects leading to unpredictable reactor shutdowns and consequently lost output); a long period over which to recover investment, increasing the risk due to uncertainty in prices on the wholesale electricity markets; higher regulatory and political risks due to the opposition of part of public opinion and some political parties to atomic energy. In the face of these additional risks, the MIT 2003 study cited above set a weighted average capital cost 25 per cent higher than for gas and coal, which pushed up the cost per MWh of nuclear power by 33 per cent.

We may observe that it makes little sense to rely on the levelized cost method in an economy with liberalized energy markets. The rationale used to establish the price of electricity, which balances income and expenditure, including the remuneration of capital, is more in keeping with regulated electricity tariffs set by the authorities. In a market economy, electricity prices fluctuate; they are uncertain, just like the price of fuel consumed by generating plants, or the price of tradable emissions permits. The solution is to use the conventional method for calculating the return on a project in terms of net present value, while taking into account the uncertainties.

The price of electricity can thus be treated as a variable, which is associated with a distribution function (e.g. a bell curve, on which the peak represents the most probable expected value and the extremities the lowest and highest values, of low probability). Similarly various values with a range of probabilities are allocated to the other variables affecting income or outgoings. Then we shake up all these data, carrying out repeated random sampling, thousands of times – using the Monte Carlo method, in reference to roulette. We thus obtain the risk profile for the investment, in other words a curve showing the losses and gains it may produce, each level of loss and gain being associated with a probability. If the curve is relatively flat the risk is high, because the probability is more or less the same for low or high rates of return, both positive and negative. If the curve rises sharply, the risk is low, with a substantial probability that the rate of return will be centred near the peak, be it positive or negative.

The merit of this probabilistic approach is that it yields a mean value (obviously essential to knowing whether the return will be positive or negative, low or high), but also an indication of the possible variances on either side of the mean. Assisted by other authors, Fabien Roques has used this approach to obtain a better comparison of baseload electricity generating technologies.[6] With a whole series of possible hypotheses – in particular a 10 per cent discount rate – their research shows that gas yields higher profits than nuclear power, at a lower risk, the latter point being due to the gains achieved by more flexible plant operation. The load factor, instead of being constant throughout the service life of plants, varies according to the market price of electricity. If the price results in a loss, production stops, starting again when the net present value is once again positive. A second interesting outcome of this work is that it puts figures on the complementary relation between gas and electricity. A portfolio of assets, with gas-fired plants making up 80% of capacity and nuclear power the remainder, yields a lower average return than an exclusively gas-fired portfolio, but entails less risk. Investors may prefer this combination, which offers better protection, particularly from high but unlikely losses incurred if gas and carbon prices are high, a situation which has no effect on nuclear power.

The competitive advantages of nuclear power and renewable energies

In suitable locations onshore wind farms display levelized costs comparable to those of nuclear plants. Neither technology releases CO_2 emissions and both are characterized by high fixed costs. However, although nuclear power has a low marginal cost (about €6 per MWh for fuel[7]), for wind the cost is zero. (The same is true of solar but, except under extremely favourable conditions, its levelized cost is way above that of nuclear.) From an economic point of view this difference is of fundamental importance, because in an electricity market the optimal price is equal to the marginal cost of the marginal unit, in other words the unit that needs to be generated to meet instantaneous demand. When instantaneous demand is at its lowest, generally in the middle of the night, only baseload plants are used. If massive wind capacity were to be installed, the night breeze would blow away gas and coal (perhaps even nuclear) during off-peak hours, reducing their load factor and raising their respective costs per MWh. In fact the loss would be even greater. Coal-fired or nuclear power plants do not ramp up to full capacity or shut down instantaneously. So slowing down or stopping output at night would reduce the power available in the early morning. To sell more electricity at times when prices are higher, it may be in the interest of baseload plant operators to bid negative prices in order to keep their plants running all night. So at certain times of the day, large scale wind capacity would result in a market price equal to its marginal cost, in other words zero, and even, at other times, in a lower market price, equal to the opportunity cost of baseload operators forgoing a reduction in output.

Not taking into account variations in demand distorts the results when calculating the levelized cost. Paul Joskow, at MIT, has shown that this method is unsuitable for intermittent renewables.[8] Only exceptionally are intermittent energies in sync with demand. The wind does not blow harder at the beginning or end of the day, nor yet during the five working days of the week, which is when power demand is highest. To simplify matters we shall suppose that peak and off-peak hours are evenly distributed throughout the year. We shall then suppose that an intermittent renewable plant produces two-thirds of its output at off-peak hours, the remaining third at peak hours, and that its levelized cost per MWh is the same as that of a baseload plant. If the country as a whole needs one additional MWh of power, the levelized cost method tells us that it makes no difference whether we invest in wind power or a baseload technology. Yet the second option is more useful because it will produce proportionately more at peak hours: with all-year-round output it operates half of the time at peak hours, the other half off-peak. So the levelized cost method is biased against investment in baseload technology. It is also worth noting that it distorts the ranking of intermittent renewable energies. As the sun does not shine at night, a solar plant generally responds in a larger proportion to peak demand in summer than a wind farm. To compare investment projects in various generating technologies, it is consequently wiser to use the net present value method to estimate income on the basis of the hourly generation profiles of plants and the electricity prices expected at different times of the day.

A third form of distortion which handicaps nuclear power is specific to Europe. The EU has set targets for renewable energies. By 2020 renewables are slated to account for 20 per cent of final energy consumption. As applied to electricity this target means that renewables should supply 35 per cent of all electricity. Measures of this sort requiring a share of renewables in the overall energy mix are commonplace. Most US states apply similar measures. But the EU is unusual in that the measure operates in parallel with a carbon price. The EU system of tradable emissions permits already adds to the cost of fossil-fuel-generated electricity, compared to nuclear power or renewables, changing their relative competitiveness in the same way as a carbon tax. For example, with a permit costing €30 per tonne of CO_2, it costs about €30 per MWh more to generate 1 MWh using coal. Adding a target for renewables to this scheme pushes the price of carbon down. The 20 per cent target for 2020 was set without adjusting the cap on CO_2 emissions decided when the Emissions Trading Scheme was originally set up. As a result the cut in emissions, made compulsory by the renewables quota, restricts demand for permits. So their price drops. David Newbery has estimated that the price of permits will be driven down by €10 per tonne by 2020, from €60 to €50.[9] To avoid this downward pressure, the cap on emissions should have been lowered to allow for the volume of CO_2 recently avoided, in such a way as to achieve the target of 35 per cent electricity from renewable sources. In conclusion, the quota for renewable energies in the EU energy mix has a dual effect. It deprives nuclear power of part of its potential market, despite its also being carbon-free, and makes it less competitive by doing less to increase the price of competing baseload technologies, due to a lower carbon price.

We need to see the electricity system as a whole in order to grasp the relative competitive advantages of nuclear power and renewables. As wind, solar and wave are intermittent energy sources, and storing electricity is very expensive, large-scale development of renewables involves building back-up capacity to make up for the lack of wind, sunlight or tide at certain times. Such capacity is far from negligible. For Ireland to meet its target for the 2020 renewables quota, it will have to install 30 GW more renewable capacity, while providing a further 15–20 GW of non-intermittent capacity as a back-up.[10] To enable such supplementary capacity to be built, the country must either agree to stupendous electricity prices (several thousands of euros per MWh) at certain times of day, or set

up capacity markets to pay utilities even when they are not producing anything. Otherwise the plant will simply not be built, because
investors will anticipate difficulties covering fixed costs due to the
insufficient load factor. Nuclear power, dogged by higher fixed costs
than gas and less flexible production, is ill suited to catering for this
new demand. All other things being equal, the more intermittent
energies develop, the more the competitiveness of nuclear power
with regard to gas will be undermined.

Looking beyond 2020 we see no sign of a possible improvement
in the competitiveness of nuclear power compared with renewables:
quite the opposite. The development of storage technologies and
ongoing learning effects for wind and solar represent serious threats.
Using batteries to store electricity is still outrageously expensive. So
far the only alternative solution to have been developed is pumped-
storage hydroelectricity. This involves using electrical pumps to raise
water from one reservoir to another at a higher elevation. Meanwhile
research is focusing on countless other possibilities. What results and
applications will research yield over the next twenty years? Without
an answer it is hard to see whether electricity storage will one day be
sufficiently affordable to be deployed on a very large scale. Realizing
such a possibility would remedy the main shortcoming of intermittent renewable energy and substantially increase its economic value,
at least for renewables for which the cost is currently close to that of
more traditional technologies. This is the case for onshore wind, setting aside the sources of distortion cited above. In the future it might
also be the case for offshore wind, and photovoltaic or concentrated
solar. The costs of these technologies have dropped substantially,
with scope for powerful learning effects. But we shall once again
concentrate on terrestrial wind power.

The levelized cost per MWh of onshore wind power was divided
by three, allowing for inflation, between the early 1980s and the
late 2000s.[11] Estimates indicate learning effects between 10 and
20 per cent.[12] However, a closer look reveals that the reduction in

the levelized cost in constant dollars stopped in 2005, and that the levelized cost has actually risen since. Is this a sign that the technology has reached maturity, with an end to diminishing costs? Very probably not, as shown by the report by the US National Renewable Energy Laboratory. The rise in costs towards the end of the 2000s is due to the increase in the price of materials and machinery, and a flattening out of performance gains. But since then performance gains have started to improve and the cost per MW of installed capacity is steady. The levelized cost across all wind speeds started dropping again in 2012, down on 2009. The NREL has also compared a dozen prospective studies looking ahead to 2030, covering eighteen scenarios in all. Most of them predict a 20–30 per cent reduction in the levelized cost. Only one forecasts that it will remain steady. These results obviously concern specific wind classes. The average performance of wind capacity in a country or region may decline over time, due to the less favourable characteristics of more recent locations, the first wind farms having occupied the spots with the best conditions. The issue of siting is the only factor driving costs upwards. However, in the future it would be more than offset by the gains derived from mass production and higher performance fed by R&D.

So nuclear has been caught in a pincer movement, so to speak. In OECD countries its high cost, particularly with regard to capital, is a handicap compared to gas. It is only competitive if a carbon price is introduced – a fairly high one at that. On the other hand, setting aside onshore wind power, it is still more cost-effective than intermittent renewables. So in principle there is every reason why it should feature in a mix of carbon-free generating technologies. But only in principle, because in practice it is sidelined and hampered by quotas for renewable energies. In other countries nuclear power is at a disadvantage when compared to cheap, polluting coal, but at least the prospects are a little better. Demand for energy is often so great that all technologies are considered. Large countries such as

China and India can plausibly hope to reduce costs through large-scale production and learning effects. Smaller nations may count on the advantage derived from keen competition between vendors of turnkey solutions (see Chapter 10).

On reaching the end of the first part of this book, readers may feel slightly bereft, having lost any sense of certainty regarding costs. There is no such thing as a 'true' cost for nuclear power, which economists may discover after much trial and error. Nor yet are there any hidden external costs, such as those related to managing waste or the risk of serious accidents, which might completely change the picture if they were taken into account. Far from reducing the cost of nuclear power, technical progress has actually contributed to its increase. It makes no sense to assert that it is currently more or less expensive, in terms of euros per MWh, to build a wind farm or a nuclear power plant. There can be no universally valid ranking order for coal, gas and the atom based on the cost of generating electricity.

But the loss of such illusions should not leave readers in a vacuum. The first part has also provided a firm basis for assessing the costs of electricity, which depend on location and various hypotheses on future developments. Consequently such costs can only be properly calculated with a clear understanding of both factors.[13] The construction cost of a nuclear power plant is not the same in Finland, China or the United States. Overall expenditure may vary a great deal depending on the influence of the safety regulator, scale effects and the cost of capital. Regarding wagers, the future prices of gas, coal and carbon dioxide will be largely decisive in the ranking of coal, gas and nuclear power. These same prices will also affect the profit margins of nuclear plants, their revenue depending on the number of hours per year during which they operate, and whether the prices per kWh during those hours are decided by a marginal generating plant burning coal or gas, or one powered by sunlight or wind. Confronted by the risky long-term wagers which investors must make to calculate costs and take decisions, even the most laissez-faire public authority will feel obliged to intervene. Concerned by the general interest, it must set a discount rate, the parameter with the greatest impact on the cost of nuclear power. This particular wager hinges on how prosperous future generations may be: the richer they are, the lower the discount rate will be, making nuclear power that much cheaper. Furthermore, there is a political choice to be made, in order to maintain a certain degree of equity between rich and poor, and between generations, a choice which influences the rate set for converting present dollars into future dollars.

What is more, analysing trends for past costs throws light on their future behaviour. Historically, nuclear technology has been characterized by rising costs. Today's third-generation reactors are no exception to this iron rule. They are safer than earlier counterparts, but also more expensive. The escalation of costs may stop, but only on two conditions: through a massive scale effect – if China chooses one type of reactor and sticks to it, it may achieve this effect – or through a fundamental change in direction of innovation, giving priority to modular design and small reactors, for instance. Failing this, nuclear technology seems doomed to suffer a steady decline in its competitiveness compared with any thermal technologies spared by taxes and renewable energies boosted by high learning effects.

Setting aside any consideration of possible accidents, it would be an economically risky choice for an operator to invest in building new nuclear power plants or for a state to facilitate such projects.

PART II

The risk of a major nuclear accident

Calculation and perception of probabilities

The accident at Fukushima Daiichi, Japan, occurred on 11 March 2011. This nuclear disaster left a lasting mark in the minds of hundreds of millions of people. Much as Three Mile Island or Chernobyl, yet another place will be permanently associated with a nuclear power plant which went out of control. Fukushima Daiichi revived the issue of the hazards of civil nuclear power, stirring up all the associated passion and emotion.

The whole of Part II is devoted to the risk of a major nuclear accident. By this we mean a failure initiating core meltdown, a situation in which the fuel rods melt and mix with their metal cladding. Such accidents are classified as at least level five on the International Nuclear Event Scale. The Three Mile Island accident, which occurred in 1979 in the United States, reached this level of severity. The explosion of reactor four at the Chernobyl plant in Ukraine in 1986 and the recent accident in Japan were classified as level seven, the highest grade on this logarithmic scale.[1] The main difference between the top two levels and level five relates to a significant or major release of radioactive material to the environment. In the event of a level-five accident, damage is restricted to the inside of the plant, whereas, in the case of level-seven accidents, huge areas of land, above or below the surface, and/or sea may be contaminated.[2]

Before the meltdown of reactors one, two and three at Fukushima Daiichi, eight major accidents affecting nuclear power plants had occurred worldwide.[3] This is a high figure compared with the one calculated by the experts. Observations in the field do not appear to fit the results of the probabilistic models of nuclear accidents

produced since the 1970s. Oddly enough, the number of major accidents is closer to the risk as perceived by the general public. In
general we tend to overestimate any risk relating to rare, fearsome
accidents. What are we to make of this divergence? How are we to
reconcile observations of the real world, the objective probability of
an accident and the subjective assessment of risks? Did the experts err
on the side of optimism? Is public opinion irrational when it comes
to the hazards of nuclear power? How should risk and its perception
be measured?

FOUR

Calculating risk

In Part I we made the tentative suggestion that the cost of accidents was low, indeed negligible, when compared with the value of the electricity generated. This introductory conclusion was based on a scratch calculation drawing on upper-case assumptions, multiplying the (ill) chance of a disaster of 1 in 100,000 years of a reactor's operation by damage costing €1,000 billion. The cost of such an accident amounts to €1 per MWh generated. Setting aside the back of an envelope, which lends itself to quick, simple calculations, we shall now look at the matter in greater detail, from both a theoretical and an empirical standpoint.

Calculating the cost of major accidents

Is the cost per MWh of an accident negligible, at less than 10 euro cents? Or is it just visible, at about €1, or rather a significant fraction of the several tens of euros that a MWh costs to generate? How does our scratch calculation, in Part I, compare with existing detailed assessments and how were the latter obtained?

Risk is the combination of a random event and a consequence. To calculate the risk of an accident, the probability of its occurrence is multiplied by the damage it causes.[1] Much like many other forms of disaster, a major nuclear accident is characterized by an infinitesimal probability and huge damage. A frequently used short-cut likens the former to zero, the latter to infinity. As we all know, multiplying zero by infinity results in an indeterminate quantity. The short-cut is easy but idiotic. The probability of an accident is not zero; unfortunately, some have already occurred. Nor yet is the damage infinite. Even the worst-case accident on a nuclear reactor cannot lead to the destruction of the planet and humankind. (Would the latter outcome, following a collision with an asteroid 10 kilometres in diameter, for example, or quarks going out of control in a particle accelerator, count as infinite damage?[2]) Mathematically, multiplying a very small number by a very large one always produces a determinate value. So nuclear risk assessments seek to approximate the two numbers and then multiply them.

In its worst-case scenario ExternE, the major European study of the external effects of various energy sources published in 1995, estimated the cost of an accident at €83 billion. This estimate was based on the hypothetical case of a core melt on a 1,250 MW reactor, followed two hours later by emissions lasting only an hour containing 10 per cent of the most volatile elements (caesium, iodine) of the core. The population was exposed to a collective dose of 291,000 person-sieverts.[3] This contamination ultimately caused about 50,000 cancers, one-third of which were fatal, and 3,000 severe hereditary effects. In a few days it caused 138 diseases and 9 fatalities. The impact on public health accounted for about two-thirds of the accident's cost. The study also assessed the cost of restrictions on farming (lost production, agricultural capital, etc.), and the cost of evacuating and re-housing local residents. This string of figures gives only a tiny idea of all the data required to estimate the cost of a nuclear accident. It merely lists some of the main parameters, in other words those that may double, or indeed multiply by ten, the total cost of economic damage. Let us now take a closer look.

In theory the extent of emissions may reach the release of the entire contents of the reactor core. The explosion at Chernobyl released the equivalent of 30 per cent of the radioactive material in the reactor, a huge, unprecedented proportion. Emissions from

Fukushima Daiichi's three damaged reactors are estimated to have amounted to ten times less than the amount released in Ukraine. The collective dose is the radiation dose measured in person-sieverts and the sum of the radiation absorbed by groups of people subject to varying levels of exposure. The collective dose depends on emissions, but also the weather conditions and population density. Depending on whether radioactivity is deposited by rain on an area of woodland or a city, the number of people exposed will obviously vary. The person-Sv unit is used because it is generally assumed that the biological effects of radiation follow a linear trend: the health effect of exposure of 20,000 people to 1 millisievert or 20 people to 1 sievert is consequently taken as being the same. This approach is based on the assumption that even the lowest level of exposure is sufficient to increase the number of fatalities and diseases, in particular cancer. It is controversial because it implies that the natural radioactivity that exists in some areas, such as Brittany in France, exposes local residents to a specific hazard. For our present purposes we shall treat it as an upper-case hypothesis, in comparison with the one setting a threshold below which ionizing radiation has no effect.

Translating the collective dose into figures for fatalities and diseases then depends on which effect one decides to use. For example, positing a 5 per cent risk factor of a fatal cancer to 100 people who have accumulated an equivalent-dose of 1 Sv means that five will be affected by the disease under consideration. The final step in assessing health effects involves choosing a monetary value for human life. Without that it is impossible to add the damage to public health to the other consequences, such as population displacement or soil decontamination. There are several methods for calculating the value of human life, based for example on the amount allocated to reducing road accidents or the average contribution of a single individual to their country's economy, in terms of gross domestic product.[4]

The assumptions used in studies of the quantity and dispersion of emissions, the collective dose received, the risk factor, the value of human life, the number of people displaced or indeed the amount of farmland left sterile all contribute to creating substantial disparities in estimates.[5] Just looking at two indicators – the number of additional cancers and the total cost of an accident – is sufficient to grasp the scale of variations. In the ExternE study cited above, the scenario corresponding to the largest volume of emissions led to 49,739 cancers and cost €83.2 billion$_{1995}$, whereas the scenario with the lowest emissions led to 2,380 cancers and cost €3.3 billion$_{1995}$. In a recent German study,[6] the low-case values calculated were 255,528 cancers and €199 billion$_{2011}$ – which corresponds to frequently quoted orders of magnitude. But the high-case figures reported by the study are far larger, with 5.3 million cancers and €5,566 billion$_{2011}$. It is unusual for experts to produce such a high estimate, with a single accident leading to millions of cancers and total damage amounting to thousands of billions of euros. However, it is close to the orders of magnitude reported in the first studies carried out in the 1980s after the Chernobyl disaster.[7] Allowance must nevertheless be made for such extreme figures, which correspond to worst-case scenarios. For example, in the German study just mentioned, the weather conditions were strong wind, changing in direction, and light rain (1 mm per hour). The rain and wind severely contaminated an area of 22,900 square kilometres (a circle about 85 km in diameter), occupied by millions of people who had to be evacuated. The most catastrophic scenarios obviously correspond to accidents at power plants in densely populated areas. Some 8.3 million people live inside a 30-kilometre radius round the nuclear power plant at Karachi, Pakistan. Worldwide there are twenty-one nuclear plants with more than a million people living within a 30-kilometre radius around them.[8]

Rather than picking a random number from the various damage assessments, the right approach would be to take these uncertainties into account, particularly the ones which affect the collective dose and risk factor. Let us suppose an accident has occurred with a given quantity of emissions. We need to plot a curve indicating, for example, that there is a 1% probability of the event causing economic losses in excess of €1,000 billion, a 10% probability of losses ranging from €500 billion and €999 billion, or indeed a 5% probability of losses below €1 billion. In conceptual terms an exercise of this sort is easy to carry out. But in practice the problem is obtaining sufficient data on variations in the determinants of damage. This is the case for weather parameters: the wind and rainfall conditions have been statistically established for each plant. But for many other factors, the scale of their variation is unknown, in which case it must be modelled on the basis of purely theoretical considerations.

There have been too few accidents in the past with significant emissions to allow observation of the statistical variations affecting their impacts, such as the frequency of cancers. We do not even know exactly how many fatal cancers followed the Chernobyl disaster. This is not so much due to a lack of epidemiologic studies or monitoring of the local population – several studies have been carried out since the accident – nor yet to their manipulation inspired by some conspiracy theory. On the contrary, the uncertainty is due to the fact that cancer is a very common cause of death and cancers caused by ionizing radiation are difficult to isolate. According to the Chernobyl Forum – a group of international organizations, including the World Health Organization – of the 600,000 people who received the highest radiation doses (emergency recovery workers, or liquidators, and residents of the most severely contaminated areas), 4,000 fatal cancers caused by radiation are likely to be added to the 100,000 or so cancers normally expected for a population group of this size. Among the 5 million people exposed to less severe contamination and living in the three most affected countries (Ukraine, Belarus and the Russian Federation), the Forum forecasts that the number of additional fatal cancers will amount to several thousand, ten thousand at the very most. This estimate is one of the lowest in the literature. For the whole population of the contaminated areas in the three countries, estimates vary between 4,000 and 22,000 additional deaths.[9] It should be noted that these figures do not take into account emissions outside the officially contaminated areas, nor in other parts of these countries, nor yet in Europe or the rest of the world. The second set of estimates is less reliable, more controversial, as radiation exposure per person is very low. Only the hypothesis of a linear relationship between dose and effect leads to additional fatal cancers outside the three areas, estimated for example at 24,700 by Lisbeth Gronlund, a senior scientist at the US Union of Concerned Scientists.[10]

If we accept the rough estimate suggested in Part I for the purposes of illustration, with a €1,000 billion loss for a major nuclear accident, we would not only be somewhere in the upper range of estimates but substantially exceeding the estimated cost of actual accidents in the past: Three Mile Island cost an estimated $1 billion[11] and Chernobyl several hundreds of billions of dollars.[12]

Calculating the frequency of major accidents

We shall now turn to the task of putting figures on the probability of a major nuclear accident. The ExternE study reports a probability of a core melt at 5×10^{-5} per reactor-year,[13] in other words a 0.00005 chance of an accident on a reactor operating for one year; or alternatively, due to the selected unit, a frequency of five accidents for 100,000 years of reactor operation, or indeed a frequency of five accidents a year if the planet boasted a fleet of 100,000 reactors in operation. Following a core melt, two possibilities are considered: either an eight-in-ten chance that radiation will remain confined inside the reactor containment; or a two-in-ten chance that part of the radiation will be released into the environment. In the first case damage is estimated at €431 million, in the second case at

€83.252 billion. As we do not know which of the two scenarios will actually happen, the forecast damage is calculated using its expected value, in other words: $0.8 \times 431 + 0.2 \times 83{,}252$, which equals roughly €17 billion. This simple example illustrates two connected concepts, which are essential to understanding probabilistic analysis of accidents: conditional probability and event trees (see box).

The main purpose of probabilistic safety assessments is not to estimate the probability of an accident for a specific plant or reactor, but rather to detect exactly what may go wrong, to identify the weakest links in the process and to understand the failures which most contribute to the risk of an accident. In short, such studies are a powerful instrument for preventing risks and ranking priorities, focusing attention on the points where efforts are required to improve safety. But our obsession with single numbers has pushed this goal into the background and all we remember of these studies is the final probability they calculate, namely *core-melt frequency*.

This bias is all the more unfortunate because the overall result is rarely weighted by any measure of uncertainty. If no confidence interval is indicated, we do not know whether the figure reported – for example 1 accident per 100,000 reactor-years – is very close to the mean value, for example an eight-in-ten likelihood that the accident frequency ranges from 0.9 to 1.1 accidents per 100,000 reactor-years, or more widely spread, with an eight-in-ten likelihood that the frequency ranges between 0.1 and 10 accidents per 100,000 reactor-years. Intuitively it is not the same risk, but in both cases the mean frequency is the same. In the second case there is some likelihood that more than ten accidents will occur per 100,000 reactor-years, whereas in the first case this risk is almost non-existent. Of the studies which have estimated the uncertainty, it is worth noting an NRC appraisal carried out in 1990 on five plants. It found, for example, that for the two pressurized water reactors at Surry (Virginia) the confidence interval for the mean frequency of 4.5×10^{-5} ranged from 1.3×10^{-4} at its upper limit to 6.8×10^{-6} at the lower end. The

Conditional probability, event trees and probabilistic safety assessment

The probability that in the event of core melt the radiation will remain confined inside the reactor containment is 0.8 (eight-in-ten chance). This is a conditional probability. It is commonly denoted using a vertical bar: p(release | melt). In a general way, A and B being two events, it is written as p(A | B), which reads as 'the probability of A given B'. Conditional probability is a key concept. In Chapter 6 we shall see that it gave rise to a fundamental mathematical formula, known as Bayes' rule, or theorem. It enables us to update our appraisals on the basis of new information. In the present case conditional probability is used as a tool for estimating the probability of various sequences of events, and for estimating the cost of the event among their number which leads to a major accident. For example, p(release | melt | cooling system failure | loss of emergency power source | protective wall round plant breached by wave | 7.0 magnitude quake). All the possible sequences form an 'event' tree, with a series of forks, each branch being assigned a probability, for example p for one branch and therefore (1–p) for the other.[14] Try to picture an apple tree growing on a trellis, and the route taken by sap to convey water to each of its extremities, one of which is diseased. The event tree maps the route taken by a water molecule which reaches the diseased part rather than taking any of the other possible routes.

Probabilistic assessment of nuclear accidents is based on this type of tree structure. It seeks to identify all the possible technical paths leading to an accident, then assigns a probability to the faulty branch at each fork. The starting point is given by the probability of a factor triggering an accident, for example a 1-in-1,000 chance per year of a quake resulting in peak ground acceleration of 0.5g at the site of the plant. The outcome is the occurrence of core melt, or the massive release of radiation into the environment following meltdown. There may be many intermediate forks, concerning both technical (1-in-10,000 chance that a pump will break down for each year of operation) and human failures (1-in-5,000 chance that an operator disregards a flashing light on the control panel).

The first large-scale probabilistic assessment was carried out in the US in the 1970s.[15] It was led by Norman Rasmussen, then head of the nuclear engineering department at the Massachusetts Institute of Technology. The study was commissioned by the Atomic Energy Commission, which was keen to reassure public opinion by demonstrating that the risks, albeit real, were actually infinitesimal. To this end it circulated a misleading summary of the study, which over-simplified its findings. To impress readers the document made dubious comparisons – not contained in the Rasmussen report – with other risks. For example, it asserted that the likelihood of a person dying as a result of a nuclear accident was about the same as being hit by a meteorite. Such distortion of the report and some of the errors it contained prompted a major controversy.[16] The Nuclear Regulatory Commission, which was set up to separate nuclear safety from the other missions allocated to the AEC, rejected the contents of the report summary in 1979. But ultimately the Rasmussen study is remembered for the work done in establishing a detailed method, rather than the values it calculated for probabilities and damages. Since then probabilistic assessment has become more rigorous and an increasing number of such safety studies have been carried out.

The first probabilistic safety assessments changed several deeply rooted beliefs. They highlighted the possible input of operators, capable of either interrupting a sequence of material faults, or in some cases making it worse. Accidents and preventive measures do not only have a technical dimension. Rasmussen and his fellow scientists showed that the loss of liquid through small breaks in the primary cooling system could also be a frequent cause of accidents, largely disregarded until then. Several years later the Three Mile Island disaster prompted new interest in probabilistic safety assessment. Since then its scope has broadened and it has grown more complex. It has taken into account additional factors which may initiate an accident, both natural and human (for example the risk of falling aircraft). Probabilistic safety assessments have now been carried out on all the nuclear plants in the US and many others worldwide. Similarly reactor vendors carry out such studies for each reactor model while it is still in the design stage.

first figure indicates that there is a 5% chance that the value of the frequency may be even greater; the second that there is a 5% chance it may be lower. In other words, there is a 90% chance that the core-melt frequency is somewhere between the two limits. However, this interval was not calculated. It was based on the judgement of various experts who were questioned.

The widespread lack of any mention of the distribution on either side of the mean may be explained by the method employed. The probabilities assigned to the various branches of the tree used to calculate the overall core-melt frequency are selected as best estimates. The final number is single, because it is the sum of a succession of single numbers. Safety specialists naturally know how to use statistics and calculate uncertainties. They do not make do with averages. But they are concerned with the details, because it is here that there is scope for improving safety, for example using a probability density function to model the failure of a particular type of pump. At this scale, the error and distribution parameters – with barbaric names such as standard deviation, mode, variance or kurtosis – are generally entered. So why are they not systematically used to obtain an overall core-melt probability expressed as more than just a single number? The first reason is that uncertainty propagation in an event tree is far from trivial, compared to addition or multiplication. It is not just a matter of adding up or combining the standard deviations at each fork to obtain the one governing core-melt frequency. The second reason is that the prime aim of probabilistic safety assessments is not to obtain a final result. Rather they focus on the details of each branch. Only in recent years have the specialists started paying sustained, systematic attention to presenting the uncertainty affecting the aggregate probability of an accident.

Non-specialists are consequently inclined to think that probabilistic safety assessments reveal the true value for accident frequency for a given reactor, whereas in fact this value is subject to uncertainty. At best it is possible to offer a confidence interval within which the probability of an accident will fall.

It is worth noting that with advances in reactor technology the probability of a core melt has dropped. For example, on its 1,300 MW *palier*, or step, EDF estimated the core-melt frequency as 7.2×10^{-6}. On the following generation, represented by the EPR, the results of safety studies carried out by Areva and vetted by the British regulator show a core-melt frequency of 2.7×10^{-7} per reactor-year,[17] lower by a factor of more than 25. In the US an Electric Power Research Institute study found that the mean core-melt frequency of the US fleet had dropped by a factor of five since the early 1990s.[18]

Divergence between real-world observation of accidents and their frequency as predicted by the models

The Fukushima Daiichi disaster revealed an order-of-magnitude difference between the accident frequencies forecast by probabilistic safety assessments and observed frequencies.[19] Since the early 1960s and grid-connection of the first nuclear reactor, 14,400 reactor-years have passed worldwide. This figure is obtained by adding up all the years of operation of all the reactors ever built that generated kWhs, whether or not they are still in operation, were shut down earlier than planned or not. In other words the depth of observation currently at our disposal is equivalent to a single reactor operating for 14,400 years. Given that the global fleet currently numbers about 500 reactors, it may make more sense to say that this depth is equivalent to 28.8 years for 500 reactors. At the same time, since grid-connection of the first civil reactor, eleven failures initiating a core-melt have occurred, of which three were at Fukushima Daiichi. So the recorded core-melt frequency is 11 over 14,400, or 7.6×10^{-4}, or an accident for every 1,300 reactor-years. Yet the order of magnitude reported by probabilistic safety studies ranges from 10^{-4} to 10^{-5}, or an accident every 10,000 to 100,000 reactor years. Compared to 1,300 that means a ten- to hundred-fold divergence between calculated and observed probabilities.

How can such a large divergence be explained? The reasons are good or bad, trivial or complicated.

The first possible reason is simply bad luck. Just because you score 6 five times running with the same die, it does not mean it is loaded. There is a 1-in-7,776 chance of this sequence with a perfectly balanced die. So experts firmly convinced of the accuracy of their models or passionate advocates of nuclear power may set aside the suggestion that the calculated frequencies are erroneous, despite being much lower. Much as with the die, 14,400 reactor-years are not sufficient to obtain an accurate picture. This reason is legitimate in principle but it does mean ignoring observations if there are only a limited number. All in all it is not very different from the opposite standpoint, which consists in discarding probabilistic safety assessments and only accepting observations. The right approach is to base our reasoning on data obtained from both observation and modelling. Faced with uncertainty, all data should be considered, whether obtained from the field or from laboratories. We shall examine this approach in greater depth in Chapter 6.

A variation on the bad luck theory is to point out that the observed frequency actually falls within the range predicted by probabilistic assessments. As we saw above, in their forecast for the Surry plant, the experts estimated a 5 per cent likelihood that the core-melt frequency would exceed 1.3×10^{-4}, in other words an accident every 769 reactor-years. The observed value of an accident every 1,300 reactor-years is actually lower than this limit value. So convinced experts have no reason to review their position: there is no divergence between observations and the model. This stance might carry some weight if core-melt frequencies were reported with a confidence interval, but this is not the case. Moreover, the previous comment still holds true: the upper and lower limits on uncertainty must move to accommodate fresh observations.

The second possible reason is that the probabilistic assessments are not exhaustive. The event trees they examine and assess do not cover all the possible scenarios. The first safety studies only focused on internal initiating events, such as a device failure. The sequences of faults initiated by an earthquake or flood which might lead to core-melt have only gradually been taken into account. The validity of calculated frequencies is restricted to the perimeter under study. If no allowance is made for the risk of a falling aircraft the frequency is lower. The studies which do take it into account estimate that it is lower than 10^{-7} per reactor-year.[20] On its own this figure is too small to significantly change core-melt frequency, which is much higher. All this example shows is that by adding scenarios the frequency gradually increases. Little streams make big rivers. The Fukushima Daiichi accident is a concrete illustration of missing scenarios. It made people realize that spent-fuel pools could cause a massive release of radioactive material into the atmosphere. Probabilistic safety assessments do not usually register a break in the water supply to these pools as a possible initiating event. At Fukushima Daiichi, much as at other Japanese nuclear plants, the possibility that two risk factors – an earthquake and a tsunami – might coincide was apparently not studied either. Readers may be surprised by this oversight. Tidal waves and quakes are frequent in Japan and the two events are connected: one triggers the other. In fact the scenario which was not considered (nor its probability assessed) was the failure of the regional electricity network, knocked out by the quake, combined with flooding of the plant, due to the tsunami. With the surrounding area devastated, the backup diesel pumps underwater and the grid down, the power plant was left without an electricity supply for eleven days. Safety assessments generally assume power will be restored within twenty-four hours.

But is it possible for probabilistic studies to take into account all possible scenarios? Obviously not. It is impossible to imagine the unimaginable or to conceive the inconceivable. Joking apart, there is an intrinsic limit to probabilistic analysis: it can be applied to risk and uncertainty, not to situations of incompleteness (see box).

The third possible reason is that every event is unique, so probability theory cannot apply. The divergence between the observed frequency of accidents and their calculated probability is not a matter of bad luck, but results from the impossibility of applying probability theory to exceptional or one-off events. This reason is intuitive but must nevertheless be discarded.

In our minds the concept of probability is associated with that of frequency, and the law of large numbers too. We all learned at school that probability is the ratio of favourable or unfavourable outcomes to the number of possible cases. We all remember having to apply this definition to the observation of rolling dice or drawing cards. We also recall that calculating a probability requires the operation to be repeated a large number of times. We need to toss a coin several dozen times to grasp that it will land on one or the other side roughly the same number of times. This frequency-based approach to calculating probabilities is the best known and it does not work without data. But there are other ways of – or theories for – analysing

Risk, uncertainty and incompleteness

These basic concepts may be explained using the example of an urn containing different coloured balls. We shall start from what is a *certainty*. It may be described using the case of an urn only containing balls of the same colour, red for instance. We know that if we pick one ball out of the urn, it will inevitably be red. The outcome is a foregone conclusion. *Risk* corresponds to an urn of which the content is known: thirty red balls and sixty white, for instance. We can no longer be sure of picking out a red ball, but we do know that we have a one-in-three chance of picking a red, a two-in-three chance of picking a white. In theoretical jargon, we would say that all the states of the world (or indeed the universe of events) are known with certainty, and for each state or event there is a corresponding probability, also known with certainty. *Uncertainty* may be represented by an urn known to contain thirty red balls, where we do not know whether the sixty others are black or white. So only the probability of picking a red ball (one-in-three) is known. On the other hand all the states of the world (picking a red, black or white ball) are known. There is no possibility of a surprise, such as picking a blue ball. Lastly, *incompleteness* corresponds to an urn full of balls of unspecified colours. We may pick a white or a purple ball, perhaps even a multicoloured one. Unlike risk and uncertainty, in a situation of incompleteness all the states of the world are not known. So probability theory cannot apply. A probability cannot be assigned to an unknown event.[21]

This presentation makes a distinction between uncertainty and risk. However, this vocabulary is not universally accepted and must be handled with care. The term 'uncertainty' is often used with a broader sense, which encompasses the notion of risk. The part of uncertainty which is not covered by the term 'risk' is then referred to as 'ambiguity' or 'non-specific uncertainty'.[22] But such quibbles are of secondary importance, the priority being to draw a line between situations in which we have probabilities for all the events under consideration, and situations in which we do not. In the second case it is necessary to make assumptions in order to assign probabilities to events for which they are unknown.

Returning to the urn containing thirty red and sixty black or white balls. A simple way of assigning a probability to picking a black ball and a white ball would be to posit that the two events are of equal likelihood, namely a one-in-two chance of picking a black or white ball from among the sixty which are not red.[23] The probability of picking a black, white or red ball, from among the ninety balls in the urn, is one-in-three (30/90). In other words, ignorance is treated by assuming equiprobability: if n outcomes are possible, and if we have no idea of their chances of occurring, we consider them to be equiprobable (equally probable) and equal to $1/n$. This approach provides a way of treating non-specific uncertainty as a risk, thus making it possible to apply the calculation of probabilities to situations of uncertainty in general.

probabilities, which do away with the need for repeated experiments, and consequently a large number of observations, to calculate frequencies. It is quite possible to carry out probabilistic analysis without any observation at all. The reader may recall the wager made by Pascal. The French thinker was puzzled about the right approach to adopt regarding the uncertainty of God's existence. Here there could be no repeated events. The existence of a Supreme Being was a singular proposition, which Pascal subjected to probabilistic reasoning.

So probabilistic logic can be applied to one-off events. The concept of probability refers to a degree of certainty regarding the veracity of a proposition. It applies for instance to the reasoning of a court judge who takes a different view of the guilt of the accused if it is known that the latter lacks an alibi or that traces of his or her DNA have been found on the body of the victim. According to John Maynard Keynes the theory of probability 'is concerned with [the] part of our knowledge we obtain [...] by argument, and it treats of the different degrees in which the results so obtained are conclusive or inconclusive'. This reference to the author of *The General Theory of Employment, Interest and Money* may surprise readers unfamiliar with the work of the Cambridge economist. *A Treatise on Probability* was one of the first works published by Keynes, but is still well worth reading even now.[24]

The theory of subjective probability opens up a second approach to probability, not based on frequency. It has been advocated and developed by three leading figures in economic science: Britain's Frank Plumpton Ramsey, already cited with reference to discount rates; Bruno de Finetti, from Italy; and an American, Leonard Jimmie Savage. These authors understand the concept of probability as the belief which an individual invests in an event, regardless of whether or not the event recurs. According to De Finetti, probability is the degree of confidence of a given subject in the realization of an event, at a given time and with a given set of data.[25] So probability is not an objective measurement, because it depends on the observer and his or her knowledge at that time. Probability is thus assimilated to the odds a gambler will accept when betting on a given outcome, odds at which he or she will neither lose nor win money. Imagine, for example, that two nuclear experts are asked to bet on the likelihood of a nuclear accident occurring in Europe in the course of the next thirty years. One agrees to odds of 100-to-1, the other 120-to-1, or 200-to-1. So according to subjective probability theory anyone can bet on anything. However, we should not be misled by the terms 'belief' and 'subjective'. The odds accepted do not depend on a person's mood or state of mind, but are supposed to be based on their knowledge. Furthermore, the person making the wager is deemed to be rational, being subject to the rules governing the calculation of probabilities. For example, he or she cannot bet three-to-one for and one-to-two against a given outcome. The theory of decision under uncertainty, a monument elaborated by Savage in the middle of the last century, assumes that economic agents comply with all the axioms for calculating probabilities: they must behave as perfect statisticians.

The fourth reason for the divergence between observations and forecasts is that the models may be faulty or use the wrong parameters. It is vital to avoid mistakes when assigning a probability to the known states of the world, and consequently when measuring the probability and associated uncertainty. Returning to what happened at Fukushima Daiichi, the six reactors at the plant were commissioned in the 1970s. We do not have access to the probabilistic studies carried out by the plant operator, Tokyo Electric Power (Tepco), at the time of the plant's construction or afterwards. But we do know some of the values taken into account by the generating company or the regulator for the risk of an earthquake or tsunami. The figures were largely underestimated. The plant was designed to withstand a magnitude 7.9 earthquake and tidal wave of several metres. On 11 March 2011 at 14:46 JST it was subjected to a magnitude 9 tremor, then swamped by a wave more than 10 metres high. So, much like Tepco, the nuclear industry is purportedly inclined to play down risks by picking values or models favourable to growth. Unless one is an adept of conspiracy theories, this explanation for the divergence between observations and forecasts is barely convincing. For many years safety authorities and independent experts have scrutinized such probabilistic studies.

Two points are of particular note in this long list of possible reasons for the divergence between the observed frequency and calculated probability of an accident. Firstly, with regard to method, we should make use of all the available instruments, combining empirical and theoretical data. Assessments of the risk of a major nuclear accident based exclusively on either data from past observations or theoretical

The wrong values taken into account for Fukushima Daiichi

When the nuclear power plant at Fukushima Daiichi was built, the risk of an earthquake exceeding magnitude 8 on the Richter scale was estimated at less than 2×10^{-5} per year.[26] This value was taken from the work of modelling and numerical simulation carried out for each plant in Japan by the National Research Institute for Earth Science and Disaster Prevention (NIED). However, historical research has identified six major quakes which have occurred on the Sanriku coast since 869. That was the year of the Jogan undersea earthquake, probably the most devastating ever known on this stretch of coastline until March 2011. The various pieces of evidence which have been gathered suggest that these quakes all exceeded magnitude 8. This means the observed annual frequency should be about 5×10^{-3}, in other words more than 200 times higher than the results calculated by the NIED.[27]

The protective seawall at Fukushima Daiichi was built in 1966. It was six metres high, a dimension decided in line with a classical deterministic principle: take the most severe historic event and add a twofold safety margin. The three-metre wave which struck the coast of Chile in 1960 was taken as a baseline value. This was a surprising choice, the Jogan quake having triggered a four-metre wave locally, a fact that was already known when the plant was built.[28] Be that as it may, forty years later, our understanding of past tsunamis had obviously made significant progress, but the initial height of the wall was thought to comply with the 2002 guidelines for tsunami assessment set by the regulatory authority.[29] Such compliance was based on an annual probability of less than 10^{-4}. Yet historical studies have established that waves exceeding eight metres have been recorded on the Sanriku coast: witness the stones set into the ground marking the points furthest inland reached by the flood. Some of these stones are

more than 400 years old. The inscriptions on them urge residents
not to build homes lower down the slope. Moreover, core samples
have revealed sedimentary deposits left by previous tsunamis. At
the Onagawa plant, on the basis of remains found in the hills one
kilometre inland, it was estimated that the 1611 quake had caused
a six-to-eight-metre wave.[30]

On the evidence of old records Woody Epstein estimated that
the average frequency of a tsunami of eight metres or more on
the Sendai plain, behind the Fukushima Daiichi plant, was about
1 every 1,000 years. He estimated as 8.1×10^{-4} the probability
of an earthquake of a magnitude equivalent to or greater than a
seismic intensity of 6 or more,[31] followed by a tidal wave of over
eight metres. Due to the layout of the plant, this dual shock would
very likely lead to flooding of the turbine building, destruction of
the diesel generators, loss of battery power and station blackout
lasting at least eight hours. This entire sequence of events would
correspond, according to Epstein, to a probability of core-melt
of about 5×10^{-4}, five times higher than the authorized limit.
Tepco based its various probabilistic studies on very low values,
very probably taken from a badly designed historical database or
unsuitable simulation models.[32]

probabilistic simulations lead to a dead end. Secondly, in practical
terms, the limitations of probabilistic assessment lead to the deployment of deterministic safety measures. As we do not know all the
states of the world, nor yet the probability of all those we do know, it is
vitally important to install successive, redundant lines of defence as a
means of protection against unforeseeable or ill-appraised events. In
short, we must protect ourselves against the unknown. We could
raise protective walls or quake-resistant structures able to withstand events twice as severe as the worst recorded case, install large

numbers of well-protected back-up diesel generators and build nesting containments – the first one in the fuel cladding itself, forming an initial barrier between radioactive elements and the environment; the largest one, made of reinforced concrete, encasing the reactor and steam-supply system.

FIVE

Perceived probabilities and aversion to disaster

The concept of subjective probability can be a misleading intro-duction to individuals' perception of probabilities. Perceived proba-bility, much like its subjective counterpart, varies from one person to the next but it does not take the same route in our brain. The former expresses itself rapidly, effortlessly, in some sense as a reflex response; the latter demands time, effort and supervision. Perceived probability is based on experience and routine, whereas subjective probability is rooted in reason and optimization. In response to the question, 'Which is the most dangerous reactor: the one for which the probability of an accident over the next year is 0.0001; or the one which has a 1 in 10,000 chance of having an accident over the next year?', most people will spontaneously pick the second answer. Yet reason tells us that the two reactors are equally dan-gerous (i.e. 1:10,000 = 0.0001). So how do we perceive risks? Are individuals poor statisticians, or perhaps not statistically minded at all? In which case, what use is the theory of decision under uncer-tainty, given that it requires us to calculate probabilities accurately? How do individuals make a choice if they do not optimize their decisions? These questions are central to forty years' work by exper-imental cognitive psychologists on how individuals assess the prob-ability of events. Understanding this work is essential, for almost all its findings contribute to amplifying the perception of nuclear risk.

Biases in our perception of probabilities

What is the connection between cognitive psychology – which is an experimental science – and economics? In fact, there is a significant link. In 2002, in Stockholm, Daniel Kahneman was awarded the most coveted distinction to which an economist can aspire: the Sveriges Riksbank prize in Economic Sciences in memory of Alfred Nobel. His work was distinguished for 'having established laboratory experiments as a tool in empirical economic analysis, especially in the study of alternative market mechanisms'. That year, the winner of the Nobel prize for economics was not an economist, but a psychologist!

Economic analysis focuses on many subjects and lends itself to many definitions: decision theory is among these subjects; it may, among others, be defined as the science of human behaviour. Economics investigates how humans seek the best means of achieving their aims. When an individual needs to take a decision under uncertainty,[1] he or she assigns more or less weight to the probabilities associated with each choice. A rational being faced with an alternative between an action yielding a satisfaction of 100 associated with a probability of 0.3, and an action yielding a satisfaction of 105 associated with a probability of 0.29, will choose the second option because its mathematical expectation is greater ($100 \times 0.3 < 105 \times 0.29$). The expected utility of the outcome is thus optimized.

The Swiss mathematician Daniel Bernoulli laid the foundations of expected utility theory. In his 1738 essay he raised the question of how to give formal expression to the intuition according to which the rich were prepared to sell insurance to the poor, and the latter were prepared to buy it. He also sought to resolve an enigma of great interest at the time, subsequently known as the Saint Petersburg paradox: why does a gamble which holds an infinite expectation of gain not attract players prepared to bet all they own?[2] The answer to both these questions is to be found in our aversion to risk. This psychological trait means that we prefer a certain gain of 100 to an expected gain of 110. This also explains why a rich person attaches less value to a sum of €100 than a poor person does, which translates into contemporary economic parlance as the declining marginal utility of income. In mathematical terms it is represented by the concave form of the utility function. (The curve, which expresses our satisfaction depending on the money we own, gradually flattens out. Bernoulli thus used a logarithmic function to represent utility.)

The connection between risk aversion and the form of the utility function may not be immediately apparent to the reader. In which case, illustrating the point with figures should help. Let us assume that €100 yields a satisfaction of one; €200 yields a proportionately lower satisfaction, 1.5 for example; €220 less still, say 1.58. I offer you €100 which you either accept or we toss a coin with the following rule: heads, I keep my €100; tails, you take the €100 and I add €120 more. Which option would you choose? The certainty of pocketing €100, or a one in two chance of winning €220? In the first case your gain is €100, whereas in the second case there is the expectation of €110 (€220 × 1/2). But what matters to you is not the money, but the satisfaction – or utility – it yields. The first case yields a utility of one, the second an expected utility of 0.79 (1.58 × 1/2). So you choose the first option, which does not involve any risk. With the resolution of the Saint Petersburg paradox, by altering the form of the utility function, Bernoulli opened the way for progress towards decision theory, which carried on to Kahneman. This was achieved through a back-and-forth exchange between economic modelling and psychological experimentation. The latter would, for instance, pick up an anomaly – in a particular instance people's behaviour did not conform to what the theory predicted – and the former would repair it, altering the mathematical properties of the utility function or the weighting of probabilities. The paradoxes identified by Allais and Ellsberg were two key moments in this achievement (see the box).

Allais, Keynes, Ellsberg and the *homo probabilis*

During an academic lecture in 1952 Maurice Allais, a Professor at the Ecole des Mines in Paris, handed out a questionnaire to those present, asking them to choose between various simple gambles, arranged in pairs. He then collected their answers and demonstrated that they had contradicted expected utility theory in what was then its most advanced form, as developed by Leonard Jimmie Savage. Their responses violated one of the axioms of the theory, which was supposed to dictate the rational decision under uncertainty. In simple terms the Allais paradox may be expressed as follows: the first gamble offers the choice between (A) the certainty of winning €100 million, and (B) winning €500m with a probability of 0.98, or otherwise nothing. The second gamble offers the choice between (C) receiving €100 million with a probability of 0.01, or otherwise nothing, and (D) €500 million with a probability of 0.0098, or otherwise nothing. The paired gambles are therefore the same, but with a probability 100 times smaller. Most of the students chose A, not B, but D rather than C. It seemed to them that the probability of winning €500 million with D (0.0098) was roughly the same as that of winning €100 million with C (0.01), whereas in the previous case the same difference of 2% between probabilities seemed greater. Yet, according to Savage, rational behaviour would have dictated that if they chose A rather than B, they should also pick C, not D. Ironically, Savage also attended the lecture and handed in answers to the questionnaire which contradicted his own theory.

A common solution to the Allais paradox is to weigh the probabilities depending on their value, with high coefficients for low probabilities, and vice versa. Putting it another way, the preferences assigned to the probabilities are not linear. This is more than just a technical response. It makes allowance for a psychological

trait, which has since been confirmed by a large body of experimental study: people overestimate low probabilities and under-
estimate high probabilities. In other words they tend to see rare
events as more frequent than they really are, and very common
events as less frequent than is actually the case.

To our preference for certainty, rather than risk, and our varying
perception of probabilities depending on their value, we must add
another phenomenon well known to economists: our aversion
to ambiguity. This characteristic was suggested by Keynes, and
later demonstrated by Daniel Ellsberg in the form of a paradox.
In his treatise on probabilities, the Cambridge economist posited
that greater weight is given to a probability that is certain than
to one that is imprecise. He illustrated his point by comparing
the preferences for a draw from two urns containing 100 balls.
One contains black and white balls, in a known, half-and-half
proportion; the other urn also contains black and white balls but
in an unknown proportion. In the second urn, all distributions
are possible (0 black, 100 white; 1 black, 99 white; . . . ; 100 black,
0 white) with equal probability (p = 1/101). So the expected
probability of drawing a white ball is one-in-two,[3] the same value
as for the probability of drawing a white ball from the first urn.
But we would rather win by drawing white (or black) balls from
the first urn.

In 1961 Ellsberg revisited Keynes' example, developing it and
making experiments. We shall now look at his experiment with
an urn containing balls of three different colours. In all it contains
ninety balls, of which thirty are red and the remaining sixty either
black or yellow. So all we accurately know is the probability
of drawing a red (one-in-three) and that of drawing a black or
yellow – in other words one that is not red (two-in-three). You
are presented with two pairs of gambles. In the first pair, (A) you
win €100 if you draw a red ball from the urn, (B) you win €100 if

you draw a black ball from the urn. Which option do you choose? If, like most people, you are averse to ambiguity, you choose A. The other pair is more complicated: (C) you win €100 if you draw a red or a yellow ball from the urn, (D) you win €100 if you draw a black or a yellow ball from the urn. The question, however, is the same: which option do you choose? The answer is also the same: aversion to ambiguity prompts most people to pick D rather than C. You know very well that you have a two-in-three chance of drawing a black or yellow ball (one that is not red). The paradox resides in the fact that the preference for A and D is inconsistent on the part of a rational person, as modelled in the classical theory of expected utility. Preferring A to B implies that the player reckons subjectively that the probability of drawing a black ball is lower than one-in-three, whereas for a red ball it is higher than one-in-three. Knowing that there is a two-in-three probability of drawing a black or yellow ball, the player deduces that the probability of drawing a yellow ball is higher than one-in-three. As the probability of drawing a yellow or black ball is higher than one-in-three in both cases, their sum must exceed two-in-three. According to Savage, the player picks C. But in the course of experiments, most players who choose A also choose D, which suggests that there is an anomaly somewhere, which the aversion to ambiguity corrects.

Just as there is a premium for taking risks, some compensation must be awarded to players for them to become indifferent to gain (or loss) with a one-in-two probability or an unknown probability with an expected value of one-in-two. Technically speaking, there are several solutions for this problem, in particular by using the utility function, yet again. It is worth understanding Ellsberg's paradox because ambiguity aversion with regard to a potential gain, has its counterpart with regard to a loss: with the choice between a hazard associated with a clearly defined probability – because the experts are in agreement – and a hazard of the same expected value – because the experts disagree – people are more inclined to agree to exposure to the first rather than the second hazard. Putting it another way, in the second instance people side with the expert predicting the worst-case scenario. Simple intuition enables us to better understand this result. If players prefer (A) the prospect of drawing a red ball associated with the certainty of a one-in-three probability, rather than that (B) of drawing a black ball, it is because they are afraid that in the latter case the person operating the experiment may be cheating. The latter may have put more yellow balls in the urn than black ones. The experimental proposition is suspect. Out of pessimism, the players adjust their behaviour to suit the least favourable case, namely the absence of black balls in the urn, comparable to the worst-case scenario among those proposed by the experts.

Kahneman's work followed on that of Bernoulli, Allais, and Ellsberg, but it also diverged in two respects.

He and his fellow author, Amos Tversky,[4] introduced two changes to the theory of expected utility.[5] Firstly, individuals no longer base their reasoning on their absolute wealth, but in relative terms with regard to a point of reference. For example, if your boss gives you a smaller rise than your fellow workers, you will perceive this change as a loss of utility, rather than a gain. The value function does not start from zero, corresponding to no wealth, subsequently rising at a diminishing rate as Bernoulli indicated with his model. A whole new part of the curve, located to the left of the zero, represents the value of losses in relation to the status quo. This part is convex (see Figure 5.1): just as we derive less satisfaction from our wealth rising from 1,000 to 1,100, than when it rises from 100 to 200, so our perception of the loss between −1,000 and −1,100 is less acute than between −100 and −200.

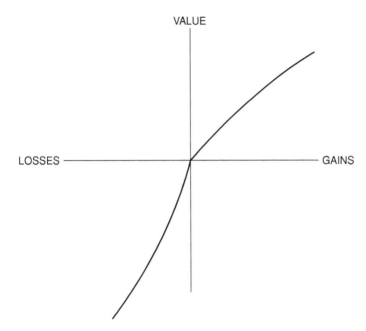

Figure 5.1 The Kahneman–Tversky asymmetric value function

Secondly, individuals are more affected by loss than gain. For example, if a professor randomly hands out mugs marked with their university shield to half the students in a lecture theatre, giving the others nothing, the recipients, when asked to sell their mugs, will set a price twice as high as the one bid by those who did not receive a gift.[6] Reflecting such loss aversion, the slope of the value function is steeper on the loss side than on the gain side. Regarding the perception of probabilities, Kahneman and Tversky revisit the idea of distortion, in particular for extreme values (overweighting of low probabilities, underweighting of high probabilities). Armed with these value functions and probability weighting, the decision-maker posited by the two researchers assesses the best option out of all those available and carries on optimizing the outcome.

Kahneman has also experimented widely and published on heuristics, the short-cuts and routines underpinning our decisions. In so doing he distances himself from previous work on optimal decision-making under uncertainty. The decision-maker no longer optimizes nor maximizes the outcome. Anomalies in behaviour with regard to expected utility theory are no longer detailed to enhance this theory and enlarge its scope, but rather to detect the ways we react and think. Here the goal of research is exclusively to describe and explain: in the words of the philosophers of science it is positive. The aim is no longer to propose a normative theoretical framework indicating how humans or society should behave. Observing the distortion of probabilities becomes a way of understanding how our brain works. This line of research is comparable to subjecting participants to optical illusions to gain a better understanding of sight. For example, a 0.0001 probability of loss will be perceived as lower than a 1/10,000 probability. Our brain seems to be misled by the presentation of figures, much as our eyes are confused by an optical effect which distorts an object's size or perspective. This bias seems to suggest that the brain takes a short-cut and disregards the denominator, focusing only on the numerator.

Psychology has also done a great deal of experimental work revealing a multitude of micro-reasoning processes, which sometimes overlap, their denomination changing from one author to the next. Economists may find this confusing, much as psychologists are often thrown by the mathematical formalism of decision theory. Readers may feel they are faced with a choice between two unsatisfactory options. On the one hand, an economic model has become increasingly complex as it has been built up with the addition of *post hoc* hypotheses, the theory of expected utility having gradually taken onboard aversion to risk, ambiguity, loss, while nevertheless remaining a schematic, relatively unrealistic representation. On the other hand, a host of behavioural regularities, identified through observation, throw light on the countless facets of the decision-making process but, lacking a theoretical basis, simply stand side by side. In one case we have a discipline which is still basically normative, in the other a science obsessed by detailed description. Building bridges between economics and psychology does not eliminate their differences. However, in a recent book targeting the general public, *Thinking, Fast and Slow*,[7] Kahneman sets out to reconcile the two disciplines. In a synthesis which rises above doctrinal differences he draws a distinction between two modes of reasoning which direct our thoughts and decisions, one automatic, the other deliberate. The first mode is swift, and requires no effort on our part nor supervision, being mainly based on association and short-cuts. The second one is quite the opposite, slow, demanding effort and supervision, largely underpinned by deduction and rules we have learnt. Supposing we submit the following problem to a group of mathematically adroit students:[8] a baseball bat and ball cost €110, the bat costs €100 more than the ball, so how much does the ball cost? The spontaneous answer is €10. But in that case the bat would cost €110, and the whole kit €120! Leave the students to think for a while or to write out the equations on paper and they will find the right answer.

By revisiting and extending the classic psychological distinction between the two cognitive systems Kahneman stops seeing heuristics and calculation as mutually exclusive. It is no longer a matter of deciding whether humans are rational or irrational: they are both.

Perception biases working against nuclear power

The overall biases in our perception of probabilities, discussed above, amplify the risk of a nuclear accident in our minds. To this we must add other forms of bias, with which economists are less familiar, but which contribute to the same trend.

A major nuclear accident is a rare event. Its probability is consequently overestimated. Much like smallpox or botulism, the general public thinks its frequency is higher than it really is. Nuclear technology is thus perceived as entailing a greater risk than other technologies. Paul Slovic, an American psychologist who started his career working on perception of the dangers of nuclear power, asked students and experts to rank thirty activities and technologies according to the risk they represented.[9] The students put nuclear power at the top of the list (and swimming last), whereas the experts ranked it in twentieth position (predictably putting road accidents first). Faced with a low probability individuals are inclined to over-reassure themselves and demand higher protection or compensation. Protecting the personnel of nuclear power plants against workplace accidents costs more than in any other field.[10] In a general way we over-invest in protection against events with a low probability, the incremental improvement being seen as more beneficial than it really is.

The risk of a nuclear accident is ambiguous. Expert appraisals diverge, depending on whether they are based on probabilistic assessments or the observation of accidents. Furthermore, probabilistic assessments produce different figures depending on the reactors or initiating events they consider; the same applies to observations of accidents, for which the definitions and consequently lists differ. Lastly there is a divergence of views between industry experts working for operators and engineering firms, and scientists opposed to the atom, such as the members of Global Change in France or the American Concerned Scientists Association. The effect suspected by Keynes and demonstrated by Ellsberg is clearly at work here. In the face of scientific uncertainty we are inclined to opt for the worst-case scenario. The highest accident probability prevails. The same phenomenon affects the controversial estimation of damages in the event of a major accident. The highest estimates tend to gain the most widespread credence.

The asymmetry between loss and gain highlighted by Kahneman and Tversky is behind a widespread effect which is less decisive for nuclear power and not as specific.[11] The main consequence of this commonplace, third bias is that it favours the status quo, the drawbacks of change being seen as greater than the benefits (there is a bend in the curve of the value function shown in Figure 5.1 near the point of reference separating the feeling of gain from that of loss). As a result local residents will tend to oppose the construction of a nuclear power plant in their vicinity, but on the other hand they will block plans to close a plant which has been operating for several years. Obviously what holds true for nuclear power is equally valid for other new facilities, be they gas-fired plants or wind farms.

The risks of a nuclear accident are also distorted by the dimension of potential damages and their impact on public opinion. With low frequency and a high impact they are among the various 'dread' risks, along with plane crashes and terrorist attacks targeting markets, hotels or buses, or indeed cyclones. The perception of the consequences of such events is such that their probability is distorted. It is as if the denominator had been forgotten. Rather than acknowledging the true scale of the accident, attention seems to focus exclusively on the accident itself. Disregard for the denominator, mentioned very briefly above, is connected to several common routines of varying similarity which have been identified by risk psychologists. Let us look at the main routines at work.

The availability heuristic is a short-cut which prompts us to answer questions on probabilities on the basis of examples which spontaneously spring to mind. The frequency of murders is generally perceived, quite wrongly, to be higher than that of suicides. Violent or disastrous events leave a clearly defined, lasting mark, in particular due to the media attention they attract. It is consequently easy to latch onto them. Chernobyl reminds us of the accident at Three Mile Island, and in turn Fukushima Daiichi brings Chernobyl to mind. It matters little that each case is different, with regard to the established causes, the course of events or the consequences in terms of exposure of the population to radiation. The spontaneous mode of thought works by analogy and does not discriminate.

The representativeness heuristic is based on similarity to stereotypes. It originated with a well-known experiment by Kahneman and

Tversky. Test participants were told that Linda was thirty-one, single, outspoken and very bright. She had majored in philosophy. As a student, she was deeply concerned with issues of discrimination and social justice, and also took part in anti-nuclear demonstrations. Then they were asked to pick a description of Linda, in descending order of likelihood: elementary schoolteacher; bookstore salesperson, attending yoga classes; active feminist; psychiatric social worker; member of the League of Women Voters; bank teller; insurance salesperson; bank teller and an active feminist. Most of the participants placed the last answer ahead of the antepenultimate one. Yet logic tells us that there is a higher probability of being a bank teller, than being a bank teller and a militant feminist, the latter category being a subset of the female bank-teller population. The representativeness heuristic prompts us to confuse frequency and plausibility. We are consequently able to find regularities and trends where they do not exist. Two successive accidents separated by a short lapse of time will be interpreted as a substantial deterioration in nuclear safety, whereas their close occurrence is merely a matter of chance. This heuristic resembles another bias which often misleads us, namely our tendency to generalize on the basis of low numbers. Rather than waiting to see how a low-probability event repeats itself, tending towards infinity or even with 100 recurrences, we immediately deduce the probability of its recurrence.

To round off this list of biases in our perception of frequencies unfavourable to nuclear power, a word on *very low probabilities*. It is difficult to grasp values such as 0.00001, or even smaller. Much as it is hard to appreciate huge figures, in the billion billions, often due to the lack of tangible points of reference to which to connect them, dividing one by several hundred thousand makes little sense to the average person. Cass Sunstein, a Harvard law professor, carried out an interesting experiment. He asked his students how much they were prepared to pay, at the most, to eliminate a cancer risk of 1-in-100,000 or 1-in-1,000,000. He also presented the problem in slightly different terms, adding that it 'produces gruesome and painful death as the cancer eats away at the internal organs of the body'. In the first case his students were prepared to spend more on saving one individual in 100,000 than on one in a million. On the other hand, playing on their emotions narrowed the difference. They forgot the denominator, despite having a basic grasp of fractions and probabilities! To an economist, the biased perception of frequencies is very odd. The way individuals react is light years away from the marginalist reasoning which underpins economic models. As an economist it is disconcerting to discover that cutting a risk from 5×10^{-4} to 10^{-4} can pass unnoticed, even if it took time and effort to achieve this shift.

In practice, if the authorities want to reassure citizens worried by nuclear risk, they will have difficulty basing their arguments on progress in reactor safety. It would apparently be more effective to emphasize the benefits. Slovic and a fellow author have noted a negative correlation between perception of risks and benefits.[12] If the benefits of a given activity are thought to be high, the corresponding risks are perceived as being low and vice versa; on the other hand, if the risks are thought to be high, the associated benefits will be underestimated. In more prosaic terms, if we like something, we will downplay the risks involved; if we dislike something, we will minimize the benefits.

Unlike very low probabilities, everyone understands zero. By playing on people's emotions it seems possible to persuade them to spend large amounts to eradicate risk completely. In the field of nuclear power, the decision by Germany to shut down its reactors following the Fukushima Daiichi disaster is a case in point (see Chapter 11). Economists have estimated the loss resulting from the decision to retire the plants earlier than planned at between €42 billion and €75 billion.

In short, however psychologists address perception biases, the latter go against nuclear power. Their effect is cumulative, one consolidating another: in this way they amplify the perceived probability of an accident. At a practical level this has two major consequences. Firstly, there is a risk of over-investing in safety. For this to happen all that is required is for the authorities to follow the trend, either because policy-makers have an interest in giving way to the electorate's demands, or because their perception of probabilities is no different from that of private individuals. Secondly, the options for alternative investment are distorted. On account of its dread nature, the perceived risk of a nuclear accident has been much more exaggerated than the risk inherent in other generating technologies. In 2010 the Organisation for Economic Cooperation and Development published a study on the comparative assessment of serious accidents (causing more than five deaths).[13] The survey covered the whole world, from 1969 to 2000. In terms of fatalities and accidents coal came top of the list, a very long way ahead of nuclear power.[14] Does this correspond to your perception, given that the list of accidents during this period of time includes the Chernobyl disaster? Very probably not, much like most other people. If the authorities base their action on perceived probabilities, their decisions may ultimately detract from the overall goal of reducing risks and loss of human life.

The decisions taken following the terrorist attacks on 11 September 2001 provide a simple illustration of the dual effect of our aversion to dread risk. During the three months following the disaster Americans travelled less by plane, more by car. The well-known German psychologist Gerd Gigerenzer has demonstrated that this behavioural shift resulted in an increase in the number of road deaths, exceeding the 265 passengers who perished in the hijacked planes.[15] As the fearsome pictures of the collapse of the twin towers of the World Trade Center receded into the past, the sudden distortion of probabilities must have been partly dissipated. On the other hand we are all affected by the long-term impact of 9/11 whenever we travel by plane. Air passengers all over the world undergo a series of trials – queuing to be checked before entering the boarding area, taking off belts and shoes, emptying pockets, taking electronic devices out of hand luggage, trashing water bottles, putting other liquids into plastic bags, forgetting keys and setting off the alarm, and being handled by complete strangers. Not to mention the rise in airport taxes to cover the extra security costs. In view of the infinitely low risk actually involved, these measures seem to have been taken too far.[16]

In conclusion, there is good reason to suppose that the discrepancy between the perceived probability of a nuclear accident and the figures advanced by the experts will persist. The work by experimental psychologists on the amplification of risks for low-probability events seems convincing. The distorting effect of the Fukushima Daiichi disaster is likely to be a durable feature, particularly as we receive regular reminders, if only when progress is achieved or shortcomings are observed in the resolution of the many outstanding problems (soil decontamination, public health monitoring, dismantling of reactors, waste processing, among others). It will also require great political determination to avoid pitfalls similar to those entailed by tightening up checks on airline passengers.

SIX

The magic of Bayesian analysis

An English Presbyterian minister and a French mathematician forged a magic key which enables us to update our probabilistic judgements, use probability as a basis for reasoning without being a statistician, reconcile objective and subjective probability, combine observed frequency and calculated probability, and predict the probability of the next event.

The Bayes–Laplace rule

Thomas Bayes was the first person to use the concept of conditional probability, for which Pierre-Simon Laplace found a more widespread application. (See the box.) We presented this concept briefly in Chapter 4 on the escalating severity of nuclear accidents, more specifically in relation to the probability of massive release of radioactive material in the event of a core melt, or in other words given that core meltdown has occurred. This probability is denoted using a vertical bar: p(release|melt). In a general way, A and B being two events, the conditional probability is written as p(A|B), which reads as 'the probability of A given B'. Or, to be more precise, we should refer to two conditional probabilities; as we are focusing on two events, we may also formulate the conditional probability p(B|A), the probability of B given A. In the case of a core melt and the release of radioactivity, p(melt|release) is almost equal to one: with just a few exceptions (water loss from a spent-fuel pool) a massive release is impossible unless the core has melted.

Bayes' rule and conditional probabilities

The Bayes–Laplace rule, more commonly known as Bayes' rule, enables us to write an equation linking two conditional probabilities. It is written as:

$$p(A|B) = p(A)[p\,(B|A)\,/p(B)] \qquad (1)$$

It reads: 'the probability of A given B is equal to the probability of A multiplied by the probability of B given A divided by the probability of B'.

It may also be written as:

$$p(A|B) = [p(A)p(B|A)]/[p(A)p(B|A)$$
$$+ p(notA)p(B|notA)] \qquad (2)$$

This formula is typically illustrated with examples from medicine. We shall use the following data for the problem:

The probability that a patient undergoing an X-ray examination has a cancer is 0.01, so p(cancer) = 0.01

If a patient has a cancer, the probability of a positive examination is 0.8, so p(positive|cancer) = 0.8

If a patient does not have a cancer, the probability of a positive examination is 0.1, so p(positive|no cancer) = 0.1

What is the probability that a patient has cancer if the examination is positive, so p(cancer|positive)?

Using equation (2), we find 0.075.[1]

Bayes' rule, set forth in the box, is the key to inductive reasoning. Let us look at how it works.

As the reader is probably more familiar with the concept of deduction rather than induction we shall start by contrasting the two approaches. Deduction generally proceeds from the general to the specific: 'All dogs have four legs; Fido, Rover, Lump and Snowy are dogs; so they have four legs.' Induction generalizes on the basis of facts or empirical data: 'Fido, Rover, Lump and Snowy are dogs; they have four legs; so all dogs have four legs.'

A simple equation enables us to grasp the inductive power of Bayes' rule. Let us suppose that event A is a hypothesis, H, and event B is an observed data, d. So $p(H|d)$ is the probability that H is true, given that d is observed. Bayes' rule is written thus:

$$p(H|d) = p(H)[p(d|H)/p(d)]$$

The conditional probability $p(d|H)$ encapsulates the essence of deductive reasoning. It indicates the probability of datum d being observed when hypothesis H is true. The reasoning starts from a hypothesis, rooted in theory, to arrive at the probability of an observation. The conditional probability $p(H|d)$ expressing inductive reasoning takes the same route but in the opposite direction. It indicates the veracity of a hypothesis, if datum d has been observed. Here, we start from the observation to infer the degree of certainty of a hypothesis.

The equation above also shows how Bayes' rule provides a means of reviewing an appraisal in the light of new information.

At the outset only the general, or prior, probability $p(H)$ is known. It may be based on objective data from the past, on scientific theory or indeed on personal belief. New data, which changes the picture, then comes to notice. Thanks to Bayes' rule we can calculate a new, posterior probability $p(H|d)$, namely that H is true now that data d has been brought to light. It depends on the prior probability $p(H)$ and the multiplier $[p(d|H)/p(d)]$. The inverse probability, $p(d|H)$, is the probability of observing data d given that H is true; it is often referred to as the likelihood. $p(d)$ is the prior probability of observing data d. The multiplier determines how much the prior probability is updated. It is worth noting, for example, that if the observation yields no additional information, then $p(d|H)$ equals $p(d)$ and the multiplier equals one, so there is no reason to update the prior probability. Intuition would suggest that if there is no relation between d and H, observing d should not change the degree of veracity assigned to H. On the other hand, when the observation is more probable if the hypothesis is true, $p(d|H)$ being greater than $p(d)$ and the multiplier greater than one, the probability will be revised upwards. In other words, if d and H are linked I must upgrade my appreciation of the hypothesis. But in the opposite case, when the observation is less probable if the hypothesis is true, $p(d|H)$ being smaller than $p(d)$ and the multiplier less than one, the probability will be revised downwards. Or in other words, if d and H conflict, I must downgrade my appreciation of the hypothesis. Lastly, it should be borne in mind that a posterior probability calculated on the basis of a new item of information may in turn be used as a prior probability for calculating another posterior probability taking into account yet another new item of information. And so on. As the new inputs accumulate, the initial prior probability exerts less and less influence over the posterior probability.

Bayes' rule thus makes it possible to calculate probabilities with only a limited number of observations. It even provides for a complete lack of data, in which case the prior probability is unchanged. For example you did not toss the coin your adversary offered, or perhaps you have never tossed a coin. If you do not know whether the coin is loaded, you will choose one-in-two as the subjective initial odds and you will stick to these odds if the game is cut short before it even starts.

Are we naturally good at statistics?

In the above we presented Bayesian analysis as a relatively intuitive mechanism for inductive reasoning and updating earlier appraisals. However, applying the rule on which it is based is tricky. In the previous section we explained that Ivy League students some-times came up with the wrong answers to much simpler probability problems. Disregard for the denominator, apparently so common, is such that one may wonder whether the average person can really grasp the concept of probability. Probability is commonly defined by a frequency, the ratio of observed cases to possible cases. Omitting the denominator renders a probability completely worthless.

Thanks to experimental psychology the focus of the classical debate on whether decision-making by humans has a rational or irrational basis has shifted to the statistical mind, raising the question of whether we are capable of reasoning in terms of probabilities.[2] The response by most experimental psychologists is categorical. Kahneman and Tversky sum up their position thus: 'People do not follow the principles of probability theory in judging the likelihood of uncertain events [. . .]. Apparently, people replace the laws of chance by heuristics which sometimes yield reasonable estimates and quite often do not.' According to Slovic our lack of probabilistic skills is a proven fact: humans have not developed a mind capable of grasping uncertainty conceptually. This view was endorsed by the well-known evolutionary biologist Stephen Jay Gould. After examining the work of the winner of the 2002 Nobel prize in economics and his main co-author, Gould concluded that: 'Tversky and Kahneman argue, correctly I think, that our minds are not built (for whatever reason) to work by the rules of probability, though these rules clearly govern our universe.'

Under these circumstances Bayesian logic seems even further beyond our reach. The case of the medical examination described in the previous chapter was presented to American physicians and medical students. An overwhelming majority answered that the chances of being ill if the examination was positive ranged from 70% to 80%, 10 times higher than the right answer, 7.5%. A survey in Germany revealed that HIV-Aids counsellors were just as confused by Bayesian reasoning. After being given the data to calculate the probability that a person who had tested positive was actually a carrier of the virus, test participants produced answers very close to one, whereas the right answer was closer to 50%. If you think you are ill and decide to have an examination, make sure you choose a doctor who is trained in statistical analysis!

In short it seems to be an open-and-shut case. As Kahneman and Tversky assert: '[In] his evaluation of evidence, man is apparently not a conservative Bayesian: he is not Bayesian at all.'[3] Participants in tests go so far as to resist attempts by experimenters to correct and instruct them. This reaction is comparable to the impact of optical effects: although we know they are optical illusions we persist in taking a bump for a hole, or in seeing an area as smaller or larger than it really is.

In the 1990s Gerd Gigerenzer firmly opposed this standpoint. According to the German psychologist humans are not deaf to statistical reasoning. Unlike Gould he upholds the idea that the human mind evolved, while integrating Bayesian algorithms. However, to be of any use such algorithms must be expressed in practical terms, close to their internal format, as is apparently the case with frequencies in their natural form, but not probabilities. (See the box.)

Cognitive science has made further progress, since the experimental work of Kahneman, Tversky and Gigerenzer, in particular with regard to language learning. Recent work seems to favour the idea of a Bayesian brain,[4] endorsing the conviction expressed by Laplace two centuries earlier in the introduction to his philosophical treatise on probabilities: 'the theory of probabilities is basically just common sense reduced to calculus; it makes one appreciate precisely something that informed minds feel with a sort of instinct, often without being able to account for it'.

Choosing the right prior probability

We explained above that the degree of prior certainty we choose to assign to a hypothesis may be based on objective data from the past, scientific theory or indeed subjective belief. It is now time to

Presenting Bayes' rule in other terms

People make mistakes in Bayesian calculations because the problem is not clearly stated. They make far fewer mistakes if data are set forth in a 'natural frequency format', instead of being given as frequencies expressed as percentages or values ranging from 0 to 1.

This approach presents the medical examination in the following way:

(a) 10 out of 1,000 patients who undergo an X-ray examination have cancer;
(b) 8 out of 10 patients with cancer test positive;
(c) 99 out of the 990 patients who do not have cancer test positive.

If we take another group of patients, who have also tested positive, how many would you expect to have cancer?

Presented in these terms one may easily reason as follows: 8 patients who tested positive have cancer and 99 patients who tested positive do not, so in all 107 patients tested positive; the proportion of patients with cancer among those who tested positive is therefore 8/107, in other words a probability of 0.075.

This problem and numerous variants were employed by Gigerenzer and his fellows in experiments on groups comprising doctors, students and ordinary people. They also developed a method for learning Bayes' rule in under two hours, which is now widely used in Germany to train medical staff.

tighten up that statement and show how this prior choice influences the degree of posterior certainty.

Bayes' rule applies equally well to statistical reasoning as to probabilistic logic. In the first case the prior value we take is based on observation. For example, a die has been rolled ten times, the six has come up twice, and we are about to roll the same die, starting a new series. The prior probability of the six coming up again (or, more simply, the prior) is two-in-ten. Before rolling any dice at all, we may also choose a theory such as the one which posits the equiprobability of any of the faces coming up. This can no longer be treated as an observation, rather a belief. It assumes that the die is perfectly balanced, which is never the case. The strict equiprobability of one-in-six is rarely observed, even if a die is rolled several thousand times. Some people have taken the trouble to check this. So by choosing the prior, we are engaging in probabilistic logic. Equiprobability is the most plausible initial hypothesis, lacking any knowledge of the properties of the die on the board. Adopting a more subjective stance we may also opt to assign a prior probability of one-in-ten to the six, because we know we are unlucky or having a bad day.

The effect of the prior is described visually in the next box. It shows that only in two cases does it have no effect: either there are an infinite number of observations or measurements, or the beliefs are vague and all the outcomes equiprobable. Between the two the prior carries a varying amount of weight.

In this example Bayes' rule worked one of its many magic tricks, reconciling perceived probability with its objective counterpart. It combines an initial perception regarding the plausibility of a hypothesis or the probability of an event with a calculated probability based on new knowledge.

Predicting the probability of the next event

Will the sun rise tomorrow? According to Laplace the answer is uncertain, having estimated the probability of it not rising to be 1/1,826,215! In this example – which earned him much mockery and criticism – he applied a general formula which he had worked out himself. His rule of succession is based on the same principles as Bayes' rule.

Illustrating Bayesian revision

Figure 6.1 describes a probability density function.[5] It expresses your prior judgement on the proportion of your compatriots who hold the same opinion as you do on nuclear power. According to you, the proportion is probably (95% chance of being right) between 5% and 55%, and its most likely value is 20%. Of course, someone else may be more sure than you are, in which case the curve would be more pointed; on the other hand a third party might only have a very vague prior conviction, making the curve very flat.

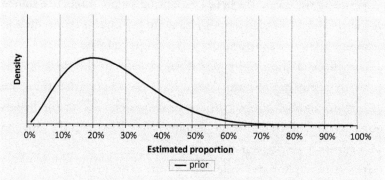

Figure 6.1 Probability density function

Let us now assume that one of your friends has carried out a mini-survey of acquaintances. Of the twenty people she has questioned, eight (40%) shared your point of view. With some knowledge of statistics you will be able to define what is known as the likelihood function, summarizing the survey's findings. The light grey curve in Figure 6.2 plots its density. Had a higher number of people been surveyed, the curve would have had a steeper peak. As we all know, the larger the number of people polled, the greater the certainty associated with poll results.

You are now ready to update your initial judgement by applying Bayes' rule. Just multiply the two previous functions. The dark grey curve in Figure 6.2 plots the new density function which expresses the proportion of your compatriots who hold the same opinion as you do on nuclear power, given the results of your friend's mini-survey.

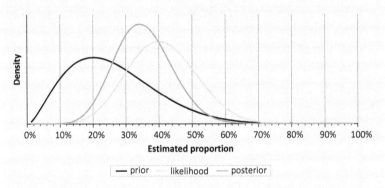

Figure 6.2 Prior distribution, posterior distribution and likelihood function

It is immediately apparent that the posterior is more certain than the prior – the dark grey curve is not as flat as the black one. This is hardly surprising, because new data result in a better judgement. It is also worth noting that observation carries more weight than the prior: the posterior peaks at 34%, a value closer to 40% than to 20%. Finally, you should bear in mind that if the survey had polled a larger number of people, the dark grey posterior curve would have been even closer to the light grey curve, which would – others things being equal – also rise to a steeper peak. The likelihood would have weighed even more heavily on the prior. Ultimately, if observations are carried out on very large samples, the event is repeated a large number of times, or a quasi-exhaustive survey is conducted, the choice of the prior no longer has any bearing on the posterior. It makes no difference.

On the other hand, what happens if the prior is changed? If your prior is subject to greater uncertainty (a flatter black curve), it will weigh less heavily on the posterior, which will resemble more closely the likelihood. The prior exerts less influence. If, at the outset, you have absolutely no idea of how many people share your views (a horizontal line from one end to the other), the prior will exert no influence on the posterior; the latter will follow the likelihood exactly – a horizontal straight line does not distort, through multiplication, the likelihood density function. The weightless prior is obtained in the same way as equiprobability when rolling dice. If you know nothing about its lack of balance, the posterior will only be influenced by each roll of the dice, not your initial belief.

The problem of succession may be stated in the following abstract terms: what is the probability of picking a red ball out of an urn at the $(n + 1)$th attempt, given that for the n previous attempts, k red balls were picked? Or alternatively, posing a more concrete question addressed in the following section, given that the global reactor fleet has experienced eleven core-melt events in 14,400 reactor-years, what is the probability of another core-melt occurring tomorrow?

Your intuitive answer to the question on the next draw is very probably k/n. Previously k red balls have been picked from the urn in the course of n draws, so you conclude that the same proportion will also be valid next time. It is not a bad solution, but there is a better one. From a mathematical point of view your answer does not work if $n = 0$.[6] So you cannot use this formula to determine the probability of the first event, for example a core-melt before an accident of this type ever happened. Using the formula means you can only base your judgement on observation. Much like Doubting Thomas, you only believe what you can see. You may, however, have carried out previous observations (though this is fairly unlikely in the case of picking balls out of an urn), or perhaps you fear that the person who set the urn on the table wants to cheat you. In short, you are not basing your decision on your prior; you are not using Bayesian reasoning.

To solve the succession problem Laplace resorted to Bayes' rule, though it was not yet known as such. Indeed Laplace reinvented it, very probably never having heard of the work done by the British minister. He started from an *a priori* judgement, assuming that only two outcomes were possible: picking a red ball or a ball that was not red. Each had an equal chance of occurring, so the probability was one-in-two. He thus obtained a formula $(k + 1)/(n + 2)$. For example, if five draws are made and a red ball is only picked once, the probability predicted by the formula for the sixth draw is $(1 + 1)/(5 + 2)$, or $2/7$, or indeed 0.286. Alternatively, if we return to the example of the sun,[7] Laplace went back to the earliest time in history, 5,000 years or 1,826,214 days earlier, making 1,826,213 successful sunrises out of 1,826,213. The probability that the sun would also rise on the following day was consequently $(1,826,213 + 1)/(1,826,213 + 2)$ and the probability of the sun not rising was $1–(1,826,213 + 1)/(1,826,213 + 2)$, or one chance in 1.8 million.

Laplace proceeded as if two virtual draws had been made, in addition to the real ones, one yielding a red ball, the other a non-red ball. Hence the simple, intuitive explanation of the origin of his formula: he adds two to n in the denominator, because there are two virtual draws; and adds one to k in the numerator, to account for the virtual draw of a red ball. From this point of view the choice of the sun is unfortunate. The merit of the prior depends on it being selected advisedly. Laplace was a gifted astronomer, yet he chose a prior as if he knew nothing of celestial mechanics, as if he lacked any understanding of the movement of the sun apart from the number of its appearances.

The choice of the prior to predict picking a red ball at the next draw is more successful. It anticipates Keynes' principle of indifference:

when there is no *a priori* reason to suppose that one outcome is more probable than another, equiprobability is the only option. If there is nothing to indicate a bias, the prior probability that a coin will land heads up is one-in-two, the prior probability of scoring a three with a roll of a die is one-in-six, and so on. A $1/n$ probability makes complete sense if no prior knowledge or expertise suggests that a specific outcome among the n possible outcomes is more probable than another.

Thanks to progress in probability theory we now have a better instrument than the Laplace formula for solving the succession problem. The solution found by the French mathematician, $(k+1)/(n+2)$, has become the particular case in a more general formula. This formula is still the result of Bayesian reasoning, but it has the key advantage of introducing a parameter which expresses the strength of the prior in relation to new observations and knowledge. For the two extreme values of this parameter, either your confidence in the prior is so strong that nothing will change your mind – so the posterior cannot diverge from the prior – or your confidence in the prior is so weak that the tiniest scrap of new data will demolish it – leaving the posterior exclusively dependent on the new data.

In this modern version the expected probability of picking a red ball in the $(n + 1)$th draw is written as $(k + st)/(n + s)$, where t is the prior expected probability – for example 0.5 for equiprobability – and s is the parameter measuring the strength of the prior. The two virtual draws, of which one is successful, added by Laplace, are replaced here by st virtual draws (where $t < 1$) of which s are successful. In other words we return to Laplace's formula if $s = 2$ and $t = 1/2$. Bear in mind that if $s = 0$, the posterior, in other words the probability of drawing a red ball in the $(n + 1)$th draw, becomes k/n. Only the observations count. On the other hand, if s tends towards infinity, the posterior tends towards the prior.[8] Only the prior counts.

The general formula, $(k + st)/(n + s)$, corresponds to the summit of a curve similar to the light grey curve in Figure 6.2. Similarly, the value t marks the top of the black curve in the same figure. So Bayes' rule does apply to functions. The prior probability and the observed probability are both random variables for which only the distribution and classical parameters (expectation, variance) are known.[9] The exact value is not known, but simply estimated by statements such as 'there is a 95 per cent chance that the target value is between 0.3 and 0.6'. The parameter s which expresses the strength of the prior may therefore be interpreted as the uncertainty of the prior. The greater the value of s, the steeper the curve; the lower the value of s, the flatter the curve (in mathematical terms $1/s$ is proportional to the variance, which measures the distribution on either side of the mean value of the prior function). Expert opinions can be finely quantified, thanks to this property. They can be queried too, for the most probable prior measurement of a phenomenon (t), but also the strength of their opinion (s). In this way two experts can state that they estimate the probability of radioactive emissions in the event of a core melt as 0.1, but one may be confident, assigning a value of 10 to s, whereas the other is much less certain, only crediting s with a value of 0.5.

An interesting feature of this way of calculating the probability of the next event is that it enables us to grasp the connection between perceived probability and acquired objective probability. At the out-set all you have is your subjective prior (the expected probability, t). Then you receive the objective information that k red balls have been picked in n draws (an expected probability of k/n). So your perception of the next draw is given by the posterior (the expected probability of $(k + st)/(n + s)$), which combines the two previous elements. In other words the perceived probability is seen as the updated prior probability taking into account the acquired objec-tive probability. This interpretation is fruitful because it provides a theoretical explanation for our biased perception of low and high probabilities.[10] There is a linear relation between the expectation of the perceived probability $(k + st)/(n + s)$ and the expectation of the acquired objective probability k/n. If $k/n < t$, the perceived probability is less than the objective probability.

What is the global probability of a core melt tomorrow?

In the wake of the Fukushima Daiichi disaster numerous scratch calculations appeared in the press to determine the observed frequency of nuclear accidents and estimate the probability of future accidents.[11] They started from the fact that four core melt events followed by a massive release of radioactive material (Chernobyl 4, Fukushima Daiichi 1, 2 and 3) had occurred with a global nuclear fleet which had operated for a total of 14,000 reactor-years. So the observed accident frequency was 4/14,000, or about 0.0003. If we restrict ourselves to Europe and its 143 reactors, we should therefore expect 1.29 accidents in the course of the next thirty years ($30 \times 143 \times 0.0003$). Of course, this number is not a probability because it is higher than one. Confusing it with a probability is tantamount to saying that in a family with four children the probability of having a daughter is 2 (0.5×4), whereas in fact it is 15/16 ($1-1/(2 \times 2 \times 2 \times 2)$)! To calculate a probability, one needs to adopt a different approach. The most straightforward explanation could be presented in the form of an exercise for a student starting a course in statistics. 'If 14,000 reactor-years were asked: "Have you had a major accident?", and four answered yes, then what is the probability of an accident over the next 30 years for a fleet of 143 units?" The answer is 0.72. This result is calculated by modelling the probability of a major accident using a binomial distribution function with the following parameters [$30 \times 143; 0.0003$].[12]

This result is frightening, because it means that it is almost certain that an accident will occur in Europe over the next thirty years, a probability of 0.72 being almost equivalent to a three-in-four chance. Fortunately, this figure can be discarded, because it is based on assumptions and scientific method which make no sense. It assumes that all reactors are identical, representing the same degree of risk regardless of their design, their exposure to natural hazards, the precautions taken by their operators or indeed the ability of their regulatory authority. It also assumes that safety does not vary over time. What was true in the past will hold true tomorrow, so no provision may be made for improved safety. According to this approach, more effective preventive measures, stricter standards, better reactor designs or even the lessons learned from past accidents have no impact on performance. Nor would it make any difference if efforts and expenditure to improve safety were dropped. In short, it supposes that the entire European fleet is in an imaginary state of permanence, perfectly homogeneous and immutable, with each reactor being replaced by an identical unit and all of them exposed to the same risk of failure regardless of their geographical situation and operations.

Technically speaking, the method outlined above is open to criticism because of the very low number of observations on which it is based. It is hazardous, to say the least, to estimate the value of a parameter statistically on the basis of just four observations!

But, in our view, the main methodological shortcoming of a scratch calculation of this sort is the assumption that our knowledge of the subject is based entirely on these observations. It proceeds as if the probability of another accident tomorrow could only be elucidated and parameterized by the past observed frequency, k/n. This reasoning focuses exclusively on observation, completely disregarding all the other learning which has accumulated on the subject. Yet tens of thousands of engineers, researchers, technicians and regulators have been working on precisely this topic for the past sixty years. It is as if the only hope of salvation was in major accident data, despite their number being extremely limited, unlike other forms of knowledge. It considers that the parameter indicating the strength of the prior (previously designated as s) has a value of zero. Such an approach is as extremist as its opposite: refusing to attach any credit to observations of past accidents to predict the probability of an accident in the future, in other words, leaving s to tend towards infinity.

A simple example may be used to illustrate how observation and other knowledge can be combined to predict future nuclear risks. There are no particular difficulties regarding observations, apart from their very limited number. This constraint may, however, be slightly reduced if we focus on the risk of a core-melt accident, of which there are eleven cases,[13] rather than the risk of core melt leading to release, of which there are only four instances. As ever, choosing the prior is tricky, but we may take advantage of the availability of probabilistic safety assessments, the results of which summarize all the existing knowledge on accidents, apart from observations. On the basis of assessments carried out in the 1990s on US reactors, we may choose to add to the data on 11 accidents in 14,000 reactor-years, a virtual observation of 1.6 accidents in 25,000 reactor-years. This virtual observation is derived from the expected value of the probability of core melt, estimated by the experts as 6.5×10^{-5} per reactor-year, associated with an uncertainty measured by a prior strength of 25,000.[14] We thus obtain values for t and s and can apply the formula $(k + st)/(n + s)$, or $[11 + (25,000 \times 6.5 \times 10^{-5})]/(14,000 + 25,000)$, which equals 3.2×10^{-4}. In other words the experts propose a mean probability of core-melt per reactor-year of 6.5×10^{-5}; and observed evidence leads to 7.8×10^{-4}. By advisedly combining the two sources of knowledge we obtain a probability of 3.2×10^{-4}. To make this figure easier to grasp, we may translate it by calculating that the probability of a core-melt accident next year in Europe is 4.4 in 1,000. This probability is less than half the value obtained from the observed frequency of core-melt accidents on its own.

It is nevertheless very high, because the approach used in this example is based on the same oversimplifying hypotheses criticized above, especially the assumption that the accident probability we want to measure has remained constant over time. But progress has been made on safety and these gains are reflected in the risk of a core melt. A large number of the accidents taken into account happened during the early years of the development of civil nuclear power.[15]

Nor is the above approach ideal, because it assumes that events are unconnected. Yet the European, or global, nuclear fleet in 2012 is fairly similar to the one that existed in 2011, in 2010, and so on. In other words, we are not dealing with a situation akin to rolling dice, in which the result of one roll has absolutely no bearing on the following one. On the contrary the occurrence of one major accident may point to others, because we are still dealing with the same reactors.[16] For example, an accident may indicate that a similar problem affects other reactors of the same design or subject to comparable natural risks. A recent study sought to remedy these two shortcomings.[17] The model it used weights accident observations according to the date when they occurred. It calculates a sort of discount rate which, with time, tends to reduce the influence of old accidents over the probability of an accident now. With this model the probability of a core-melt accident next year in Europe is 0.7 in 1,000, less than one-sixth of that calculated with the previous approach.

How may we conclude this second part devoted to risk? By emphasizing the pointless opposition between experts and the general public, with both parties accusing the other of rank stupidity. The experts, with their sophisticated calculations, have allegedly made massive mistakes estimating the frequency of major accidents and the associated damage. Locked up in their laboratories, their certainty has purportedly blinded them to events that are glaringly obvious, namely the recurrence of disasters since Three Mile Island. On the other hand the general public is supposedly guilty of yielding exclusively to its fear of disaster, stubbornly clinging to its rejection of calculated probabilities. Brainwashed by a stream of disaster scenes and incapable of basing the slightest decision on statistical evidence, people's reactions are ruled by emotion and nothing else; they are ostensibly quite unable to see that coal or hydroelectric dams constitute risks every bit as serious as nuclear power plants. So you may choose sides, denigrating either the experts or the general public! However, there is no contradiction between analysing on paper sequences of events that may potentially lead to a core melt, and observing accidents and their causes. Furthermore, theory provides ways of combining and associating such knowledge. It enables us to find rational explanations for the irrational, which becomes much less or not at all irrational. We have a better grasp of how probabilities are distorted, either through simple heuristics or gradual acquisition of Bayesian methods, depending on one's school of thought. What was once perceived as irrational loses that connotation once it is seen to conform to identified mechanisms. A fuzzy border now separates rational decision-making from other forms of choice. Is it irrational to take decisions under uncertainty without allowing for risk aversion? Surely it would in fact be irrational to go on denying the existence of such aversion? When Maurice Allais presented Leonard Jimmie Savage with a puzzle, the latter's answer contradicted the results of his own theory. When he appears as a guest-speaker in Israel, Daniel Kahneman avoids travelling on Tel Aviv buses for fear of an attack. In so doing he is fully aware that his actions are dictated by perceived, rather than calculated, probability.

The loss of bearings which fuels discord between experts and the general public, opposing the rational and irrational, is most uncomfortable. It raises a terrifying question: should government base its decisions on perceived probabilities or on those calculated by experts? In the case of nuclear power, the former are largely overestimated, a situation which is likely to last. It would be foolish to treat the attitude of the general public as the expression of fleeting fears which can quickly be allayed, through calls to reason or the reassuring communication of the 'true' facts and figures. If government and the nuclear industry did share an illusion of this sort, it would only lead to serious pitfalls. The reality test, in the form of hostile demonstrations or electoral reversals, may substantially add to the cost for society of going back on past decisions based exclusively on expert calculations. On the other hand, the airline security syndrome will inevitably spread to nuclear power if the authorities only pay attention to public perception of probabilities. If the propensity to invest in nuclear safety is not brought under control, many expensive new protective measures will accumulate, without necessarily having any effect.

PART III

Safety regulation

An analysis of the American, French and Japanese cases

The accident at Fukushima Daiichi starkly revealed the deficiencies of safety regulation. How is public confidence in nuclear power to be maintained if safety standards are badly designed or simply not enforced? The disaster in Japan resulted from a conjunction of natural forces, but it probably would not have caused so much damage had there been a clearer division between the regulatory authorities and the nuclear power companies they were supposed to be supervising. How then is safety to be effectively regulated? In the absence of powerful, independent, transparent and competent regulatory authorities, nuclear power will not be able to progress worldwide.

Nuclear power is regulated long before work starts on building plants. Investors must obtain a licence from the government or regulatory authority tasked with safety. The design of reactors is subject to a whole series of standards and principles laid down by the public authorities. For construction of the plant to be authorized it must comply with these 'specifications'. During the construction project the regulator must check that the relevant standards are being implemented. It must subsequently intervene all the way through the operating life of the plant, from initial grid-connection to final decommissioning. It monitors the operator's compliance with the safety regulations it has established. So a safety failure with the potential to cause an accident is not necessarily only the failure of the organization which built or is operating the plant, which may not have complied with regulatory safety requirements. It may also be due to shortcomings in the regulatory framework itself, its loopholes or fuzzy definitions, lack of supervision and inadequate sanctions. But in the nuclear power industry it is not easy to draw a line between good and bad regulation, between proper and improper enforcement. A nuclear reactor is a complex system. It is difficult to define and assess its safety level. This depends on the design of reactors, their maintenance, the way they are operated and their geographical location. It is impossible to reduce the safety level to a single variable. But supposing for a moment that a probabilistic criterion – for example a core-melt frequency of less than 0.000001 per year of operation – could fulfil this role, there would be no way of observing it directly. Nor would it be easy to define precise technical guidelines to ensure this safety level was actually maintained. The regulation of nuclear safety is necessarily based on a large number of criteria and standards.

It is much easier to perform an economic analysis of safety regulation.[1] Such analysis highlights the overall problems that need to be solved, advocates regulatory, legal and institutional solutions, checks that the measures already in force are satisfactory, and shows why public intervention is necessary and the form it should take. In this way it goes far beyond simply estimating the impact of safety measures on costs. Why then are self-regulation and civil liability not sufficient to guarantee an adequate safety level? Why must the safety regulator be independent from both industry and government? Is it necessary to set quantitative safety goals, such as risk thresholds? Would it be preferable to establish detailed standards to which engineering firms and operators must conform, or rather to set overall goals for performance? Economic analysis of regulation shows that safety is not an exclusively technical concern. There are other institutional and organizational solutions – often less expensive than adding certain redundant devices – which may substantially increase the level of nuclear safety.

SEVEN

Does nuclear safety need to be regulated?

What an odd question! Surely everyone accepts the need to regulate nuclear safety? Only economists would think of querying something so obvious! Naturally we have no intention of claiming that the need for state regulation in this field is a recent discovery. The value of economic theory resides in the analytical process it offers for this purpose. In terms of methodology it always starts from opposition to state intervention per se. Such intervention is always open to question and the first thing an economist will ask is why the market is not sufficient in itself to solve the problem. This does not necessarily reflect an ideological preference, on his or her part, for the invisible hand or outright rejection of public intervention, but simply the knowledge that economic theory has identified specific conditions in which the market is not an effective means of securing the general economic interest, in other words maximizing wealth for the whole of society.[1] Externalities, such as pollution, or a public good, such as national security, are the main impediments to market efficiency. If there is no market failure, there is no justification for public intervention. But economists also know that the state – be it embodied by planners, regulators or legislators – has weaknesses of its own, and that public intervention is not perfect. It is easy to summarize what economic theory prescribes with regard to regulation: resorting to the visible hand of the state is justified if, and only if, the defects of public intervention are less than those of the market it sets out to correct. In short, the benefit of public intervention must exceed its cost, otherwise *laissez-faire* is the only option and one must make do with an inefficient market. (Unless, of course, the means can promptly be found to reduce the cost and inefficiency of the visible hand of the state.)

When it comes to nuclear safety, the market does not provide operators with sufficient incentives to make the necessary efforts. The signals it sends are too weak. On the demand side of the electricity market, consumers are exposed to a relatively low average risk of accident. They are not spontaneously inclined to pay for all the necessary safety efforts, in particular the protection of local residents, who are exposed to much greater risk. Consumers are primarily concerned about the price of electricity, which is seen as a commodity. On the supply side, it is in the collective interest of both operators and reactor vendors to invest in safety. Another disaster would damage their image and future prospects. But individually each company stands to gain by doing nothing (or very little, as we shall see below). It can maximize its gains by pocketing the collective benefits of a lower accident-risk without additional expenditure. In keeping with this rationale all the companies would tend to behave like stowaways, but if so there would no longer be a ship to carry them. To deal with this two-sided failure, the most cost-effective form of regulation would be to establish rules on civil liability. But full insurance against accidents must be possible for this to work. Unfortunately, as we shall see, this is not the case for nuclear power.

Inadequate private incentives

The economically optimal level for nuclear safety is determined in the same way as efforts to mitigate pollution. The same principles apply as those presented in Chapter 1 with regard to reducing carbon-dioxide emissions. The level of safety efforts is optimal when the marginal social cost of protection is equal to the marginal social benefit of the damage avoided. Beyond this level, additional efforts to improve safety cost more than the additional benefit they yield. Below this level additional efforts can still be made, their cost being lower than the benefit they procure.

Left to itself a market balances private costs and private gain. An operator will invest in safety as long as the resulting profit exceeds the cost entailed. This cost roughly corresponds to the social cost. Setting aside a few emergency services devoted to nuclear risk, the operator shoulders the full cost. In France the government even charges operators for the police officers tasked with supervising nuclear power plants and fuel transport.[2] On the other hand, an operator only receives part of the benefit from the safety measures it deploys, for example in terms of the industry's image. Its efforts to improve safety being trimmed to suit the limited benefit it receives, they will necessarily be inadequate.

Though inadequate, it will still make some effort on safety. The private incentives for operators are far from negligible. Improving safety contributes to reducing the number of breakdowns; in turn, fewer breakdowns mean higher electricity production, so more revenue. As we saw in Chapter 1, the load factor is critical for the profitability of a nuclear power plant, due to its very high fixed costs. Drops in output or temporary reactor shutdowns are very expensive for an operator. There is every incentive to restrict them as much as possible. Furthermore, in the event of a core melt, even without the release of radioactive material to the environment, the generating company loses its means of production and the value of the asset is wiped out. An operator which only owns one reactor will go bankrupt. Even with several in its fleet it may well suffer the same fate, having lost the confidence of consumers, banks, small investors and even its workforce. The risk of disappearing is a powerful incentive for an operator to concern itself with safety. So it would be foolish to imagine that nuclear operators are actively hostile to prevention and regulation. This point is important for two reasons. Regulation would be much more expensive and a great deal less effective if nuclear operators stood to gain by blocking initiatives and getting round measures introduced by the regulator. In addition, government sometimes fails in its duty to protect the general public: when confronted with a toothless regulator, operators are not exposed only to temptations that jeopardize safety.

However, it would also be a mistake to conclude that, for lack of anything better, self-regulation would be an acceptable solution. Our concern is merely to emphasize that market forces and safety are not wholly antagonistic. Self-regulation may set in motion a virtuous circle in order to reduce what is known as 'free-riding'; witness the case of the Institute of Nuclear Power Operations (see box).

So the question is not whether self-regulation can take the place of state intervention, but rather the extent to which it may play a complementary role. Self-regulation streamlines the flow of information and the dissemination of good practice among operators, the latter no longer restricting themselves to the single channel connecting them to the safety authority. The larger the number of operators, the greater this advantage: they currently number more than twenty-five in the US. Self-regulation can partly fill a vacuum too. National regulators are trapped inside their respective borders; they can neither inspect nor stigmatize operators outside their jurisdiction, nor yet act against black sheep behaving in a way that threatens the global industry as a whole. To do that would require an international federation of operators, playing the same role as the INPO but worldwide. A World Association of Nuclear Operators, dedicated to the safety of nuclear power plants, does now exist, but its operating rules are a far cry from the US equivalent. The peer inspections it implements are neither systematic nor mandatory; results are only reported to the operator being inspected; there is no scoring system or ranking, nor any sense of stigma associated with shortcomings. This pale replica of the INPO was set up after the Chernobyl accident. The Fukushima Daiichi disaster could have given rise to an increase in its powers,

The Institute of Nuclear Power Operations: a case of successful collective regulation

After the accident at Three Mile Island on 28 March 1979 the reputation and credibility of all the nuclear operators in the United States were seriously damaged. They realized that the image of the nuclear electricity industry was a common good and that the existence of just one black sheep constituted an economic threat to them all. On the strength of this realization they decided to set up a trade federation to promote progress and excellence in safety. The INPO came into existence seven months after the accident. Marking a new departure, it relied on peer pressure to oblige operators, in particular those with a poor record, to improve their safety performance. At two-year intervals mixed teams, comprising INPO employees (currently about 400) and safety experts working for operators other than the power plant being inspected, assessed the safety of each plant. Since the INPO was first started, some 13,000 peer-assessors have contributed to the work of these teams. Their appraisals are reported and discussed at an annual gathering, devoted exclusively to this topic, for the CEOs of nuclear operators. Poor performers are singled out and must remedy any detected deficiencies. If they fail to improve safety conditions they run the risk of being ostracized by the rest of the trade and barred from the INPO.

The INPO is a success.[3] It has contributed to continuously and significantly improving the safety of the US nuclear fleet, while reducing the gap between the overall average and poor performers. This is not a cover-up, with cosmetic safety measures acting as a front for communication and lobbying objectives. At first sight an economist is inclined to view such an achievement as an anomaly. Economic theory explains that corporate coalitions are by nature unstable. As the free-rider phenomenon also operates over time, the INPO should supposedly have folded once the shockwave of Three Mile Island had passed. An operator which persists in substandard performance avoids expenditure while benefiting from the positive collective image built up by its fellows, and from the lower probability of another accident in the US. Coalitions can only be sustained if there is an effective mechanism offering incentives and imposing sanctions on deviants. Peer pressure, a force identified by sociologists, does not seem to carry enough weight. In fact it is underpinned by economic mechanisms. Firstly, a form of financial solidarity comes into play among US nuclear operators if one of their number suffers an accident. It is in their interest to institute mutual supervision, as they are under a legal obligation to contribute to compensation paid out for damage caused by a fellow operator. Secondly, INPO assessments affect the level of compulsory civil liability insurance premiums. The better an operator performs, the less it contributes to Nuclear Electric Insurance Ltd, which is jointly owned by nuclear generating companies. NEIL requires the organizations it insures to be INPO members, giving added weight to the threat of exclusion: an operator excluded by its peers will struggle to obtain insurance or will have to pay a much higher premium. Lastly, the INPO is supported by the US Nuclear Regulatory Commission. It submits inspection reports, annual updates on assessments and its ranking of operators to the NRC. If poor performers repeatedly fail to remedy shortcomings, it may threaten intervention by the regulatory authority. The INPO is not authorized to impose fines, nor yet to order a reactor to be shut down, but on the other hand it can persuade the NRC to sanction those who fail to toe the line. As with most self-regulation mechanisms, the effectiveness of the INPO is dependent on the presence of public regulation in the background.

but no one seized the opportunity. Nuclear operators which adopt an uncompromising approach to safety consequently remain at the mercy of black sheep operating plants tens of thousands of kilometres away.

Civil liability

From a legal standpoint the rules on civil liability are designed to compensate victims for damages. Inspired by considerations related to morality and fairness, such rules come into play after an accident. But an economist sees the rules on civil liability as an incentive. They encourage potential wrong-doers to take preventive action. In theory they bring about an optimal level of effort. A potentially liable economic agent seeks to minimize spending on *ex ante* prevention and *ex post* compensation for damage. It is therefore in its interest to stop preventive action if an additional measure costs more than compensating for any potential damage. The law of civil liability thus appears to offer an alternative to regulation. Rather than some authoritarian regulator laying down standards of behaviour and monitoring compliance, an economic agent has an incentive to behave virtuously. Public intervention can thus be restricted to the work of the courts which assess the value and order the payment of compensation to victims. As those liable for the damages may be insolvent, civil liability is often backed by a legal obligation to take out insurance. But even as cumbersome a system as this usually costs less than public regulation, which is why economists prefer it and recommend it whenever possible.

A system of this sort cannot take the place of regulation to guard against nuclear accidents: much like self-regulation, it can only play a complementary role. The financial limit on operators makes it impossible for civil liability to play an exclusive role. Liability must be unlimited, in order to provide an incentive for optimal preventive efforts. Unfortunately, in practice, the cost of the damage caused by a major accident can exceed the value of generating companies' assets. Disaster leads to bankruptcy, leaving third parties only partly compensated. This means that the operator is not being given sufficient incentive to take the necessary preventive measures in relation to the economically optimal level.

The problem of solvency can be overcome by a mandatory insurance mechanism, but this raises another obstacle: the impossibility of insuring the full risk of a major nuclear accident.[4] Major accidents are too infrequent for the average risk to be determined with sufficient accuracy. Nor is there sufficient certainty that the limited number of accidents and incidents will compensate an insurer for the occasions when it will have to pay out very high compensation. Confronted with a major accident, insurers and re-insurers may in turn be made insolvent. The annual insurance premium, not including margin and overheads, must be equal to the probability of an accident in the course of the coming year multiplied by the cost of the damage. As the probability of an accident occurring next year is equal to that of it occurring in any other reactor-year, the insurer must build up a reserve ahead of the event. However, if the accident occurs next year, the insurer will not have received a sufficient number of premiums to be able to compensate victims. The initial premiums, paid during the first few years of coverage, would therefore have to be high enough to constitute a reserve equal to the cost of average damages, raising the cost of the premium for the insured. Lastly, premiums will be too expensive for operators to pay if the size of the reserve is based on worst-case, rather than average, damages.

Given these various obstacles, civil liability can only play a secondary role. It is imperative for it to be associated with public safety regulation, to which it serves as a useful complement, acting as an incentive on operators to make up for the gaps and mistakes of regulation. The regulator cannot dictate every aspect of the behaviour and action of an operator and its workforce. Even if the regulator could do so, it would be unable to check compliance with its many requirements. In economics the fact that the regulator is relatively powerless is referred to as information asymmetry. The regulator does not possess all the information it needs – particularly regarding costs and performance – to regulate a firm. Nor is it able to check how much effort a firm makes to comply with its orders. The firm is better informed, but it is not in its interest to be entirely open towards the regulator without something in return. Telling all would be tantamount to shooting itself in the foot, the immediate consequence being more costly regulation. So regulation is necessarily imperfect when compared to the ideal situation of an all-knowing authority. The regulator inevitably makes mistakes. Practically speaking, a safety regulator may not establish a standard for an important safety criterion, for example if it can neither observe nor check this criterion. Lacking adequate information the regulator may also set a technical standard at too low a level. If the operator is subject to rules on civil liability, it is in its interest to make up for at least part of the regulator's shortcomings, introducing an in-house rule on the missing safety criterion or raising, on its own accord, the severity of the standard applied to the whole power-plant workforce. The higher its civil liability and the greater its assets, the more a firm will feel the incentive to make up for such shortcomings.

Civil liability for nuclear damage, in practice

In practice civil liability for nuclear-generation companies is usually capped. The extent of liability is generally slight in comparison to the cost of a major accident. In France, for instance, EDF's total liability amounts to €91.5 million. In the United Kingdom the upper limit is £140 million. Unlimited liability is exceptional. In the European Union it only applies in four Member States. But three of them – Austria, Ireland and Luxembourg – have no nuclear power plants.

Only German operators are required by law fully to compensate accident victims regardless of the extent of damage.

The low limit on civil liability is mainly a legacy of the past. It only makes sense in the light of the other characteristics of this regime, which is very particular compared to other sectors. In the event of an accident, the operator of a nuclear power plant is deemed liable regardless of how it has behaved. It is liable even if it has not committed any form of negligence, and has complied with all the regulatory requirements. Under this regime of 'strict' liability, there is no burden of proof. Furthermore, operator liability is exclusive: it must compensate for any damage caused by the negligence of a supplier present on-site or due to faulty design on the part of an equipment manufacturer. Responsibility for an accident may be shared, in terms of what actually happened, but only the operator is legally liable. These two characteristics, which are unusual in industry, offer an additional incentive for operators to maintain a high level of safety, entailing greater expenditure. Furthermore, this system secures quicker, more extensive compensation for victims.[5] This was in fact the goal pursued by early legislators framing nuclear law, when these terms were imposed on operators in the 1960s. In return, operators obtained a provision setting limits on their liability. They also pointed out that there was in any case an upper limit on the mandatory insurance associated with their liability, simply because insurers at that time were unable to offer more extensive coverage. In economic terms the system negotiated at this point increased incentives on the one hand – through strict, exclusive liability – while reducing them on the other by capping liability.

This limited-liability regime is obviously related to governments' determination to encourage the development of the nuclear industry. In the late 1950s initial debate on nuclear legislation in the US emphasized that it was critical to its vital national interests to develop nuclear energy and protect the industry against as yet unforeseeable demands for compensation.[6] Subsequently the 1963 Vienna

Convention on Civil Liability for Nuclear Damage underlined that 'unlimited liability [. . .] could easily lead to the ruin of the operator'.

Today the nuclear industry is no longer in its infancy, nor yet nuclear risk insurance. It is time to raise the upper limit on civil liability, or perhaps remove it altogether. Indeed the process has already started. The UK government, for example, plans to raise the cap on operator liability to £1.2 billion, eight times its current level. In the next few years France will probably set a new maximum limit at €700 million, a more than sevenfold increase. The highest limit applies to all US generating companies. The 1957 Price-Anderson Act, which has been revised several times, sets the maximum limit at $12.6 billion. This amount includes an operator's financial liability for its own plants ($375 million per site), which must be insured by a pool of private insurers. What is unique about the system is that if damage exceeds this amount, the other operators must pay. As mentioned above, each operator is collectively liable in the event of an accident on any reactor in the fleet. This liability takes the form of a payment, after the accident, which may be as much as $117.5 million for each reactor it owns. With 104 nuclear power plants currently operating, this collective mechanism thus provides for third-party compensation of up to $12.2 billion.

A subsidy in disguise?

If a major accident does occur in the US, leading to damages in excess of $12.2 billion, the US taxpayer will have to pay, with Congress, the insurer of last resort, drawing on the federal budget to supplement third-party compensation. Can this be construed as a form of subsidy and on what scale?

Opponents of nuclear energy are adamant that the upper limit on liability constitutes a subsidy:[7] the insurance premiums paid by generating companies would be higher if the cap were removed. This is indeed the case. Nuclear advocates counter that there is no subsidy unless an accident leading to damage exceeding the cap really occurs. Prior to such an eventuality taxpayers pay nothing. This too is true. Rather than fighting over how to define a subsidy, let us return to the basic economic principles outlined in Chapter 1. Theory prescribes that the decision-maker should pay the full cost of his or her action, and pocket the entire gain. When there is a gap between the private and public values of these two amounts, it must be filled by a series of taxes or subsidies which internalize external effects. The question is consequently whether the external cost of the accident should be partly or completely internalized. Economists favour the second solution, so that optimal quantities of goods are produced and consumed. For example, if the price of electricity generated using coal does not reflect the cost of carbon-dioxide emissions, too much electricity will be consumed and too much will be invested in this technology. Similarly, if the price of nuclear electricity makes inadequate, or no, provision for the cost of accidents, the incentives for consumers and investors in nuclear power will be too great.

How large is the residual externality, in other words the externality covered by neither the operator nor the consumer of nuclear electricity because of the cap on liability (see Chapter 1)? Or to use a term which is more straightforward but laden with connotations, how big is the hidden subsidy? Naturally the answer depends on the cap itself. If it is very high, exceeding for example the worst conceivable damage, there is no difference between limited and unlimited liability. A note of caution, though: there is no question of comparing maximum liability and the actual cost of an accident. Even the US limit falls far short of the damage caused by the Chernobyl or Fukushima Daiichi disasters. An accident in the US entailing $100 billion in damages would cost the taxpayer $87.4 billion. But this amount does not measure the residual externality. Allowance must be made for an accident's probability too. The subsidy is equal to the gap between the cost of the insurance required to cover the entire risk, and the cost of insurance only covering the maximum liability. To calculate this gap involves making assumptions about the damage distribution function. Unfortunately very few full estimates have been made: two in the US, one in France. In the US the gap is $2.3 million per reactor-year, according to old studies by academic economists,[8] or $600,000 per reactor-year, according to the Congressional Budget Office in its 2008 report on nuclear power.[9] Allowing for the size of the US fleet, these amounts correspond to an annual subsidy about a hundred times larger to the industry as a whole. In the case of France,[10] the disparity in the annual cost of insurance between the liability of EDF, limited to €91.5 million, and unlimited liability ranges from €140,000 to €3.3 million per reactor-year, depending on various assumptions as to accident probability and costs (making an upper-range annual subsidy worth €500 million for the whole French fleet). If we compare these amounts to the price per MWh of nuclear electricity, they are very low, about $0.07/MWh, or 0.1% of the levelized cost,[11] for the Congressional estimate, and €0.45 per MWh, or 0.75% of the levelized cost, for the highest French estimate.[12]

The low level of the preceding figures should not come as a surprise. To illustrate a particular point in Chapter 1 we made a scratch calculation, which found a cost of €1 per MWh. This value necessarily marks the upper limit of the subsidy provided by limited liability. It is equivalent to assuming that operators would not compensate any victims and that the cap on liability is set at zero. The gap between fully and partly internalizing the cost of accidents is always lower than the first term of this disparity.

Of course the residual externality can be inflated by making extreme assumptions on the probability of an accident and the cost of damages. In Part II we cited a study, commissioned by Germany's Renewable Energy Federation,[13] which reported an extremely high risk. It found, for example, that the probability of a terrorist attack was one-in-a-thousand per reactor-year, with upper-range damages costing several thousands of billions of euros. Under such conditions the subsidy would soar, exceeding even the full cost of generating electricity. Liability in Germany is unlimited, but the mandatory financial guarantee underwritten by private insurance or comparable means is limited to €2.5 billion per plant. The authors of the study claim that if the financial guarantee was unlimited, it would cost – depending on the various scenarios and assumptions they studied – from €139 per MWh to €6,730 per MWh, between twice and a hundred times the price of electricity![14]

By setting an upper limit on the operator's civil liability, the legislator is more or less certain to make a mistake, as it does not know the exact probability of the worst-case accident, less still the cost of the resulting damage. Would it not be preferable to put an end to this confusing situation by decreeing that the liability of nuclear operators is unlimited? There would be no need for any more calculations. Moreover, from an economic point of view, this seems the best solution. After all academics specializing in insurance and nuclear law have advocated doing just that. We shall rapidly demonstrate that a reform of this nature would be appropriate but very expensive to implement. To start with, we need to return to the two approaches to analysing liability mentioned in the introduction: one, economic, based on incentives for operators to improve safety; the other, legal, hinging on compensation to victims in the event of an accident. In an incentive-driven system, unlimited liability must be recommended, for it is always beneficial. If there is no safety authority or it is too lax, removing the cap on liability will prompt the operator to increase safety efforts. Such efforts will not attain their optimal level due to the finite value of its assets, but they will come much closer. Whenever regulation is too strict, the regulator imposes safety measures the marginal cost of which exceeds their marginal benefit. At first sight unlimited liability makes no difference to this situation. Regulation alone dictates the safety efforts which exceed the optimal level. Here too, reform can in fact be beneficial, bearing in mind that the regulator – which neither sees nor knows all things – may overlook some aspects of safety. Liability corrects this shortcoming: with unlimited liability efforts will come much closer to the optimal level than if it is limited.

Regarding compensation of victims, removing the cap on liability only has an effect if, at the same time, the legislator requires the operator, through insurance or a comparable mechanism, to obtain a financial guarantee which is also unlimited. Without this provision, victims will only receive compensation in the event of an accident up to the value of the operator's assets. In Germany, as we saw above, liability is unlimited but the financial guarantee is capped at €2.5 billion. Above this amount victims are compensated out of the assets owned by the bankrupt operator. If that is not sufficient, the taxpayer must pay. Implementation of the financial guarantee is impeded by the constraints described above regarding the degree to which nuclear risk can really be insured. The operator needs a market with insurers of adequate size and sufficient number. In practice few insurance companies specialize in nuclear accidents. Furthermore, they are generally organized on a strictly national basis, which limits the pooling of risk, competition and, ultimately, supply. So implementing an unlimited guarantee would fail due to insufficient capacity or excessive cost. It would reveal the shortcomings of the market for insurance and its derivatives; or, failing that, with help from creative financiers,[15] it would lead to premiums so expensive that operators could not afford them (at levels close to those estimated in the German study cited above). Predictably, unlimited liability underwritten by an unlimited guarantee is advocated by the opponents of nuclear power.

To conclude, reform of nuclear civil liability is needed. It should rest on three pillars: unlimited liability, capped financial obligations and pooling of risk at a European level. The first pillar is essential due to its positive effect on incentives, forcing them to rise to meet the glass ceiling constituted by liability, at a height determined by the value of the assets belonging to the person liable for damage. The cap on financial obligations is justified by the catastrophic nature of major nuclear accidents and the structures of the associated insurance market. The first two pillars correspond to the German model. The recommendation to introduce Europe-wide pooling of risk is inspired by the US example.

EIGHT

The basic rules of regulation

An engineer's view of safety regulation

Nuclear safety is primarily a matter for engineers, and that is just as well. A reactor operates at a crossroads between many disciplines, including chemistry, mechanical engineering, physics, automation, computing, neutronics and thermodynamics. To design and safely operate these technological monsters requires theoretical and practical knowledge of which engineers have a better grasp than managers or administrators. An accident may occur when a chain reaction goes out of control or a break appears in the cooling system. So the parameters which must be monitored are the fuel and moderator temperature coefficients, excess radioactivity, the neutron life cycle, capture cross-sections for neutrons of varying energies, calorific capacity and thermal conductivity, and radiation resistance of cladding. In short, a series of values with which accountants and financiers are wholly unfamiliar.

If you open a book on nuclear power written by an engineer, you will find the key principles and full details of how a reactor works, with a section on safety. This describes two possible approaches: a deterministic approach based on the defence-in-depth concept; or a probabilistic approach based on risk calculation. The first one dates from the 1950s, the second took shape in the late 1960s. For many years they were presented as rivals, but the quarrel of the ancients and moderns is now largely behind us. The probabilistic approach, discussed in Chapter 4, is based on identifying fault sequences which have the potential to initiate a major accident. The deterministic approach considers a whole list of plausible incidents and accidents, but without assigning them a probability. It frames rules, either to avoid such events purely and simply, or to mitigate them, but without trying to calculate the scale of the reduction. For example it is a basic rule that a failure on a single device must not be able to cause an accident on its own. Defence in depth is closely linked to the deterministic approach, because it involves raising a succession of barriers to prevent the release of radioactive materials into the environment. Furthermore, the dimensions of each barrier include a safety margin.

Engineers have designed and specified three main lines of defence: the cladding on fuel rods, the structure containing the primary cooling system and reactor vessel, and the concrete containment building which houses the entire system. Up to the mid-1960s this final barrier was thought to be impassable, unless it was hit by a missile.[1] A major accident leading to the massive release of radioactive material was not considered plausible. But the first theoretical calculations showed that it was possible: meltdown in the reactor core, following a break in the cooling system, would open a break in the pressure vessel and rupture the final barrier formed by the outer containment building. This was the so-called China syndrome, popularized by the eponymous film. Unfortunately the term is misleading: China is not at the antipodes in relation to the US; the nuclear reaction, if it carried on into the depths of the Earth, would stop when it reached the central core. The purpose of the first large-scale probabilistic assessment in the US was to calculate the frequency of such an event (see Chapter 4).

For some time the probabilistic and deterministic approaches were seen as alternative options, one taking the place of the other. Once it became possible to estimate probabilities, an approach which sought to determine the right dimensions of system components on the

basis of constraints such as maximum pressure, corrosion, temperature or indeed seismic intensity looked obsolete. Criticism also
focused on the effectiveness of a deterministic approach, because it
operates blindly. It provides no indication of what should be pri-
oritized, whether, for instance, it is more important to double the
thickness of the containment shell or the number of back-up pumps
on the primary cooling system. However, it gradually emerged that
probabilistic safety assessments were not a universal panacea either,
being unable to encompass all the parameters and causes of an accident. In particular, it is very difficult to assign probabilities to human
error or building faults. As we saw in Chapter 4, a probability cannot
be calculated in a situation of incompleteness, in other words when
all the states of the world are not known. A deterministic approach
is the only way of countering 'unknown unknowns', in other words
when you do not know what is unknown.

A deterministic approach is also a key component in non-
preventive defence in depth. As human and material weaknesses
cannot all be eliminated, safety measures must detect them in good
time and stop them. They must be prevented from cascading into a
core melt. Lastly, as the worst cannot always be avoided, safety must
plan and organize action to contain the accident and limit its impact,
for example by setting up rapid-action forces or taking measures to
evacuate residents. For thirty or forty years nuclear engineers have
debated, designed and worked out in detail these three aspects of
defence in depth – prevention, supervision and action.

That safety is primarily the concern of engineers does not mean
it should be their exclusive preserve. On the contrary, safety should
involve many other trades: physicians, psychologists, public-safety
specialists, experts in crisis-management and logistics, among others. Technicians, team leaders and managers play a key role in accident prevention inside nuclear power plants. There is now broad
consensus regarding the crucial importance of organization and the
human factor in risk management. Engineers may lack the necessary

competencies in these fields, much like economists, so we shall not venture any further down this path. On the other hand, safety comes at a cost and must be regulated, two domains on which economic analysis has focused for many years. It seeks to clarify the ends and means of implementing regulation, and to characterize good and bad regulatory practices.

Japanese regulation, an example to avoid

I must start by apologizing to my Japanese friends for being so blunt, but the serious shortcomings of nuclear-safety regulation in Japan reveal several essential basic principles.[2] In a word, the regulator must be independent, competent, transparent and powerful. These four characteristics have in the past all been cruelly lacking in Japan's Nuclear Industrial Safety Agency.

The shortcomings of nuclear regulation in Japan go back a long way, but it took the accident at Fukushima Daiichi to bring them to public attention. Specialists in nuclear safety and reactor operations were fully aware of these weaknesses. A scientific journalist recalls the following exchange, in the course of a conversation long ago with the head of a foreign safety agency.[3] 'So, where do you think the next nuclear accident will happen?' 'In Japan.' 'Why?' 'Because their system of control and supervision of nuclear safety is not up to scratch, and their safety authority isn't independent enough. On the contrary it is governed, to too great an extent, by political, industrial and financial priorities. I don't trust Japan's nuclear-safety system.'

In June 2007 a mission comprising a dozen foreign experts in safety regulation visited Nisa to carry out a peer review of its activities. Such missions are frequent. They are organized by the International Atomic Energy Agency at the request of governments and national authorities. Specialists refer to the process as the International Regulatory Review Service. The visit to Japan gave rise to a public report which gave the impression that the Japanese regulator was doing a pretty good job. Good marks were awarded, substantial progress was underlined. There was however some criticism, barely perceptible to anyone not familiar with IRRS reports on other countries. It noted, for instance, that some safety incidents were not followed by corrective measures due to 'limited use of resources for evaluating operating experience, and lack of systematic inspection and enforcement of licensees' activities by Nisa'. Those who took part in the mission complied with the rules of Japanese courtesy, which make it difficult to voice criticism, both face-to-face and in a public report.

The Fukushima Daiichi disaster uncovered a whole series of recurrent, serious misdemeanours committed by various operators. This information, which had previously escaped notice, revealed gaping holes in the supervision carried out by the safety regulator. Seven out of Japan's ten generating companies admitted to having knowingly deceived the regulator, falsifying the results of safety tests and reports on maintenance and repairs on their nuclear power plants.[4] Among their number, Tepco, the operator of the Fukushima Daiichi plant, was the most frequent offender.[5] In 2002 Nisa revealed that Tepco had omitted to report a whole series of faults observed on its containment buildings.[6] To begin with, the operator admitted to twenty-nine falsifications, finally owning up to about 200 between 1977 and 2002. In 2006 it admitted having censored primary-cooling-system temperature recordings. In 2007, when an accident occurred at the Kashiwazaki-Kariwa plant, Tepco initially denied that any radioactivity had been released, subsequently admitting that several thousand litres of contaminated water had been discharged into the sea. The same year the firm acknowledged having failed to report six emergency shutdowns at the Fukushima Daiichi plant. The *Japan Times* has alleged that just ten days before the disaster on 11 March 2011 Tepco sent yet another falsified report to the regulator.

Fukushima Daiichi also revealed the scale of conflicts of interest in Japan's nuclear village, highlighting shortcomings, inconsistencies and failures to implement safety regulations.

Revolving doors and failures

Revolving doors are common practice in the Japanese administration. For officials who transfer to industry, this process is known as *amakudari*, or descent from heaven. Much as the Shinto gods coming down to Earth, senior public-sector officials at the end of their career are invited to take up honorary or executive positions in business. In the past nearly seventy high-ranking Ministry of Economy, Trade and Industry (Meti) officials have joined the senior management of generating companies.[7] In 2011 thirteen of them were on the boards of various power operators. The *New York Times* reported that there was a position as vice-president at Tepco reserved as a retirement sinecure for a top-grade bureaucrat.[8] The head of the Agency for Natural Resources and Energy was the last official who was supposed to enjoy this benefit. The agency is a branch of Meti; the Japanese safety authority, Nisa, is affiliated to it, its budget and staff being dependent on it. ANRE Director-General Toru Ishida moved to Tepco in January 2011, initially working as an advisor before obtaining the reserved position as vice-president. The Fukushima Daiichi disaster derailed this plan, bringing the practice to public notice. Mr Ishida was forced to resign a month later.[9] Amakudari helps utilities stay on good terms with officials in charge of energy and obtain favourable decisions. The prospect of a prestigious, well-paid job is a sufficient incentive to convince some people to do the occasional favour. Here is just one example. In 2000, as part of Tepco's in-house inspections, a General Electric engineer, Kei Sugaoka, discovered that Tepco had falsified data. He reported this to the ministry in charge of energy and nuclear safety. For two years he received no response, and his warning was not followed up. All that happened was that Meti passed on his name to Tepco.

Fukushima Daiichi brought to light a large number of failures in safety regulation. They were detailed in the very thorough reports on two inquiries, one conducted by the government,[10] the other by the Diet (parliament).[11] Published after the accident, they are most instructive. Their analysis of the disaster draws attention to the mistakes, negligence and lack of preparation of all parties. None of the government, the civil service, or Tepco are spared. Point by point the two reports show how their respective short-comings led to loss of control over the nuclear power plant and disastrous mismanagement of the ensuing crisis. Both reports also focus on the underlying causes: backtracking over the main deci-sions on safety regulation, particularly measures to protect against earthquakes, flooding and station blackout. For safety regulation in Japan it was typical for changes in the regulations either to be scrapped altogether, amended to reduce their impact, delayed or never implemented. Three brief illustrations will suffice.

Shortly after it was set up, Nisa was supposed to frame a base-line document charting long-term changes in regulatory practice. In the end the report was only written and published ten years later.[12] The Guideline for the Reactor Site Evaluation, which was established in 1964, is still in place regarding construction permits for nuclear power plants.[13] In the US and most other countries nuclear power plants must be capable of coping with an eight-hour outage. This threshold was set following numerous incidents on the US fleet in the 1980s. In Japan the long-standing requirement for plant designers and operators was thirty minutes. Various working groups addressed and reported on the issue, ulti-mately concluding that there was no need for it to be changed.[14]

The anecdotes in the box on 'revolving doors' are appalling, but they are all due to the way safety regulation is organized in Japan. Even on paper the institutional system there cannot work, for the simple reason that Nisa lacks the full attributes of a nuclear safety authority. It only carries out part of the necessary regulation work, enjoys no real independence from policy-makers, and also supervises other hazardous industrial facilities. In this respect it cannot be compared to the modern model embodied by the NRC in the US, or the Autorité de Sûreté Nucléaire in France. Safety regulation in Japan is spread over several bodies. Nisa works alongside the Nuclear Safety Commission.[15] The latter reports directly to the Prime Minister and is supposed to supervise and check up on Nisa. But the NSC is not really empowered to investigate or sanction Nisa. The NSC is also supposed to duplicate some of its work, in particular carrying out inquiries before issuing operating licences, and framing regulatory directives and guidelines. However, it has no mandate to investigate operators. This 'reserve' regulator is headed by five commissioners, assisted by several hundred officials. Inspections, which are a key component of safety, are partly carried out, by legal provision, by a third body, the Japan Nuclear Energy Safety Organization (JNES). Nisa entrusts work to this technical support department, but has no authority over it. As the IRRS mission to Japan briefly noted, all the functions and responsibilities expected of a safety authority are present in the Japanese regulatory framework, but they are unfortunately dispersed. Their responsibilities are consequently diluted and pooling of information is inefficient.

Nisa is not strictly speaking an independent authority, rather an administrative body that is part of ANRE, which in turn is a branch of Meti, a powerful ministry. Nisa does not have its own budget, nor even autonomous personnel. There is no *de facto* separation from the organization tasked with energy and the economy. Indeed, most of its staff belong to ANRE. It is commonplace for personnel to move from an office supervising safety regulation to Meti departments tasked with nuclear affairs. Others transfer to or from the Ministry of Education, Science and Technology. Exactly the same situation prevails at the NSC, where staff are managed in a similar way. The NSC reports to the Cabinet, which decides policy on energy and trade. This institutional set-up does not

guarantee an airtight seal between safety regulation and the promotion of nuclear power. Moreover, the lack of any legislation requiring
complete transparency in the work of the three safety organizations –
NSC, Nisa and JNES – exacerbates the problem. Very few of the discussions, decisions, reports, minutes, inspections and projects are
brought to the attention of the general public, the media and local
authorities. There is no way for them to monitor progress on regulatory work and its results, or to determine whether efforts are
influenced by political imperatives or interest groups. It all goes on
behind closed doors.

No legislative or judicial power counterbalances the pressure on
safety exerted by the executive. In Japan the government appoints
Supreme Court judges. In turn the Supreme Court supervises the
office in charge of the team tasked with assessing, promoting and
sanctioning less senior judges. The same office, itself made up of
judges, vets all job allocations. According to J. Mark Ramseyer, Professor of Japanese legal studies at Harvard Law School, the appoint-
ment system in Japan ensures that sensitive cases will be settled, even
in courts of first instance, in line with the political priorities set by
the government.[16] As a former judge at the district court explained
to the *New York Times*,[17] 'Judges are less likely to invite criticism
by siding and erring with the government than by sympathizing and
erring with a small group of experts.' District courts have received
about fifteen complaints about safety defects, due in particular to
the proximity of nuclear power plants to seismic fault lines and non-
compliance with prevailing standards. The cases were lodged by local
opponents to projects to build new reactors or restart existing ones.
In only two cases did the courts rule in favour of the plaintiffs, but
their decision was overturned by the appeal court.

The Diet does not counterbalance government influence over
regulation either. Japan is a parliamentary democracy and the prime
minister is appointed by the lower chamber, of which he or she is
a member. In practice the leader of the party holding a majority is

elected prime minister. As the largest party in many majorities, the Liberal Democrats (LDP), held power almost without interruption from 1955 to 2009. It dominated the various assemblies and ruling coalitions. A separation exists between executive and legislative powers, but in political terms, they have marched in step for decades. In a democratic regime, parliament controls the authorities tasked with regulating network industries and public health. It is an essential characteristic of nuclear safety agencies, because their work extends into the long term, a responsibility which is generally better suited to law-makers than the executive. Japan is an exception in this respect, the Diet exerting no control over Nisa's work. On the contrary, the latter body reports to the NSC, itself answerable to the prime minister.

The Japanese regulator is a captive to industry

There are two sides to the independence enjoyed by a safety authority. We have just examined its position in relation to the executive. Our concern here is to put regulation out of the reach of the many, shifting goals which may interfere with nuclear safety, priorities such as maintaining living standards thanks to the price of electricity, or sustaining the trade balance by exporting nuclear materials and technology. The other, even more crucial, side hinges on independence from industry, primarily engineering firms and operators. The regulator must not adjust its actions to suit the interests of the companies it regulates. This would produce the same level of safety as with self-regulation, which is inadequate even under an unlimited-liability regime.

Since the work of George J. Stigler in the 1960s, economic theory has taken an interest in the risk of the regulator acting in the interest of those it regulates. This University of Chicago economist discovered an astonishing phenomenon. The price of electricity in US states where it was set by the regulator was no lower than in states where utilities were free to decide for themselves. Stigler then asked two questions, previously disregarded by economists, blinded by a conciliatory view of regulation in the general interest: who benefits from regulation? And why? His answer was that 'regulation is acquired by the industry and is designed and operated primarily for its benefits'.[18] To explain this bias he cited the dominant position enjoyed by industry in relation to other interest groups. Taxpayers, consumers or indeed people who suffer damages are more numerous than companies, yet they have fewer resources. It is more difficult for them to form a collective group. The theory of regulatory capture took shape with these preliminary ideas, but it has since progressed. We shall return to this point later, but in the meantime this sketchy account should be sufficient to understand relations between Japan's safety regulator and the operators of nuclear power plants, relations which the report on the Diet investigation rightly referred to as 'incestuous'.[19]

Questioned by members of the Diet, the NSC head Haruki Madarame said:

> The nuclear safety regulations until today have been based on a convoy system of the regulatory authority and utilities. The utilities proposed the least expensive safety standards, which in turn were approved by the authorities. This led to a vicious cycle in which the utilities did nothing and justified their inaction by claiming that the government had approved the safety standards.

He admitted that there are consequently many shortcomings in safety guidelines. 'Though global safety standards kept on improving, we wasted our time coming up with excuses for why Japan didn't need to bother meeting them', Mr. Madarame said.[20]

The Japanese regulator adjusted its behaviour to suit operators' concerns: witness the lamentable discussions between Nisa and the industry on preventive action on major accidents. They started in 2007, following the IRRS mission. The aim was to consider a new regulation specifying preventive measures required to meet international standards. The position of the Federation of Electric Power Companies was perfectly clear. It may be summed up in three points: avoid work to upgrade plants which would interrupt their operation; prevent stricter requirements which would force reactors to be shut down; and ensure that the regulation would not have a negative impact on current or subsequent litigation. The regulator accepted these imperatives and concluded that safety levels were adequate. The head of Nisa wrapped up the talks by saying that he shared industry's concern about litigation and its impact on output. He added that it might be necessary to convene a formal committee, but that first he wanted to settle the matter in hand. Ultimately these talks led to no changes until the accident at Fukushima Daiichi, and without the ensuing investigation no one would have been any the wiser.

Obviously there is nothing inevitable about regulatory capture by industry. As we have a better understanding of this process than in Stigler's day, we now have more effective solutions to counter it. The predominant influence of industry, compared to other interest groups, is due to unequal access to regulation. The financial resources at industry's disposal naturally spring to mind. But setting aside means, economic theory shows that the representation of interests is systematically distorted in favour of small homogeneous groups comprising potential losers.[21] Their homogeneity makes it easier to form a cohesive group; their small number is a powerful incentive for each member to act, and also makes it easier to identify those shirking their obligations; losers are more pugnacious than winners due to the endowment effect. You may recall the example, cited in Chapter 5, of mugs being randomly handed out to half the students in a class. The lucky ones set a higher selling price on their mugs, than their unfortunate counterparts were prepared to pay. But the authorities are empowered to deal with this disparity between interest groups: they can broadcast information widely, appeal for expressions of interest, invite stakeholders to make themselves known, officially recognize certain groups, make consultation procedures compulsory, encourage independent expert appraisals. In France there is a legal requirement for a local information committee to be set up for each nuclear power plant, with guidelines for its composition. It comprises policy-makers and the representatives of various organizations: environmental watchdogs, trade federations, chambers of commerce, public health bodies, among others. Officials and the operator take part in meetings and committee work, but only in an advisory capacity. France's Autorité de Sûreté Nucléaire supports the committees financially and ensures that the information they receive is as comprehensive as possible. It also encourages committee members to take part in plant inspections and to resort to outside expertise, distinct from advice offered by itself or the operator.[22]

Regarding regulation, industry draws its strength from the information advantage it enjoys, a situation encapsulated in the information asymmetry concept, which we introduced in Chapter 7. Regarding economic regulation, such as setting the tariff for using a transport or telecommunications network, the solution is to pay a company to reveal its real costs. Similarly to bonuses given to CIOs to ensure that they genuinely uphold shareholder interests, it is necessary to award a bonus to the most successful regulated companies. This principle – which is complex to implement and rarely ideal – is designed to prevent companies from inflating their costs, which saps productivity. On the one hand the regulator loses, by awarding the company a rent in exchange for the information it discloses, but on the other hand it has the benefit of a lower tariff. Overall the net gain for society is positive. In the case of nuclear regulation, the regulator also tries to avoid excessively high safety costs. But this is a secondary consideration. Above all it seeks to prevent operators from lying about their shortcomings. The nuclear safety authority must know whether incidents occur, whether their cause has been identified, and whether corrective measures have been taken. It must be in a position to assess a plant's safety performance and check compliance with its requirements. Far from rewarding regulated companies, it is simply a matter of monitoring and sanctioning them in the event of deficiencies. To know, to inspect and to sanction are the three priorities for safety regulation. Which is why the safety authority must have competent staff and the means to enforce the dissuasive sanctions at its disposal. A nuclear safety regulator which has neither top-notch technical and scientific expertise nor real powers will not achieve a level of safety significantly better than self-regulation.

To achieve effective safety regulation, powers of inspection and sanction, underpinned by the requisite skills, are certainly necessary but not sufficient in themselves. The regulator must be prepared to exercise such powers too. In modern economic theory, the regulator is an economic agent much as any other: it is moved by its own interests and pursues an individual goal – which is not spontaneously in the general interest, contrary to the model presented by classical public economics. It will act in the general interest – in more concrete terms it will try to fulfil its legally defined mandate – providing it is in someone's personal interest to do so: for example, to advance one's career, for fear of sanction, to enjoy the benefits of a larger or more highly qualified team, to occupy more comfortable premises, among others. In short, a regulator must also be supervised and given incentives. Its own interests must be brought into line with that of the law-maker, distancing it from that of the regulated. To this end a whole range of instruments may be deployed to combat corruption and conflicts of interest (banning revolving doors in regulated companies, operating as a collegial body, making it compulsory to report any meeting with any company or its management).

In conclusion, Japanese regulation failed because it was trapped by industry in a pincer movement. On the one hand this was a classic case of a regulator allowing itself to be captured by the utilities it was supposed to be regulating. But in another respect it was more unusual, because the authority's lack of independence from government also brought it under the influence of industry. The political system in Japan is tightly meshed with the interests of utilities, energy-intensive industries and nuclear engineering firms. So written between the lines of the Nisa mandate was the imperative neither to hinder electricity production nor yet to impede promotion of nuclear power. Safety was never its prime concern, less still the main focus of its action. It acted as a fully paid-up member of the *genshiryoku mura*, or nuclear village, an expression hatched to describe the select club formed by the stakeholders in Japan's nuclear industry: businesses, but also the relevant administrative bodies and scientists, and of course policy-makers. The village concept here reflects the loyalty owed by members to their common cause. Nisa was built in the village, not outside.

NINE

What goal should be set for safety and how is it to be attained?

The above review of safety regulation in Japan illustrates the recommendations of economic analysis on how an authority should be organized, and how such prescriptions are justified. But economic analysis also focuses on regulatory goals and instruments. In this section we shall draw on the examples of regulation in the United States and France. Naturally they both have their shortcomings and they are very different, yet both may be taken as good models.

Let us start with a reminder of the economic principles guiding the setting of goals and the choice of instruments. Economics is useful for discarding hollow slogans such as 'nuclear safety is our absolute priority' or 'nuclear safety is priceless'. Catchphrases of this sort suggest that there is not, or there should not be, any limit to safety efforts.

The first limit established by economic theory relates to determination of the optimal level of safety efforts on the basis of marginal costs. The incomplete nature of data reduces the practical value of this response to the question of when safe is safe enough. Very little is known about the marginal costs of safety efforts and even greater uncertainty affects the marginal costs of avoided damages. However, this is not specific to nuclear accidents. Economists have difficulty determining the optimal level of carbon-dioxide emissions or safety on oil-rigs. It is equally tricky to estimate the right discount rate, or put a value on loss of human life or damage to the natural environment. In practice economic calculation very rarely has any say in setting health and safety goals, generally decided by scientific and technical debate, and political process.

The second limit relates to the maximum level of safety efforts, which results from the law of substitution. From an economic standpoint there can be no absolute measurement of the value of a technology; it can only be estimated in relation to competing technologies. In the case, for example, of two rival technologies, the value of the better one is equal to the gain it procures for society compared to the less efficient technology. Over the long term the market achieves a form of Darwinian selection, discarding less successful technologies. The natural economic limit on safety efforts is the one which forces nuclear power out of the market because it has become too expensive compared to alternative technologies. This limit becomes apparent when attempts are made to extend the service life of ageing reactors. If the additional safety work required by the regulator to extend its licence exceeds a certain threshold, operators stand to gain from investing in new means of production.

Having set a goal for regulation, economic analysis then looks at how it can be achieved at the lowest cost. The value of this approach is obvious: savings are made by minimizing expenditure to achieve a given level of polluting emissions or a given safety objective. The money thus saved can be used to mitigate even more pollution or increase safety further – doing more with the same amount – or it can be used for something else.

To minimize costs, economic analysis recommends the use of standards based on performance rather than technology. The latter type of standard focuses on the characteristics of an installation, such as the thickness of concrete, or the number and start-up time of emergency pumps. The regulator prescribes standards and checks compliance. With performance-based standards the regulator simply defines criteria and levels, for example the resistance of a reinforced concrete containment to the start of a core melt, or the longest acceptable duration of a failure of the secondary cooling system. It is up to the regulated party to choose the right measures to achieve the necessary performance level. This provides an incentive for the nuclear operator to select and fine-tune effective, less costly measures, reducing expenditure and increasing margin. From the point of view of the general interest, performance-based standards have the dual advantage of reducing information costs and protecting innovation. By delegating the choice of the appropriate component or device to the operator, the regulator spares itself the effort of collecting information and expertise. But it is important to understand that it is not simply transferring costs to the operator. The operator incurs lower costs because it already has the information. Furthermore if it can see ways of achieving performance goals by developing new processes, it will invest in R&D work, which may ultimately benefit the community.

The story of nuclear regulation started without any explicit goal. It has gradually taken shape, alongside the design and construction of nuclear power plants. Means having preceded ends, we shall start by looking at the issue of standards before that of goals, proceeding in chronological order.

Technology versus performance-based standards in the United States

Performance-based standards, guided by probabilistic safety assessments, now play a central role in nuclear regulation in the US, the goal being to manage and contain costs. But for a long while the balance tipped in the opposite direction and nuclear safety in the US was beset by mountains of prescriptive regulations. Between 1967 and 1977 the pace of annual publication of regulations, implementation guidelines and other documents setting forth regulatory doctrine increased by a factor of twenty-five. In the early 1970s there were less than ten such publications; by the end of the decade the full catalogue contained almost 150 items.[1] Indeed regulatory inflation and its exclusively prescriptive focus, in terms of technical options and details, were instrumental in slowing down the construction process (see Chapter 1).

Slow progress is a prime characteristic of regulation by technology-based standards. The pitfalls associated with the application of the Nuclear Regulatory Commission's fire-protection standards are symptomatic of this approach. In 2010 there were still almost fifty reactors which did not comply with these regulations. The standards were drawn up after a fire at Browns Ferry nuclear power plant, which rapidly went out of control, putting reactor 1 out of service for more than a year. Setting aside Three Mile Island, this failure was certainly the most severe yet to occur in the US. It is well known because the event that triggered it seems so absurd only a newspaper cartoonist could have imagined such a tale: a candle flame set light to polyurethane foam sealing material, propagating from there to the adjoining electrical cables. This occurred in the cable-spreading room, below the control room, through which control cables passed on their way to the reactor building. Two electricians were applying inflammable foam to stop air leaks from the adjoining room. To check the seal round the cables one of the electricians lit a candle and placed it beside the stopped holes. Coming too close it set light to the foam. The fire then spread into the cables and from there all the way down the line. A sequence of errors followed. Many safety systems were damaged, including the cooling system, and a core-melt accident was narrowly avoided.

To prevent similar accidents the NRC set out to establish new standards. One required operators to separate the circuit supplying the primary cooling system from its secondary counterpart by six metres (at Browns Ferry they were almost side-by-side). Failing this, operators must fit automatic fire-suppression systems, fire barriers or fireproof cladding that would protect cables for three hours. The operators thought these measures were excessive and extremely expensive. A series of legal proceedings started, accompanied by protracted hostilities between operators and regulator. In 1982 the Connecticut Light and Power Company went on the offensive, claiming that the NRC had failed to provide adequate technical justification for its fire-protection regulations. The District of Columbia Court of Appeals ruled in favour of the safety authority. Some operators opted to apply only part of the new regulations, others not at all. In the face of this refusal to comply with its demands the NRC finally announced at the start of the 2000s that it would no longer tolerate any violation of its standards. However the industry managed to have the deadline postponed, until new regulations came into force in 2004. They have still not been applied. Deadlines have been extended several times. The most recent one requires compliance by 2016. If all the parties fulfil this requirement it will have taken almost forty years for the fire-protection regulations to be deployed on the entire US fleet.

My grasp of the technicalities of nuclear safety are such that I cannot pass judgement on the validity of the 1980 fire-protection standards. Were the measures impracticable, at least in some cases? Was their cost excessive compared to the avoided risk? Were all the delays the fault of a few operators, determined to limit costs, which forced the regulator to retreat? Whatever the answer, this example is emblematic of the dead end to which nuclear safety regulation leads when it is based exclusively on detailed technical prescriptions. The complexity and diversity of reactors is so great that it is necessary to draw up huge catalogues of standards. The cost of their *ex post* verification comes on top of the expense of framing the standards. The cost of a single check is low, but as they pile up, it soars. Take for example the building industry, with its myriad standards, which confuse both operators and regulator: it is impossible for all the rules to be applied, let alone checked. And even if they were, there would still be a major problem: technology-based standards induce a passive attitude to safety in the industry, dispelling any sense of responsibility. In other words, compliance with regulations is no guarantee of safety. This was one of the key lessons learnt from Three Mile Island: full compliance with the detailed technical rules would have done nothing to prevent the accident.

Awareness of the many shortcomings of technology-based standards made it easier to switch to a new approach to regulation based on performance. Its development was fuelled by the boom in probabilistic safety methods and the adoption, in 1986, of the first quantitative safety goals. Risk-informed and performance-based regulation, better known by its acronym RIPBR, has since taken over as the dominant approach.[2]

A regulatory guide published in 2002 perfectly illustrates the new approach, describing how the NRC assesses 'licensee requests for changes to a plant's licensing basis'.[3] The guide starts by recounting the US authority's convictions regarding the merits of probabilistic risk assessments. Such studies enable the authority to improve safety, but also to better direct its efforts and reduce pointless regulatory constraints on operators. As Richard A. Meserve, NRC Chairman when the guide was published, explains, 'The aim, of course, is to use risk as the tool for dissecting and reforming our regulatory system so that the NRC focuses on risk-significant activities, thereby both enhancing safety and reducing needless regulatory burden.'[4] The guide then explains the authority's attitude to requests by operators for changes, according to the reactor's overall level of safety performance and how any changes may alter such performance. Core-damage frequency and large-early-release frequency values are used to define risks. But they are also used to characterize various situations when the licensing-basis change requested by an operator may entail '*safety degradation*'.[5] The key idea is that the NRC may accept a change leading to a slight incremental risk providing the plant's overall safety performance is high, but not if it is poor. For example, if the change increases the core-damage frequency by less than 10^{-6} per reactor-year, and the overall frequency is lower than 10^{-5} per reactor-year, the licensing-basis change is acceptable. On the other hand, it is not acceptable if the total core-damage frequency is close to or higher than 10^{-4} per reactor-year. Several areas of acceptance or refusal are thus defined depending on how the results of the probabilistic risk assessments compare with the various thresholds.

George E. Apostolakis was sworn in as an NRC Commissioner in 2010, for a four-year term. Professor of Nuclear Science and Engineering at the Massachusetts Institute of Technology and a keen advocate of quantitative risk assessment, Apostolakis maintains that this guide constitutes a breakthrough. Probabilistic risk assessments are no longer used simply to pinpoint negative features, revealing previously unidentified failures. They also 'pay attention to the "positive" insights, i.e. that some of the previously imposed safety requirements can be relaxed because either they do not contribute to safety or they contribute a very small amount that cannot be justified when it is compared to the corresponding cost'.[6]

However, performance-based nuclear-safety regulation is by no means a panacea. Much of the performance can only be observed indirectly, by probabilistic means. It may not actually be achieved and it is not always possible to measure exactly and rigorously the uncertainty affecting it. Of course, verification becomes easier with time. It will be possible to confirm or invalidate some aspects of safety performance measured during the reactor-design phase, once it starts operating. Much as with forensic medicine, dismantling reactors and exploring their entrails will also provide new evidence as to the weakness or solidity of certain components. But even this ultimate phase will never be sufficient to reconstruct the whole picture.

The shortcomings in the verification of performance mean that regulation based exclusively on performance must be ruled out. Even in the US, which has gone furthest down this path, regulation still has a dual basis. Let us return to the most recent episode in the fire-prevention saga, when a new regulation was adopted in 2004. Rather than revising its technology-based standards, the authority proposed to take a risk-informed, performance-based approach. The operators of the forty-seven reactors which are still not compliant must either opt to apply the standards or to take ad hoc measures on the basis of fire-propagation models and probabilistic safety assessments. The latter option enables them to concentrate on the parts of the plant which display the highest risks. The vast majority of the operators have indeed taken the second route. As a result some US nuclear power plants comply with certain fire-prevention rules, whereas others disregard them. Some operators are actively committed to risk-informed regulations, whereas others are more 'passive' in their attitude to the new approach.[7] Technology and performance-based standards now coexist in the US and are sometimes combined. Indeed the prevalent model is hybrid. As we shall now see, the same applies to its objectives, with US nuclear safety regulation pursuing both qualitative and quantitative goals.

Choosing a goal for overall safety: words and figures

On 11 July 1977 the French Industry Minister, tasked with nuclear safety, sent a letter to EDF mentioning for the first time a quantitative safety goal: the overall probability of a reactor initiating unacceptable consequences must not exceed 10^{-6} per reactor-year.[8] On 21 August 1986, after talks lasting more than five years, the NRC issued a statement setting an upper limit on any additional health risk to members of the community in the vicinity of a nuclear power plant. The additional risk should not exceed one-in-a-thousand of the fatality risks resulting from other causes. A comparison of these two dates would suggest that France was quick to adopt quantitative safety goals. In fact the minister's letter has still not come into effect, whereas the US has steadily increased its reliance on quantitative goals for safety regulation.

The 1986 NRC statement followed the recommendations of the Commission on the Accident at Three Mile Island, also known as the Kennedy Commission. It set four objectives, two qualitative, two quantitative. We shall cite all four, as they illustrate key principles:

> Individual members of the public should be provided a level of protection from the consequences of nuclear power plant operation such that individuals bear no significant additional risk to life and health;

> Societal risks to life and health from nuclear power plant operation should be comparable to or less than the risks of generating electricity by viable competing technologies and should not be a significant addition to other societal risks;

> The risk to an average individual in the vicinity of a nuclear power plant of prompt fatalities that might result from reactor accidents should not exceed one-tenth of one percent (0.1%) of the sum of prompt fatality risks resulting from other accidents to which members of the US population are generally exposed;

> The risk to the population in the area near a nuclear power plant of cancer fatalities that might result from nuclear power plant operation should not exceed one-tenth of one percent (0.1%) of the sum of cancer fatality risks resulting from all other causes.[9]

These principles are based on good common sense. In a word, nuclear risk must not diverge from the norm. To start with, this may be compared with other health hazards in general: for people living close to power plants, who are obviously more exposed, the acceptable risk – with a ratio of one-in-a-thousand (one-tenth of 1%) – scarcely exceeds the normal level of risk. It may then be compared with the hazards involved in alternative electricity-generating technologies, in particular coal: the safety level required of nuclear power should neither favour nor handicap this technology.

Looking more closely, this list of goals also raises many questions: why is there no mention of costs or risks other than those affecting public health? Why are quantitative and qualitative goals mixed up?

Are these goals in any sense legally binding? Why were they issued by the regulator, not the legislator? We shall start by providing precise answers to these questions, with contextual details reflecting the specificities of US safety regulation. Then we shall offer some more general, analytical answers.

The four goals introduced in 1986 are still top priorities for safety regulation in the US. As fundamental principles they answer the question of what safe enough really means. Yet they only address the nuclear hazards affecting public health and are a poor translation of the NRC mission: 'to licence and regulate the Nation's civilian use of radioactive materials to protect public health and [. . .] protect the environment'.[10] In a press conference in March 2012 NRC Chairman Gregory Jaczko regretted the fact that safety goals did not deal with 'significant land contamination and displacement, perhaps permanently, of people from their homes and their livelihoods'.[11] He expressed the hope that they would be changed to ensure that, under the US regulatory framework, an accident such as the one at Fukushima Daiichi would be unacceptable, even if, as he emphasized, radiation had not had any immediate health impact. At present such impacts are, in a sense, acceptable, because the four goals established by the NRC focus exclusively on risks to public health. While on the matter of oversights, it should be noted that this answer to the question of what safe enough really means completely overlooks the concept of cost or savings. The choice of the one-in-a-thousand ratio is arbitrary. It is not the result of any cost assessment and less still of any cost–benefit analysis. Furthermore, the ratio is the same for all the nuclear power plants, identical for Palo Verde, in the Arizona desert, and Zion, close to Chicago. No allowance is made for population density around reactors, whereas the economic benefit of safety efforts substantially increases with the size of the local population protected.

Could the NRC have restricted its list to just the first two basic goals? Residents living close to nuclear power plants are a subset of the US population. As such their health is protected too. Of course, there is no question of them enjoying less protection than other Americans. It would be a mistake to suppose that the specific mortality thresholds concerning them are appreciable. These thresholds in fact translate into figures the idea of not being 'a significant addition' to existing risks, asserted in the qualitative goals. Without some firm basis, any attempt to gauge the extent of a phenomenon, be it significant or not, is either quite impossible or simply subjective. In the present case the figures provide a firm basis. Given the annual rate of accidental death and the annual rate of death by cancer in the US, the limits placed on additional deaths among local residents due to nuclear power plant operations are, respectively, 5×10^{-7} and 2×10^{-6}, or 5 and 20 persons per 10 million residents. According to the NRC, if the figures were any higher they would constitute a significant addition to the risks affecting local residents and as such would not be acceptable.

Introducing quantitative goals also reflects the concern, following Three Mile Island, to make the goals pursued by the regulator more explicit. The 1986 statement was preceded by a large number of reports and workshops devoted to safety goals, focusing in particular on choosing quantitative criteria to specify them. These criteria seemed necessary to clarify terms used to qualify risks, such as 'unreasonable', 'undue', 'intolerable' or indeed 'unacceptable'.[12] They were consequently seen as supplementing, rather than replacing, qualitative goals, it not being possible to quantify all aspects of safety. When it was possible, safety was still subject to great uncertainty. The NRC took care to stipulate that selected quantitative goals could not form the exclusive, nor even prime, basis for decisions on granting licences or on regulations. Moreover, it soon emerged that the goals must be underpinned by subsidiary benchmarks. The additional mortality thresholds proved difficult to use as a basis for standards and practical rules implemented by operators. In a memorandum dating from 1990 the NRC introduced two new limits: a core-damage probability lower than 10^{-4} per reactor-year and an overall mean frequency of a large release of radioactive materials to the environment of less than 10^{-6}.[13]

The NRC set the subsidiary benchmarks, just as it did for the fundamental goals. They were adopted by the five commissioners (who make up the Commission). So the goals were not prescribed by Congress. The fundamental goals set in 1986, in particular the requirement that there be no significant additional risk to life, did not reflect any legal obligation imposed by Congress. It is also worth noting that the NRC decided not to make its fundamental and subsidiary goals binding. It cannot sanction operators which fail to comply with them. It sees the goals as guidelines, enabling it to frame tighter standards, which may on the contrary be binding.

The reader may be surprised by this approach, but Congress lacks the necessary technical expertise to set a quantitative goal. It would have to allocate substantial resources to determining the right thresholds. Moreover, this effort would have to be repeated at each update, the thresholds being likely to vary over time in line with changes in the understanding of accident risks. Qualitative goals, such as a 'tolerable' or 'reasonable' risk, are obviously of a more permanent nature. The legislator may also stipulate how the regulator should go about setting quantitative goals, according to what procedure, striking a balance in this way between contradictory factors. It may also check *ex post* that the regulator's goals do really correspond to its wishes. In a further example of savings on information costs and labour division, the regulator may ask its administrative services to draft proposals for possible quantitative goals, selecting the ones which best reflect the legislator's concerns and wishes; then ask its staff to transform the goals into operational rules; finally checking that they are really being implemented.

The combination of quantitative and qualitative goals is justified by their respective shortcomings and advantages. Without quantitative goals the regulator cannot separately assess how efficiently an operator achieves a particular goal, and at the same time how effectively it minimizes the cost entailed. If such and such a safety expense is pinpointed by an operator, is it trying to achieve the goal or just concealing its inability to identify the most cost-effective means? The regulator needs to know whether achieving a goal is very expensive, or whether the operator is artificially inflating the cost by wasting resources! This is clearly impossible if the stated goal is a 'tolerable' or 'reasonable' level of safety. Without quantitative goals the regulator enjoys greater discretionary powers. Obliging it to set a threshold for a particular risk is tantamount to tying its hands. It will be less at liberty to demand over-ambitious safety efforts, yielding to pressure from environmental pressure groups, or alternatively efforts that are too feeble to satisfy industry. There is less danger of regulatory capture by interest groups. Lastly, without quantitative goals it is difficult to put technologies on an equal footing. Thanks to quantitative risk thresholds safety performance in the nuclear industry can be compared to that of other hazardous activities, in particular coal- and gas-powered energy.

But setting quantitative goals does not solve all the problems either, so by necessity they must be backed up by their qualitative counterparts. Defining a risk threshold leads to a focusing effect. Concerned with a particular figure, the administrative services of both regulator and operator may disregard other goals, despite their importance for safety, such as staff training or new knowledge production. It is impossible to quantify many of the factors determining nuclear risk and the corresponding mitigating measures. So there is a danger of making insufficient allowance for them. Above all, verification problems are a further obstacle to meeting goals regarding additional mortality or the probability of large-scale contamination. It is not just a question of checking the speed of motor vehicles on a road. There are no radar speed-guns, with a low margin of error, for measuring nuclear risk. The limit here is a probability and it cannot be observed. Nor is it always easy to interpret. For example, a threshold corresponding to a core-melt probability of less than, say, one-in-ten-thousand per reactor-year seems at first sight to be clearly defined. But what does core melt mean? Slight damage to the zirconium-based cladding round the fuel rods? Partial meltdown? The formation of corium, a molten mixture of parts of the nuclear-reactor core? And interpreting the threshold itself is no easy task. Does it correspond to a mathematical expectation? Or is it an interval, such as the core-melt probability must be, with a nine-in-ten likelihood, lower than the limit of one accident in 10,000 reactor-years? The issue of whether it is possible to verify the goal persists even after an accident. The date of a failure within the relevant interval cannot be anticipated on the basis of the calculated core-melt frequency. If an accident occurs during the first few years of a fleet's operation, this does not mean that the limit has been passed, no more than if the accident had occurred much later.

Much as for performance-based standards, the limited scope for verifying quantitative goals explains why they are not legally binding. The regulator does not require the operator to prove that it has achieved a goal and is not in a position to sanction it in the event of non-compliance. Quantitative goals, in particular core-melt frequencies, which are the most commonly used goals of this sort, are used as guidelines rather than as benchmarks. The regulator uses them to focus the action of its administrative services, which in turn use them to direct operators' safety efforts.

The only binding quantitative goals concern personnel exposure to ionizing radiation under normal plant-operating conditions. This exception confirms the previous rule. The radiation dose to which operatives are exposed, on-site or in its vicinity, is relatively easy to monitor thanks to dosimeters. In the United Kingdom, just as in the rest of the European Union, 'employees working with ionizing radiation', through access to certain parts of the plant, must not receive an annual dose exceeding 20 millisieverts.[14]

A French approach in complete contrast to the American model

France is well known for its long, diverse tradition of codifying rules and its over-zealous officials. Almost everything must be put down in writing as law, the Conseil d'Etat supervises the enforcement of a very extensive body of public law, and officials draw up and implement large numbers of regulations. Yet this stereotype does not apply to nuclear safety. The first major item of legislation dates from the mid-2000s.[15] There are only a limited number of ministerial orders and rulings. Surprisingly enough, French regulation has been very sparing in its use of explicit goals and technical standards.

The Autorité de Sûreté Nucléaire, France's nuclear safety authority, is an administrative body which reports to the Industry and Environment Ministries. It was set up in 2006. The Transparency and Nuclear Safety Act[16] stipulates its mission: ASN is tasked with defining technical requirements for the design, construction and operation of civil nuclear power plants, necessary to uphold safety, and protect public health and the environment. Before issuing an operating licence ASN checks that the operator has taken the necessary organizational measures 'to prevent or limit *sufficiently* the risks or drawbacks which the installation presents'.[17] The regulator has not subsequently indicated what 'sufficiently' means. The only explanation provided by ASN regarding its objective is that it 'ensures that the safety of French civil nuclear facilities is continuously improved'. This improvement concerns both the safety of existing reactors and that of subsequent generations. ASN justifies this approach by the fact that safety can never be taken for granted and that scientific and technical knowledge are constantly evolving. Incidents and accidents on reactors in France and elsewhere throw light on further shortcomings too. Analysed in detail they give rise to a valuable return on experience, contributing to improved safety in existing and new plants. Continuous improvement is facilitated by mandatory safety visits to nuclear power plants every ten years. This periodic review of reactor safety, imposed on the operator by the 2006 act, enables ASN to introduce new technical provisions, which in particular make allowance for advances in knowledge. The ten-year check-up is extremely thorough, shutting down the reactor for several months.

The goals set forth in the technical directives adopted in 2000 for the European Pressurized Reactor, the fruit of Franco-German cooperation, are not much more explicit.[18] They simply stipulate that the core-melt frequency must be lower than for existing reactors and accidents leading to the release of material must be 'practically eliminated'. Clearly this wording is open to interpretation. Is the aim to eliminate almost all accidents? What unspoken goals does the word 'practically' conceal? Are accidents to be made impossible, by raising a series of physical barriers to prevent any radioactive material from escaping into the environment?[19]

The only officially stated quantitative safety goal dates back to the previously cited administrative document of 1977. On 11 July the Industry Minister, tasked with nuclear safety, sent a letter to EDF specifying that the overall probability of a reactor initiating unacceptable consequences must not exceed 10^{-6} per reactor-year.[20] This letter had no effect at the time, and it has had even less effect since, because it was soon followed by a sort of correction. In a second letter the minister specified that the threshold carried no regulatory weight and that EDF was under no obligation to demonstrate compliance using probabilistic assessments.[21] The threshold was in fact no more than a back-of-the-envelope calculation.[22] The following reasoning underpinned the letters penned by officials at the Service Central des Installations Nucléaires:[23] France planned to build a fleet of fifty reactors scheduled to operate for forty years; if the probability of a serious accident was 5×10^{-4} per reactor-year, an accident during the service life of the fleet was foreseeable: this was out of the question. The expected probability of an acceptable accident must therefore be about one-in-hundred or one-in-thousand, or to steer a middle course, a probability of 10^{-6} per reactor-year. Much as for its US counterpart, the 1977 letter constituted a general guideline. However, unlike the NRC, regulation in France did not adopt it. The safety authority has no intention, no more now than in the past, of defining a benchmark indicating a good enough level of safety. The safe-enough concept is entirely foreign to the French conception of safety. The explicit goal set by ASN is continuous progress.[24]

The idea of ongoing progress is difficult to reconcile with specific, detailed, technology-based standards. Indeed, less than thirty-five guidelines and rules have been established since 1980, mostly only a few pages long.[25] In contrast, the goal of continuous progress is reflected in an overall performance-based standard, enshrined in the 'baseline' concept. This is an essential part of French regulation. In practical terms it involves compiling all sorts of safety requirements (technical standards and specifications, general operating rules, good practice), from a wide range of sources (ministerial orders establishing safety rules, ASN guides, operator practices), for each reactor category. So there is a baseline for each *palier* (900 MW, 1,300 MW and 1,450 MW). The baseline changes to reflect the few new ministerial regulations, extensive return on experience and a large number of scientific and technical studies. The relevant baseline is used during the periodic safety reviews carried out by ASN, to detect non-conformity and identify areas in which progress is required, even if current compliance is demonstrated. Whatever happens, a review ends with a list of items for which performance must be improved. The following review will measure progress as a function of the previous and existing baselines. This system is obviously made easier by the relative homogeneity of the French nuclear fleet and the presence of a single operator, EDF, which centralizes data on the safety of each reactor and can compare performance between individual reactors, plants and *paliers*. The company can thus oversee the overall trend towards improvement, between various types of reactor and plants, in order to ensure that progress towards greater safety is evenly spread throughout the fleet.

Setting large numbers of detailed standards is also ill suited to good quality technical dialogue between operator and regulator, the latter acting as both supervisor and expert. In this second capacity the regulator addresses its counterpart on an equal footing. Technical exchanges resemble academic discussions and confrontations. The expert seeks to make his or her conclusions as accurate as possible, convincing the other party of their sound basis. The aim is to find an original solution not previously considered or, more modestly, to improve a solution others have suggested. Exchanges between safety experts – regardless of whether they work for ASN, EDF or other bodies – take the form of debate between peers. As this other characteristic of regulation in France is part of a long-standing tradition, some historical background is needed to explain and appraise it.

Until work started on building the first *palier* of its fleet of reactors, nuclear safety regulation in France played a very minor role. Only in 1973, with the launch of a large-scale programme to build the existing fleet, was the first centralized body established to administer nuclear safety. Reporting to the Industry Ministry, it consisted of five engineers and drew largely on the expertise of the Commissariat à l'Energie Atomique (CEA). This science and technology research organization, set up by General de Gaulle in 1945, designed France's first prototype reactors and had a complete department, with staff of about a hundred, specializing in safety. Ministry officials referred to this department the safety reports submitted by EDF as part of its application for licences to build and operate each of its new nuclear power plants. These reports were then studied by a committee known as the Groupe Permanent Réacteurs. It consisted of a dozen highly qualified specialists from EDF, CEA and the Ministry. Even allowing for these two additional inputs, there were very few people regulating the safety of projects and licensing them. All the more so given the rapid rate of procedures, with two to six licensing applications filed every year, each one described in a nuclear safety report long enough to reach the office ceiling if stacked.

But the prime concern of this proto-safety regulator was to avoid any delays to the nuclear programme.[26] It realized that detailed regulations were beyond its reach and counter-productive. To draw up standards required some practical grasp of building and operating a plant. The nuclear safety administrators only acquired these skills gradually in the process of carrying out technical reviews of installations. Reflecting its scanty resources or deep-rooted convictions, France's first nuclear authority adopted a critical stance regarding regulation based on written standards and conformance. It espoused the doctrinal views of F. R. Farmer, an official working for the UK Atomic Energy Authority's Safety and Reliability Directorate. In 1967 he called for greater care to avoid being guided by the pressures of administrative or regulatory commodity to produce formulae or rules in the light of which safety would be tested.[27] He was afraid that designers and operators would only concern themselves with conformance and neglect more searching thought on the effects of their efforts to achieve fundamental safety.

In its early days France's safety regulator benefited from US experience in two ways. The reactors built at this stage by EDF had been developed by Westinghouse, so the technology had already been tested on an industrial scale. Several units had been built in the US and their safety examined, assessed and codified in standards by the NRC. French experts could thus draw on this knowledge base, with its mass of existing data. France's regulator also learnt from the difficulties encountered by its US counterpart. It was consequently keen to avoid the instability of this regulatory framework and its standards, and its negative impact on construction deadlines. The French saw US regulation as an example to avoid, enabling it to sidestep similar teething problems with nuclear safety. But things could easily have been very different. France initially tried to develop its own gas-cooled, graphite-moderated reactors. The decision to shelve this home-grown technology in favour of another, under foreign licence, was a difficult and lengthy process (see Chapter 10),[28] which delayed the launch of France's large-scale nuclear programme. Had it persisted with research on gas-cooled reactors, it would have saved time, perhaps leading to a very different safety setup.

As for the organization of technical exchange and expertise, the situation in the 1970s foreshadowed the present arrangement. The CEA department specializing in nuclear safety has been hived off to form the Institut de Radioprotection et de Sûreté Nucléaire (IRSN). It now fields a team 2,000 strong. IRSN is a research institute but it also provides technical support for ASN, carrying out in particular the safety assessments of installations on which the regulator bases its decisions. ASN itself is a remote relation of the centralized safety department established in 1973. It still draws on the work of permanent expert committees, partly manned by EDF representatives. The Permanent Reactor Group still exists. It is very active and much in demand at ASN. It remains an outstanding body, distinguished by the skills of its members and the quality of technical debate.

The big changes have happened elsewhere. Nowadays technical dialogue no longer occurs behind closed doors. The general public can obtain and consult IRSN expert appraisals. ASN publishes a statement each time it refers an issue to one of the permanent expert committees. Committee reports are published too. The make-up of the expert committees has been extended to include views other than those of specialists working for the nuclear industry. Scientists from abroad and university researchers may now contribute to expert appraisals. Such transparency and diversity are completely at odds with the form of expertise, out of the public eye and among people with the same background – or more bluntly nucleocrats – which characterized the period when France's nuclear programme was developed.

A word in passing on the term 'nucleocrat', because it is an opportunity to dismiss two widespread pre-conceptions. Originally hatched by Philippe Simonnot, who writes for the French daily Le Monde, as the title of a book published in 1978,[29] this portmanteau word refers to a small clique of bureaucrats and leaders of the nuclear industry in cahoots to make France a great nuclear power. They belong to the same world, because 'for the most part [they] are graduates of Ecole Polytechnique and belong to the same elite: the Corps des Mines, Corps des Ponts et Chaussées, in other words two career paths which attract the best brains from Ecole Polytechnique [. . .] CEA is packed with people belonging to the Corps des Mines, EDF with their counterparts from the Corps des Ponts'. The first misconception is not that engineers belonging to these two *corps* played a decisive role. They were indeed prime movers in France's technical and economic expertise on nuclear power, as well as actively promoting its development with the government. Rather, the mistake lies in the idea that the government had no say in such developments nor in their overall direction. The nucleocrats allegedly usurped the powers of policy-makers, the latter becoming mere puppets in their hands. In fact, throughout the second half of the twentieth century, the two arms of French government – the Presidency and the Cabinet – were in the front line, taking full responsibility for the nuclear programme.[30] The second misconception is that the nuclear lobby and central government faced little opposition. On the contrary, in the 1970s France's anti-nuclear movement was one of the most powerful in Europe.[31] Simonnot's book bears this out, much like all the other literature combating nuclear power. Opposition took many forms, backed by trade unions, politicians, environmental watchdogs and leftwing extremists. It led to various acts of violence, such as the 1977 attack on the home of Marcel Boiteux, then head of EDF, or the death of Vincent Michalon, an anti-nuclear campaigner, during a demonstration at Creys Malville which was violently repressed.

Regulator and regulated: enemies or peers?

The ongoing technical dialogue between EDF and the safety authority, now ASN, should not be interpreted as a form of collusion or conniving between regulator and regulated. Such a simplistic view of the theory of regulatory capture should be discarded. The world is neither all white – no capture – nor all black, with the regulator enmeshed in industry's net. Modern economic theory on interest groups sees collusion between the authority and one of the stakeholders as a risk.[32] It has established, for example, that the risk is greater with specialist authorities supervising a small number of companies. A sectoral regulator – overseeing sectors such as telecommunications or air transport – remains in contact with the same companies, and it is hard for officials wishing to transfer to the private sector to capitalize on their acquired expertise anywhere else than in the firms they once regulated. The phenomenon is all the more acute when there are only a few players. Furthermore, with fewer companies the regulator has more limited sources of information. In contrast, competition authorities intervene in all types of market, generally only once. They supervise a merger or sanction abuse of a dominant market position, one day in the fine chemicals industry, the next day in office furniture. They can easily draw on information provided by competitors too. So the risk of capture is potentially higher for a nuclear safety authority, greater still when faced with just one company operating nuclear power plants, as in France. But just because the risk is potentially higher does not mean that it is realized. We may conclude that greater vigilance is required, with more substantial safeguards.

Modern economic theory on interest groups also provides for a trade-off between regulatory capture and information asymmetry. One way of limiting the first factor is to distance the regulator from regulated companies. But limiting contacts and connections between regulator and regulated also reduces the flow of vital information to the former. The regulator may lock itself up in an ivory tower, but it will be struck dumb by ignorance. The knowledge published in books or reports is not enough to work out standards. Similarly, undercover inspections are not up to the task of checking conformance. In the US at least, NRC inspectors are present at all times in power plants. They live on the spot, with an office on-site. Resident inspectors can provide first-hand information on reactor-safety conditions and performance. At the same time, rubbing shoulders on a daily basis with plant personnel and other families living nearby increases the risk of a loss of independence with regard to the operator. The two go hand-in-hand.

It would also be a mistake to over-simplify the aims and behaviour of the regulated company. It is commonplace to highlight cheating and resistance to the application of standards. After all, any company aims to maximize its profits. Reducing expenditure on safety imposed by the regulator by delaying or falsifying compliance is one way of cutting costs and boosting margin. No one is in any doubt that as a short-term strategy this may pay off. The story of the Millstone nuclear power plant in Connecticut, which belonged to Northeast Utilities, amply illustrates this point. It was studied in minute detail by a researcher and a professor at Yale School of Management,[33] demonstrating that in the mid-1980s the management deliberately adopted a low-cost, low-safety strategy. Spending on safety, and other items, was reined in. Safety performance was gradually degraded, but for some time, during which the reactors were operating at full capacity, the regulator was fooled. In 1996, after several incidents and warnings, the NRC forced Northeast Utilities to shut down its three plants. The share price plummeted, losing 80 per cent of its value. The oldest reactor was never restarted, the other two started operations again but after more than two years lying idle. The company itself failed and its assets were sold off. Shareholders lost substantial amounts of money, but management earnings soared. In the course of several years of excellent financial performance, achieved by cost-cutting, managers received several million dollars in bonuses. Unlike the shareholders, management suffered no losses when the reactors were shut down and the company failed; some of them simply had to retire early. This example illustrates the concept of moral hazard, brought to public awareness by the financial crisis of the late-2000s. Management takes greater risks, contrary to the interests of shareholders which it is supposed to uphold, not having to take full responsibility for the consequences. In modern economic theory large companies do not maximize their long-term profit, they simply tend to do so. On the one hand we have shareholders who are naturally concerned about the long term – a realistic assumption in the case of industrial and infrastructure assets – and on the other, management, with other aims and preferences: increasing their personal wealth in a few years or all the way through their career, more or less pronounced risk aversion, quest for social status and utility. Between the two parties, a contract seeks to reconcile management's interests with those of shareholders, for example through bonuses, but with only limited success.

One does, therefore, come across members of the management of electrical utilities who, unlike their counterparts at Northeast Utilities, care about safety just as much as their shareholders, if not more. Witness the Onagawa nuclear power plant, managed by Tohoku Electric Power, a regional utility. One of its former vice-presidents, Yanosuke Hirai, has become a legend in Japan. Onagawa is about 100 kilometres north of Fukushima Daiichi. Located closer to the epicentre of the quake on 11 March 2011, the force was even greater though the wave was the same height. The reactors were shut down in the normal way and no damage was registered. The plant withstood the shock, whereas the two nearby towns were devastated. It even served as a refuge for several hundred local people who had been made homeless. This was by no means a matter of luck, rather the result of the conviction and obstinacy of one man, Hirai san, who died in 1986. In the account that former colleagues gave to the press, he instigated the construction of a 14.8-metre dyke designed to protect the plant against a tsunami. Sure enough, it proved most effective against the Sendai tidal wave. Hirai also convinced the board of his company to install special pumps for the cooling system, to cope with the drop in sea level immediately before a tsunami. Yet no regulations required the company to take these measures. According to his colleagues, Hirai was driven by a powerful sense of duty.[34] He thought it essential to take responsibility for the consequences of one's acts. He was reportedly the sort of person who did not believe that everything would be all right as long as one complied with standards. His aim was more than just compliance. He was the sort of engineer who goes beyond regulations and makes the necessary checks to get to the root of the problem.

Much has been published in economic literature on the behaviour of companies doing more than the legal requirements, particularly with regard to the environment. Many reasons are cited. As in the case of Onagawa, management may have a strong sense of social or ethical responsibility. More commonly, and setting aside any considerations about the psychological make-up of management, companies may do more than just comply with standards and regulations because it is in their interest to do so. There are plenty of powerful incentives such as the threat of stricter legislation, the need to improve their image, the better to recruit more highly qualified young executives or to raise funds more easily. In the case of nuclear power, the most powerful stimulus is undoubtedly the operator's responsibility with regard to its workforce and the neighbouring community. The operations manager at a nuclear power plant reports to his or her superiors at head office, but is also accountable to fellow workers, whose families live nearby. Asked why he spent so much more on safety than was required by the regulations, the head of a Swiss plant would answer: 'Because we live here!'

The same mechanisms and factors explain why the regulator and a regulated company can sustain a dialogue and cooperate without straying into collusion. There is more to a company's behaviour than just bribing or duping the authority, rejecting its requests or achieving minimal conformance. When it comes to technical dialogue there is an additional reason: the need to share the cost of producing information and knowledge. The plant manager at the Diablo Canyon nuclear power plant, questioned by researchers from the University of California, Berkeley,[35] explained that he always welcomed NRC inspectors in the same manner. 'They [NRC inspectors] seem to think we invariably cover-up. They come in here with that idea. When they come in [to inspect], this is what I do.' Pulling out a pad and a pen, he leaned forward and began to write. 'I say to 'em, "Here's a list of our four or five most serious problems," and hand it to 'em. "Go see if we aren't right. And let me know if our solutions aren't working." They don't expect this. And they go away and look. We try to be better than they are at finding and fixing problems.'

This attitude is at odds with the conventional US approach to regulation. In the past, and to a lesser extent now, whether it is a matter of policy on safety, the environment or telecommunications, regulator and regulated have regarded one another as enemies, not peers. There is little mutual trust between them. Such wariness is due in particular to the weight and nature of the US judicial system. Industry often disputes regulatory decisions and measures. Up to the 2000s one-third of the regulations issued by the Environmental Protection Agency were disputed in the courts. Before judge and jury, the two parties, assisted by an army of lawyers and experts, vigorously defended their respective positions, fighting every inch with questions to friendly and hostile witnesses. Anything said or written before the complaint could be used by the opposite party. The best course of action was great caution at all times, particularly before the event. A climate of this sort is obviously not conducive to technical dialogue between NRC administrative staff and the management and safety experts of utilities.

In a more general way, political scientists attribute the antagonistic relations in the US between regulator and regulated to a deep-rooted distrust of the state: citizens need to be protected by the courts against its power of coercion. Conversely, political scientists ascribe the consensus-based regulation found in France and mainland Europe to the model of an informed elite and a benevolent state. Study of national systems and different modes of regulation gave rise to abundant literature in the last two decades of the twentieth century. The stream seems to have dried up since, the differences having become less noticeable. The European and US models have moved closer together.[36] Cooperation between industry and the authorities in the framing and application of new regulations has developed in the US, whereas on the other side of the Atlantic a more judicial approach to regulation has gained ground.

Pros and cons of American and French regulation

Let us start by briefly summarizing the similarities and differences, discussed in the preceding sections, between safety regulation in France and the US.

Basic principles apply on both sides of the Atlantic: the nuclear safety authorities are powerful and competent, independent and transparent. Yet the institutional environment is very different: the US regulator acts under the close supervision of Congress and the courts, whereas its French counterpart is comparatively free in this respect. ASN submits an annual report on its activity to the lower chamber of the French Parliament. Debate remains courteous and the hearing attracts only limited attendance. Very few MPs take an interest in the topic, let alone understand its finer points. Civil or administrative courts have almost no say on the matter. The executive, in contrast, is much more actively involved. The government enjoys far-reaching legal powers for intervention, though in practice it makes little use of them.

The institutional balance of power, with its respective strengths and weaknesses, applies to nuclear safety regulation in the US and in France. We have also seen that the two industries and the installations under supervision are very different too. The NRC must monitor a large variety of reactors and a fair number of operators. Collective self-regulation, through the good offices of the INPO, lightens this burden. In France a more uniform fleet and a single operator facilitate safety checks and performance assessments. But the regulator must take greater care to avoid capture. Overall, regulation has learnt to cope with the particular features of the industry it supervises.

The issue on which there is a major divergence between regulation in the US and France concerns allowance for costs and the role of economic factors. On the one hand we find quantitative goals, regular use of probabilistic assessments, concern about containing costs and effective allocation of efforts; on the other, poorly defined goals and few regulatory prescriptions,[37] with priority given to technical dialogue and no reference to cost-benefit analysis. Clearly we are dealing with two approaches to regulation founded on very different principles, with the US seeking the level at which safety is safe enough, whereas in France the aim is to achieve continuous progress.

Despite such significant differences, the safety regulation systems in both countries are frequently cited as examples. They constitute a baseline for specialists. The regulatory community pays just as much attention to statements by the NRC as it does to ASN. They both influence the course of debate in the various international forums on nuclear safety. But despite this peer recognition we must not overlook several intrinsic defects which have become increasingly visible in recent years.

We shall start with the shortcomings of US regulation. It is exemplary in its management of safety costs, both with respect to the limits it places on the assigned goals and its efforts to define effective measures for achieving those goals. On the other hand, the cost of drafting regulations is very high, which hinders change, delays implementation and reduces responsiveness.[38] The attempt to impose fire-protection standards, described above, is an extreme case, but it is a good illustration of an overall pattern of regulation, litigation and more regulation. To start with, the NRC sets forth new requirements. Then a stakeholder – either an operator or non-government organization – lodges a complaint before a court. In a third step, several years later, a federal judge issues a ruling, at which point the NRC must adjust its requirements. This syndrome is particularly frequent in the case of measures to upgrade existing installations to allow for return on experience following incidents or accidents. Since a decision in 1987 by the District of Columbia Court of Appeals, US regulation operates with two separate categories. The first one corresponds to the standard of 'adequate protection' of public health and safety, which is a legal requirement.[39] The safety requirements enshrined in the initial licensing process for the construction and operation of nuclear power plants, for example, belong in this category. This first set of obligations applies to all plants and the NRC enjoys full discretionary powers for their prescription. The second category comprises all the measures the NRC deems reasonable to limit damage. It must justify them by cost–benefit analysis, demonstrating a substantial gain in safety. So this category covers all the regulatory measures which go beyond an adequate level of protection. They are mandatory, but there is scope for operators to negotiate and adapt the manner in which they are deployed. Each time the NRC frames a new requirement it must choose the right category, a constant source of conflict. Operators accuse the NRC of arbitrarily choosing the first category when costs are high, whereas parties opposed to or critical of nuclear power condemn use of the second category, because making allowance for costs boils down to limiting everyone's safety.

Disputes over the appropriate category oppose the administrative services and the Commission, and also take place between the commissioners themselves. Witness the efforts to introduce stricter safety regulations following the Fukushima Daiichi disaster. The NRC set up a taskforce to highlight the lessons learned which were relevant to the safety of the US nuclear fleet. It recommended a whole range of actions, in particular three urgent new measures: hardened vent designs to prevent hydrogen explosions; instrumentation for spent-fuel pools; and a series of strategic actions to cope with extreme events (portable emergency diesel pumps, emergency intervention team). The staff thought these three mandatory requirements were necessary to secure adequate protection of public health and safety. The then NRC Chairman, Gregory Jaczko, endorsed this move, voting in favour of it when it was tabled before the Commission. However, Commissioner Kristine Svinicki, well known for her pro-industry stance, voted in favour of downgrading all these measures to the second category. The three other commissioners expressed mixed preferences depending on individual measures. Ultimately, a majority decided to put instrumentation on spent-fuel pools in the second category, delaying implementation of this measure till cost–benefit analysis could be completed. On several occasions Jaczko found himself in the minority, alone against the four other members of the Commission. Advocating a hard line requiring additional safety improvements without further delay, he was confronted by the relative inertia of his fellows, often irritated by his style of management. Jaczko finally resigned in May 2012.

In comparison to the US regulator, its French counterpart is more like light cavalry. It travels fast, when necessary, and is neither encumbered by the heavy armour of legal or procedural constraint, nor hemmed in by countless goals and standards. The principle of continuous progress governs its actions without being linked to any specific safety goal, particularly a quantitative one, or to cost–benefit analysis. There are, however, some disadvantages to the extensive discretionary powers invested in the French regulator, raising a series of problems for the years to come.

First of all, this regulatory model requires an enlightened regulator. Until recently ASN has been represented by André-Claude Lacoste, a man of fine character. A graduate of Ecole Polytechnique and the Ecole des Mines, he spent a large part of his career in industrial safety. He took over as head of the Direction de la Sûreté des Installations Nucléaires in 1993 and was in charge of nuclear safety for twenty years, initially under the aegis of the Industry Ministry, then at ASN. Indeed this body was to some extent his brainchild. He managed to convince the policy-makers of its necessity and worked tirelessly to affirm its independence and make its workings transparent. Lacoste's successor, appointed by the French President, is one of his former deputies, a graduate of Polytechnique and member of the Corps des Mines. On taking office in 2012, Pierre-Franck Chevet said that he intended to follow in his predecessor's footsteps. And there is every reason to suppose he will do so. But there is no guarantee that at the end of each six-year term the incumbent president will choose another enlightened regulator.

Secondly, pressure on safety costs is bound to increase. By 2015 two-thirds of the reactors currently operating in France will be at least thirty years old. Spending on the necessary safety and upgrade work will rise, because to continue operations parts will have to be replaced. Some of them, such as steam generators, are large and very costly. At the same time, French policy-makers are firmly opposed to any increase in administered electricity tariffs, keen to maintain living standards and industrial competitiveness. Several times in the past ten years the government has refused to allow electricity prices to make allowance for the full increase in costs, whether caused by rising gas prices, spending on improvements to the grid or subsidies for renewable energies. In principle the pricing system is supposed to reflect the full cost, but in practice this rule does not apply. EDF cannot count on being able to pass on to the consumer the full cost of spending on safety and upgrades. The regulator will have to make allowance for this new factor and methodically weigh up the economic consequences of its prescriptions.

Thirdly, the lack of quantitative goals adds yet another unknown to the tricky equation of plant retirement. The date for the final shut-down of reactors needs to be anticipated as accurately as possible in order to ensure that new capacity – nuclear or not – can take over, satisfying demand without undue disruption. The process of deter-mining this date is already fraught with much uncertainty. Should calculations be based on a forty-, fifty- or sixty-year service life? The whole picture could change almost overnight: the government may suddenly change its mind on the pros and cons of nuclear power; safety inspections may discover serious defects; or a technological breakthrough may substantially reduce the cost of alternative energy sources. With no specific safety goals, the degree of improvement demanded by ASN constitutes a sizeable unknown. All one can say is that it lies somewhere between two extremes. ASN may make do with barely perceptible, yet continuous improvement: for exam-ple, a reactor must be slightly safer as it enters its thirties or forties than it was in its late twenties; alternatively, ASN might require the safety performance of ageing reactors to be brought into line with the European Pressurized Reactor. In the latter case, this would entail substantial compulsory investment. Let us suppose, for example, that the reactors belonging to the 900 MW *palier* had to be fitted with as many redundant systems as their more recently designed 1,300 MW counterparts. The cost of work might even exceed the gain yielded by additional electricity sales from extended operation. The opera-tor would have no option but to shut down the plant completely. Raising the level of safety necessarily stops when the gain expected from electrical revenue is absorbed. This state of affairs benefits nei-ther the consumer nor EDF shareholders. Continuous progress, with no limit set by a specific goal or cost–benefit analysis, leaves wide open the question of how the economic surplus should be shared out between consumers, the generator and potential beneficiaries of the lower probability of an accident. The regulator alone decides how far it should go one way or the other. But a decision of this importance on the distribution of wealth should not be its responsibility, but that of policy-makers.[40]

The principle of unbounded, continuous progress may ultimately create the impression that safety is never adequate. Inevitably, various parties will try to up the odds. Hearing an operator assert that safety is its absolute priority or the regulator maintain that safety is 'never safe enough'[41] makes us forget that the resources available for safety are necessarily limited. Public opinion and policy-makers may end up losing sight of the fact that there comes a time when raising the safety level means closing existing plants which are fully operational. Anti-nuclear campaigners have realized this and make a point of insisting that safety is never adequate. Having no specific safety goals leaves the door wide open for ill-conceived political decisions dictated by the imperatives of fleeting alliances, and subject to local or national haggling between parties. The political decision to close the Fessenheim nuclear power plant – which we shall analyse in Chapter 11 – perfectly illustrates this danger.

On paper the respective shortcomings of nuclear safety regulation in the US and France could be remedied by borrowing from the other's strong points. The US authority lacks freedom of movement, its French counterpart enjoys too much latitude: on the one hand continuous progress is impeded, on the other it lacks direction. But the ideal balance for either organization cannot be achieved at the drop of a hat by importing ready-made solutions. Our case study shows that in both cases national institutions and the lessons of history exert considerable influence on both the form and content of nuclear safety regulation. Change can only be slow and gradual.

In conclusion, regulating the safety of nuclear power is a trade that deals in uncertainties. The better to tirelessly eliminate its defects, we must understand and accept that it is necessarily imperfect.

Identifying the rules to set for operators is no easy task: their effects are hypothetical and it is often impossible to verify their enforcement. Ideally, we should be completely sure about the measures to be taken, their impact on safety and their implementation, but that is beyond our reach. Much like any other public intervention, nuclear safety regulation is, and will remain, imperfect. The perfect regulator does not exist, no more than zero risk. But this is not a reason to down tools. On the contrary it should be seen as an incentive for greater vigilance and an ongoing quest for improvement.

Economic analysis helps us to understand why some forms of regulation are less imperfect than others; it highlights the root causes on which attention must focus to identify potential hazards and find remedies. Four essential, universal pillars are needed to contain the risk of regulatory capture: giving the regulator extensive powers to inspect and sanction; endowing it with adequate resources to secure and consolidate its skills; guaranteeing its independence from government and industry; imposing the transparency of its actions. The example of Japan is a reminder of the pitfalls to which regulatory capture may lead.

Substantial progress towards improved safety can also be achieved by changing the legal framework and balance of power. Shareholder structure, governance and management incentives all feature among information that must be taken into account by safety authorities, prompting them to exercise closer or more remote supervision. Stakeholders in the enterprise can provide the regulator with valuable support, counterbalancing shareholders and management, who may be too concerned with short-term goals. Staff may act as whistle-blowers and the local community can bring pressure to bear if the operator slackens its safety efforts, providing the regulator makes it easy for residents to access information. In short, through the overarching design of regulation and its fine-tuning, economics provides an essential complement to the scientific and technical prescriptions of engineers. Moreover, in financial terms, these additional solutions cost almost nothing. Those who stand to gain from bad governance will of course lose out. Circumscribing their resistance sometimes requires a massive political effort, but no money, unlike a thicker concrete containment.

Our certainty about the best way of regulating the nuclear industry is founded on economic analysis applied to the United States, France and Japan. But what of the rest of the world? Setting aside the majority of OECD countries, we are dealing with an unknown quantity. How does nuclear safety work in China, India, South Korea, Russia or Pakistan? Not very well, in all probability. Regulation is almost certainly far from perfect in these countries and regulatory capture extremely widespread. In the absence of public studies it is difficult to be more specific, but there seems good reason to fear that there may be many other cases similar to Japan.

PART IV

National policies and international governance

Politics is a possible route for taking decisions under uncertainty. Faced with the controversial findings of experts, it is up to public policy-makers to choose and act. It should consequently not come as a surprise to discover that politics plays a predominant role in decisions on nuclear power. Considerable uncertainty weighs on its competitive advantage, risks and regulation. Politics is also a way of providing and managing common goods. Only through mechanisms of public governance can safety and non-proliferation be secured. But, in contrast with this concept of strategically minded governments boldly advancing into the fog or labouring for the general interest, we are sometimes confronted with a more prosaic picture of public decision-making, a process not so much guided by scientific experts and legal advisors, as by the support of lobbies and vote-seeking. The pressure brought to bear on governments by 'green' parties or industrialists also explains many nuclear-policy decisions.

Regardless of where it originates, the decisive weight of politics is illustrated by a trivial observation: countries have adopted and are still pursuing very different courses on the atom. Germany, which invested in nuclear power at an early stage, is now attempting a rapid exit; in neighbouring Austria not a single reactor has ever generated any electricity and the constitution bans nuclear power. France, on the other hand, is still banking on nuclear power, but wants gradually to reduce its share in the energy mix. Meanwhile, Switzerland and Belgium aim to gradually phase out nuclear power altogether. The former Soviet Union, the United States and the People's Republic of China have developed civilian and military uses for the atom. In contrast, Japan and South Korea have both built large nuclear fleets but possess no weapons. Israel, however, probably does, but has built no power plants. Whereas some countries are phasing out nuclear power, others, such as Turkey and Vietnam, are signing up, driven by various motives ranging from energy independence to national defence, through climate change mitigation and international prestige.

This diversity highlights the fact that the decision to develop or retire nuclear power is taken by national governments. Research centres, electricity generating companies and equipment suppliers in each country obviously attempt to influence the political decision. But they do not hold all the necessary cards. After the accident at Fukushima Daiichi, Germany's nuclear industry had to comply with the decision by Chancellor Angela Merkel speedily to shut down the country's nuclear power plants. Despite the heavy losses this decision imposed on them, Germany's three electricity utilities – Eon, EnBW and RWE – could not oppose this choice. Countries may be subjected to diplomatic and commercial pressure from abroad, urging them to adopt or shelve nuclear power, but ultimately it is their decision. In the early 2010s the Czech Republic decided to add two new reactors to the existing plant at Temelin, disregarding vigorous protests by its Austrian neighbour.

Why have some countries decided in the past, and are still deciding now, to develop nuclear power? Why are others phasing out this technology? How do they go about adopting nuclear power and subsequently retiring it? The first two chapters of this final part aim to explore these questions.

The subsequent two chapters focus on supranational governance. The European Union, the inception of which was closely connected to atomic energy, has become a patchwork of energy mixes and policies. It is a classic illustration of the difficulties of framing and implementing policy on nuclear power, which without necessarily being common to all Member States is at least compatible between them.

We then turn to nuclear governance by treaty, and the question of proliferation linked to trade in nuclear raw materials and equipment. The Treaty on the Non-Proliferation of Nuclear Weapons came into force in 1970. It was based on a bargain between nuclear and non-nuclear countries, exchanging access to civilian applications for a commitment not to pursue military goals. The International Atomic Energy Agency is tasked with promoting nuclear power and monitoring installations for possible abuses. Its dual role is subject to great tension: the more international trade in nuclear goods develops, the greater the risk of proliferation, which in turn requires stricter governance of action to monitor possible diversion to military applications.

TEN

Adopting nuclear power

About thirty countries worldwide have built one or more nuclear power plants. Some fifty others have expressed an interest in the technology and asked the International Atomic Energy Agency (IAEA) for practical assistance developing a project. What prompts them to start generating nuclear electricity? Are their motives the same as those of their predecessors?

We shall start by presenting the countries which currently generate electricity using nuclear technology. About ten former soviet socialist republics belong to this category. They include Armenia, Lithuania and Ukraine, and satellites such as Bulgaria, Hungary and the Czech Republic. The choice to invest in nuclear power was above all made by Moscow. Three other major nuclear countries – the United States, the United Kingdom and France – belong in the same category as the Soviet Union. They all adopted nuclear power at an early stage, combining civilian and military applications. India and China joined the game later, but have also developed civilian and military applications. In contrast, Canada, Japan, South Korea and Germany have large nuclear fleets too, but no weapons.[1] There follow a large number of countries with only a small number of reactors. Did you know that Mexico, Argentina, Brazil, Taiwan, Belgium, Switzerland, Sweden, Spain, Finland, the Netherlands and South Africa all own nuclear power plants? To this list of small-scale players we should add Pakistan and Iran. Unlike the others, the development of civilian nuclear power here is closely linked to military ambitions. Pakistan used the development of civilian nuclear power as a blind and Iran has developed an uranium enrichment programme far in excess of its needs for power generation.[2] Counting the former Soviet Union as a single unit, there are currently twenty-one countries which have successfully developed nuclear power.

The above list shows there is no systematic link between possessing atomic bombs and building nuclear power plants. Indeed, most of the countries generating nuclear electricity have not developed such weapons. The military dimension of the atom is nevertheless essential to understanding the background to this technology's development and deployment.

Atoms for peace

Atomic energy was born of science and warfare: science because nuclear physicists played a key part in finding applications for nuclear fission; warfare because, after the atrocities which scarred Europe and Japan, atomic energy contributed to hopes of peace.

A letter from Albert Einstein to Franklin D. Roosevelt in August 1939 is testimony to the contribution of scientists. The physicist drew the President's attention to the possibility that uranium might be used to produce bombs of incomparable force. He implied that Germany, which had just invaded Czechoslovakia, had already understood the possible military significance of nuclear fission, which had recently been discovered. His warning gave rise to the Manhattan Project, the code-name for the US programme to develop nuclear weapons during the second world war, with assistance from Canada and the UK. Under the leadership of the physicist Robert Oppenheimer, the project brought together a host of US scientists and distinguished refugees from Europe. Thanks to its work, the US became the first country to deploy atom bombs, dropped on Hiroshima and Nagasaki in 1945. Through its civilian applications, this military programme also meant that the US was the first country to connect a nuclear reactor to the power grid and to generate electricity.[3]

The end of hostilities heralded a period of collective enthusiasm about the potential of civilian nuclear power, high hopes which now look unfounded. At the time it seemed to have two key assets: being abundant and cheap, this new source of energy could fuel economic growth in industrialized nations and the developing world; its expansion, thanks to scientific cooperation between advanced countries and international supervision of fissile materials, could be achieved while preventing widespread nuclear proliferation.

A famous speech by Dwight D. Eisenhower, entitled Atoms for Peace, reflected this conviction. Addressing the United Nations General Assembly on 8 December 1953, the 34th US President drew on ideas and proposals which had been under discussion for several years.[4] He urged the UN to pursue two goals: reducing the destructive potential of the nuclear stockpile which was starting to build up; and expanding the atom's civilian applications. By this time the US had already lost its monopoly of the bomb. The UK and the Soviet Union were now in the running, with France not far behind. Several tens of tonnes of enriched uranium and plutonium suitable for use in weapons had already been accumulated, whereas just a few kilos was enough to produce a bomb. Eisenhower realized that many, perhaps all, countries would ultimately acquire the scientific and technical knowledge needed to build their own weapons. With the prospect of global nuclear armament, it was time to find and apply remedies to counter the coming arms race. The solution he advocated was to divert efforts away from the atom's military applications and to concentrate on civilian uses. Today a shift of this nature seems barely credible, because just the opposite occurred: some states, such as India, used development of this energy source as a basis for obtaining nuclear weapons. But that was the conviction underpinning the Atoms for Peace initiative and the proposals it set forth. Eisenhower advocated setting up a sort of international bank, on the one hand receiving fissile material to prevent its destructive uses, and on the other distributing it for peaceful purposes, in particular as a source of abundant energy. Hence the close connection between efforts to combat proliferation and to promote nuclear power.

Were such contradictory aims the result of cool calculation or utopian thinking? Many commentators have claimed that Eisenhower's proposals were no more than realpolitik. In compensation for shifting attention from military uses countries would enjoy economic growth fuelled by the civilian applications of the atom in medicine, farming and above all energy. Cooperation on science and technology by countries which had already tamed nuclear fission, primarily the US and USSR, would speed up development for those just starting out. By opting not to compete with the superpowers for control of nuclear weapons, these countries would enjoy the benefits of nuclear power sooner. That was the deal and it was certainly a little idealistic. As the US President emphasized:

> The United States knows that peaceful power from atomic energy is no dream of the future. That capability, already proved, is here – now – today. Who can doubt, if the entire body of the world's scientists and engineers had adequate amounts of fissionable material with which to test and develop their ideas, that this capability would rapidly be transformed into universal, efficient, and economic usage.

This idyllic vision is the other side of the nuclear threat, that 'dark chamber of horrors'. Convinced of their natural symmetry, Eisenhower argued that the benefits the atom could bring to humankind were just as great as its destructive power. The apocalyptic description of nuclear ills in his speech served to highlight the promise of peaceful applications.[5]

Ultimately it makes little difference whether this offer was a cynical ploy or entirely sincere. Either way the linkage between the struggle to prevent global nuclear armament and promotion of nuclear power produced lasting effects. An immediate outcome of

Eisenhower's initiative was the setting up of the IAEA, which subsequently played a key part in the spread of nuclear power worldwide. The Agency must strive 'to accelerate and enlarge the contribution of atomic energy to peace', as well as being tasked with limiting the development of military applications by monitoring installations. The Treaty on the Non-Proliferation of Nuclear Weapons, signed eleven years later (see Chapter 13), had the same goal, to contain the spread of nuclear weapons while encouraging that of nuclear power.

It was not until India's first nuclear test that the Atoms for Peace doctrine began to be questioned. The underground explosion in the Thar desert in 1974 was carried out using plutonium from a research reactor built with Canadian assistance and technology. The test made Pakistan, its hostile neighbour, all the more determined to obtain nuclear weaponry. It achieved its aims thanks to solid scientific and technological skills gained through the international cooperation advocated by Eisenhower. Starting in the late 1950s, Pakistan had received scientific and technical assistance from many countries, including the US, Canada and the UK.[6] China's backing, in the form of military technology under the pretence of an agreement on civilian nuclear cooperation, was decisive too.

This brief summary of the early days of nuclear power should help the reader to understand why a single international body, the IAEA, should be tasked with monitoring nuclear installations while at the same time promoting them, and why a treaty on non-proliferation should encourage exchanges between nuclear scientists and engineers. What now seems a contradiction in terms made perfect sense at the end of the second world war, in the aftermath of Hiroshima and Nagasaki and then during the cold war.

This period is also a reminder of the two-sided nature of nuclear research and technology. To design and produce atom bombs or nuclear power plants involves building large-scale research facilities and training hundreds of physicists, chemists and engineers. Similar resources and skills are needed, at least in part, whether the end result is civilian or military. Top scientists worked on both, either in parallel or alternately. Major atomic institutes, such as the US Atomic Energy Commission, developed civilian and military applications. Of course, advocates of Atoms for Peace were aware of this duality, but they were convinced that the pursuit of military goals could be effectively prevented by control of fissile materials and installations.

The international cooperation on science and technology established and promoted by Washington did speed up and extend adoption of nuclear power by many countries. By 1960 the US had already signed cooperation agreements in this field with forty-four countries, ranging from Algeria to Yugoslavia. The Soviet Union was almost as active, reaching bilateral agreements with seventeen countries, mainly within its sphere of influence (e.g. Bulgaria, German Democratic Republic, Romania). At the beginning of the 1960s there were almost 200 research reactors worldwide, most of which had been imported, wholly or in part, from the US or the USSR.

Pioneers and followers

The countries that pioneered development of nuclear power were also the ones that led the way on research into the atom bomb. The first to master the use of nuclear power to generate electricity were the three nations involved in the Manhattan Project, the US, Canada and the UK, soon followed by the USSR, which tested its first atom bomb in 1949. France only caught up with this group some time later, after resurrecting its research capability, which had been mothballed during the German Occupation.

In terms of technology the pioneering countries each took a separate route, but all of them made allowance for military factors. In the US the uranium-enrichment plants, built to produce weapons, facilitated the development of light water reactors for generating electricity. Experience using this type of reactor to power nuclear submarines also helped. Meanwhile, other countries initially chose technologies using natural uranium as fuel. They saw this as a way of by-passing Washington's monopoly of enrichment. Natural-uranium technology, used in conjunction with graphite or heavy water as a moderator to reduce the speed of neutrons sufficiently to sustain a nuclear chain-reaction, could meet military demand for plutonium while producing energy. In fact, for some time, electricity was seen as a by-product. The priority for the UK and France, which had opted for this technology, was to design a reactor which would produce spent fuel with a high plutonium content, rather than a high output in kWh per tonne of uranium consumed. Military considerations influenced even the technology chosen by Canada,[7] which gave up the idea of nuclear weapons at an early stage. It developed a heavy-water reactor, having gained experience of this type of moderator during the second world war. As part of the Manhattan Project, Canada produced one of the very first prototype heavy-water reactors, manufacturing the moderator to supply US arms factories.

The pioneering countries were not the only ones to develop civilian nuclear power as a sideline to military research. China, for instance, carried out its first nuclear test in 1961, only starting to build its first nuclear power plant twenty-three years later. It is worth noting that all the nuclear-weapon states have also developed atomic energy.[8] Their decision to develop civilian applications was largely determined by military capability.

The case of such countries also throws light on the three main reasons for adopting nuclear power: national prestige, energy independence and the development of science and technology. Indeed, nuclear ambitions may exacerbate such motives. Take France, for instance. In 1945 General de Gaulle established France's Commissariat à l'Energie Atomique (CEA) to develop research and technology related to the atom. This decision, much like many others he took, was intended to restore France's lost grandeur. He firmly believed that scientific excellence and technological prowess were one of the main sources of the nation's prestige. 'France cannot be

France without grandeur', he wrote in his wartime memoirs, and this meant contributing to technical progress, for 'a state does not count if it does not bring something to the world that contributes to the technological progress of the world'. By the time he returned to power in 1958, CEA's investment in equipment and research was beginning to produce results. De Gaulle was clearly determined that France should bolster its independence with nuclear weapons. In the context of the escalating cold war he sought to steer a separate course from that taken by the US or the USSR. He approved plans to build an enrichment plant at Pierrelatte, in the Rhône valley, opening the way for the subsequent construction of a fleet of light-water reactors.

Developing nuclear power was seen as essential to France's continuing growth. It would supply electricity to industry and contribute to exports of equipment. As De Gaulle put it, 'Being the French people, we must achieve the rank of a great industrial state or resign ourselves to decline.' Making up for France's lack of energy resources was also a priority. It had little oil or gas, and coal was expensive to mine, with only limited reserves. The oil crisis in 1973 underlined the importance of energy independence as a justification for developing nuclear power. Indeed, it prompted measures to speed up the French programme: most of the existing fleet was built between 1970 and 1985.

Advances in science and technology are essential for energy independence too. Though less frequently cited as one of the factors prompting a country to adopt nuclear power, science and technology weighs heavily in the balance. In economic terms technological innovation is a response to both supply and demand. Reducing a country's dependence on oil, gas or coal imports responds to a public, political imperative, rather than consumer demand. But the pressure is nevertheless still on the demand side, and it must be met by supply. Innovation comes out of research institutes and university laboratories, not factories like ordinary goods. In the case of nuclear power the supply side involves colossal human and material resources. Research in nuclear physics is the archetypal big science, which came to the fore after the second world war. All its demands – in terms of budget, machinery, labour and research – are huge. France's Court of Auditors has estimated that CEA spent nearly €10 billion$_{2010}$ on research into civilian nuclear electricity in 1957–69, a sum equivalent to the cost of building the first fourteen reactors in the French fleet operated by EDF. In relation to the whole period from 1957 to 2010, and all the reactors, CEA's research spending amounted to half EDF's outlay building the entire fleet.[9] A very large proportion. Furthermore, nuclear research requires highly qualified staff and specific equipment only produced in small amounts. As a result it is not easily redeployed in other fields of innovation. Taken as a whole, these factors have turned nuclear scientists, engineers and technicians into a force driving the growth of nuclear power (and resisting moves to phase it out), regardless of any variations in demand. To this must be added the massive resources at EDF's disposal – in terms of both engineering skills and operating staff – and of course the industrial assets deployed by the boiler-maker Framatome and electrical engineering firm CGE (later Alstom), tasked with developing giant turbo-generators for the 1,300 MW reactors. Anti-nuclear campaigners are fully aware of the pressure exerted by science and technology, when they condemn the allocation of funds to nuclear research and seek to reduce the budgets of bodies such as CEA.

France is an interesting case in another respect, for it may be seen as the last of the countries to pioneer civilian nuclear power, and the first of the large followers. Much like the US, Canada and the USSR, it started research early on and set its own course, developing gas-cooled, graphite-moderated reactors.[10] However, in keeping with other follower countries, France ultimately opted to import foreign technology, when it reached the stage of large-scale industrial deployment (see box).[11] Its fleet consists of pressurized water reactors, the first of which were based on a model developed by Westinghouse. France went on paying licence fees to the US firm until 1991, by which point the technology in use had become entirely French.

Why did France give up gas-cooled, graphite-moderated technology?

If De Gaulle was so concerned about grandeur and standing up to US hegemony, what prompted France to adopt US nuclear technology?

We should start by pointing out that the decision to scrap gas-cooled, graphite-moderated technology was taken by Georges Pompidou, who took over from De Gaulle as President in 1969. It is unlikely that his predecessor would have agreed to this move.[12] Both were keen to promote French industry and foster industrial champions, but Pompidou was more open-minded when it came to private enterprise, more concerned about bringing his country's industry into line with international competition. The fact that the nuclear engineering company Framatome was not publicly owned was not a critical obstacle for Pompidou. Moreover, in the late 1960s, pressurized-water reactors were seen as *the* technology of the future for winning overseas contracts. In 1969 Siemens and AEG were awarded an initial contract to build a pressurized-water reactor in the Netherlands. Shortly afterwards the authors of the CEA-EDF nuclear action plan noted: 'It is sad to see [German companies] building a plant in Holland, despite the fact that Germany's nuclear industry started much later than in France.'[13]

It should also be borne in mind that collaboration with Westinghouse was already well established. National pride blinded observers to the fact that Framatome (short for Société Franco-Américaine de Constructions Atomiques) had been set up in 1959. Westinghouse was one of its initial shareholders, holding 15 per cent of its stock, alongside Schneider, Merlin Gerin and the Empain group.[14] Prior to winning the contract to build the nuclear power plant at Fessenheim, the starting point of the French nuclear programme, Framatome had equipped the Franco-Belgian plant at Chooz and another one at Tihange in

Belgium. Before it finally sold out in 1981, Westinghouse's share in the company had risen to 45 per cent. Framatome went on paying licence fees to the US firm for another 10 years.

Lastly, the gas–graphite technology was thought to be more expensive than its light-water rival. Many comparative studies were carried out, in particular by EDF, more concerned than CEA about obtaining the best cost per kWh. There was heated dispute between the two organizations over which technology to choose. CEA wanted to seize the opportunity to capitalize on its skills and past research, whereas EDF contested the former's growing importance in civilian applications of nuclear power and its industrial development. Naturally both parties did their best to convince successive policy-makers to choose their preferred technology. Ultimately the pressurized-water option supported by EDF prevailed.[15]

Many countries benefited from transfers of technology and know-how from pioneer countries, subsequently graduating to greater technological independence. Germany built its first industrial reactors under licence from Westinghouse and General Electric, but, just as in France, its equipment industry gradually rose to stand on its own two feet. The same was true of Japan and India. China has built, on home ground and under licence, almost all the various types of reactor that exist. It has put its own stamp on Franco-American technology, working upwards from its first nuclear power plants at Daya Bay. It seems likely that it will appropriate and transform the third-generation technology it has imported more recently, with the Areva EPR and Westinghouse AP1000. South Korea has gained its independence too, with its own pressurized water model, after building its early reactors under licence from Canadian, French and US firms. Taking its cue from France, Germany and Japan, South Korea has evolved from importing technology to exporting its own nuclear equipment. The Doosan conglomerate supplied the steam-supply systems for two AP1000s built in China; the Korea Electric Power Corporation won the contract to supply four reactors to the United Arab Emirates. China is progressing along similar lines and has stated on several occasions that it wishes to take part in international tenders for nuclear power plants.[16]

As for the smaller countries, among the new entrants, such as Switzerland, Brazil, South Africa and Taiwan, their first steps in nuclear power were not preceded by massive investments in research nor followed by the launch of a national nuclear industry. These countries have nevertheless built up solid teams of physicists and established high-quality laboratories. They have also taken care to combine domestic content with orders for foreign reactors, in order to support local firms and create jobs. With regard to their motives, these players all want to reduce their energy dependence and boost their prestige, particularly in science and technology.

Aspiring nuclear powers

The countries which now hope to adopt nuclear power are very similar to small past entrants. Their arrival will speed up a trend in the acquisition of nuclear power by non-OECD countries which started with Argentina and South Africa. Their motives are a combination of energy independence, desire for grandeur, and in some cases hidden military ambitions. They do not plan to make nuclear power the key component in their energy mix, nor yet to develop their own technology. Indeed they often buy turnkey plants. The only new development is the appearance of an additional motive, the quest for carbon-free generating technology.

A review of the aspiring nuclear-power countries will enable us to look at these characteristics in greater detail. The IAEA has listed about fifty countries, on the basis of expressions of interest for the advice it offers newcomers.

Most of the aspiring nuclear powers are countries which do not stand a chance of joining the club in the next twenty years. For example, the IAEA list includes the Republic of Haiti, Jamaica, Bahrain, Bangladesh, Tanzania and Sudan. A substantial budget and a powerful electricity grid are pre-conditions for building a nuclear power plant. If we follow the advice of José Goldemberg and exclude all those with gross domestic product lower than $50 billion and grid capacity of less than 10 GW,[17] the list of candidates only contains fifteen names: Algeria, Belarus, Chile, Egypt, Indonesia, Kazakhstan, Kenya, Malaysia, Philippines, Poland, Saudi Arabia, Thailand, Turkey, Venezuela and Vietnam.[18]

What distinguishes them from past entrants is the large number of countries with significant oil and gas reserves.[19] The recent arrival of the UAE is emblematic in this respect. Following a call for tenders completed in 2009 and awarded to a South Korean consortium, four reactors have been ordered. Oil states draw attention to rapidly increasing electricity demand, particularly to power sea-water desalinization plants. However, such demand could very well be met by gas, which is plentiful in many cases. The energy-independence argument rings hollow. In fact, these candidates see nuclear power as a means of coping, in the very long term, with dwindling hydrocarbon reserves. Furthermore, they often have difficulty bringing domestic oil and gas prices into line with international rates. Iran and Nigeria are examples of the popular outcry prompted by attempts to reduce subsidies. Using nuclear power to generate electricity is consequently a way of preserving export revenue.

The final point made by countries with rich hydrocarbon reserves relates to climate change. This too may seem something of a paradox, but should be taken as reflecting a determination to improve their international image and reputation rather than any powerful commitment to combat global warming. In a general way it seems odd that doubtful or even serious aspiring nuclear powers should cite climate change as a motive. Some countries, such as Chile and

Turkey, are far from having exploited the full potential of their hydraulic resources. Others, such as Kenya, have substantial biomass potential. Above all, almost none of them have made any ambitious commitments to cut greenhouse gas emissions. Poland is an exception to this rule. As a member of the European Union it is a party to Community policy on climate change and must meet its targets for reducing carbon emissions. At present 92 per cent of Polish electricity is generated using coal. The option of importing large amounts of Russian gas to diversify its energy mix is not on the cards as the country has no desire to depend on its powerful neighbour. In 2005 this combination of factors led the government to adopt nuclear power.[20] A call for tenders for the first two reactors was due to be issued in 2012, but was postponed when it emerged that Poland may have large shale-gas reserves. The priority is currently to explore that possibility.

Of course, in the case of Poland and other candidates, nuclear power is a less effective way of achieving energy independence than local resources, be they hydrocarbons or renewables. The countries will have to import the fuel. In the past some new entrants – Germany, the Netherlands, Japan, Brazil, China, India and Pakistan – have invested in uranium enrichment plants, reducing their dependence on imports of raw uranium. This is a relatively minor constraint, ore reserves being fairly evenly spread between developed countries, such as Australia and Canada, and less politically stable sources, such as Kazakhstan. Countries now planning to build nuclear power plants will find it almost impossible to enrich their own uranium. Global installed capacity already far outstrips demand and for a new plant to break even in a single country it would need to serve about twenty reactors. Under the circumstances, plans to build such a plant may be taken as signalling military ambitions, or at least interpreted as such by the international community, with the risk of outside pressure, followed by sanctions.

To round off this review of aspiring nuclear-power countries let us look at Turkey, the most advanced nation after the UAE to seek to join the nuclear club. Work on building the first power plant at Akkuyu, in the south, is due to start in 2014. It will mark the culmination of a process which started in the early-1970s. Turkey first expressed a wish to embark on nuclear power years ago. A whole succession of development plans foundered. Calls to tender were issued, but were cancelled or never completed. With strong economic growth since the early 2000s, enhancing its financial position and boosting demand for electricity, the various obstacles have been overcome. Access to nuclear power is also testimony to the political determination to restore the nation's glorious past, a desire borne out in international relations, with Turkey adopting an increasingly assertive stance as a key regional player. Nuclear power will help boost its prestige, dispelling the image of a backward country. In terms of energy independence the motives are less clear. On the one hand, nuclear power will enable it to reduce imports of Russian gas, which currently account for 30 per cent of electricity output. But at the same time, the first nuclear power plants in the Turkish fleet will be funded, built, owned and operated by Atomstroyexport, a subsidiary of Russia's nuclear giant Rosatom.[21]

ELEVEN

Nuclear exit

Several dozen countries are eager to adopt nuclear power, yet others, such as Germany or Switzerland, are trying to phase out this energy source. Why are nations which once banked on the atom now pulling out? It seems to make no sense, particularly as others, following the example set by the United Kingdom, are still determined to renew their fleet. Even France seems to be in a quandary: just a few years ago it started building a new reactor; now it has decided to reduce the share of nuclear power in its energy mix.

For countries already equipped with nuclear power plants, the first step towards phasing out nuclear technology is to stop further construction. A small number of countries have taken the plunge: Germany, Switzerland, Belgium, Spain and Sweden.[1] The next question is what to do with existing plants. Should they be shut down as soon as possible or is it preferable to wait till the safety authority or utility decides they no longer fulfil the conditions for safe or cost-effective operation? In short, a choice between swift or gradual retirement. Germany took a decision on both issues in just a few months, making it a good example for study. France is equally interesting, on account of its decision to trim its sails. We shall analyse both cases in detail. What is interesting is that some of the political motives are similar.

German hesitation over a swift or gradual exit

Germany started to consider phasing out nuclear power in the mid-1980s. Part of public opinion lost confidence after the Chernobyl disaster. The country's last nuclear power plant to be built, which was nearing completion in 1986, was subsequently shut down after three years' operation. Environmental campaigners in Rhineland-Palatinate took the case to court, which ultimately cancelled the plant's licence. The Social Democrats (SPD), once advocates of nuclear power, changed sides, adopting the same position as the Green party. The latter gained a lasting toe-hold in the Bundestag and some regional assemblies. Meanwhile, the realists prevailed over the fundamentalists. The battle against the state, which had been one of the Green party's priorities, was gradually sidelined in favour of mobilization for environmental conservation and against nuclear power. Well organized and electorally effective, the Greens evolved into the world's most powerful environmental party.

At the end of the 1990s, after sixteen years during which the federal government had been dominated by the Christian Democrats (CDU), the SPD won the general election and formed a coalition to govern with the Greens. It was no longer a question of promising the end of nuclear power; it was time for action. There were many obstacles, particularly of a legal nature, because the validity of the licence contracts issued to the operators was not limited in time and expropriation was out of the question. Ultimately, an agreement was negotiated with the utilities providing for the scheduled shutdown of plants.[2] It was ratified in 2002 by an amendment to the Atomic Energy Act. This established a quota for residual production by each plant, which once used up would lead to final shutdown. The last nuclear reactor was due to be turned off in about 2022. In exchange the government made various commitments to the operators, undertaking not to introduce any new taxes and only to prevent the use or transport of waste for technical reasons.

The CDU opposition condemned the scheduled phase-out of nuclear power. It promised to extend the operating life of reactors on returning to power in order to limit any increase in electricity prices and to leave a reasonable amount of time to deploy a new energy plan based on renewables. The German Right saw nuclear power as a transition technology that was necessary until such time as wind farms, solar panels, biogas units, energy-efficiency measures and high-voltage transmission networks could be rolled out. The aim was not to promote the construction of new reactors, simply to delay the closure of existing ones. German advocates of nuclear power had few illusions regarding a possible resurgence of this technology in their country. Given the influence of the Greens, new projects would never be able to overcome local and regional opposition. Indeed, a majority of German public opinion opposed a return to this source of energy.

Following the general election in 2009,[3] the CDU and its Liberal (FDP) allies set about implementing the projected nuclear transition. The Atomic Energy Act was accordingly amended once more in December 2010, three months before the accident at Fukushima Daiichi. It fitted into the larger framework of an Energykonzept designed to halve national electricity output by 2050 and triple the amount of power generated by renewables. The final phase-out of nuclear power was set for 2036, with the shutdown of Neckarwestheim 2, the last plant still operating. The closure date of each plant was determined in the same way as in the 2002 amendment: operators would be awarded a residual production quota, only this time it was larger, amounting to about 1,800 TWh.

German utilities grudgingly acknowledged the new law, which further encroached on their profits. They complained that the extension was too short. Every year they would have to pay a special tax on the uranium and plutonium they consumed, amounting to just over €2 billion. They would also have to pay several million euros a year into an energy-transition fund. The overall cost of about €30 billion was high but ultimately made sense. Extending the operating life of a nuclear power plant would boost the operator's profits, once most of the initial investment had been paid off. Of course, the extension entailed additional costs to maintain the level of safety and reliability, but they were generally far less than the revenue from additional operation. Allowing for work amounting to €500 million on each reactor, a variable cost of €12 per MWh, and assuming that the cost of building the fleet had been fully depreciated, J. H. Keppler estimated the total cost of generating the residual amount authorized by the quota to be about €30 billion (roughly €17 per MWh).[4] This sum must be set against revenue which could amount to €90 billion, on the assumption of an average market price of €50 per MWh over the relevant period. So the €30 billion in taxation would halve the gain the operators derived from their reactors' extended operating life. The utilities' lack of enthusiasm was all the more understandable given that the initial operating life of the reactors, used to calculate depreciation in their accounts, had been forty years. The new timetable for nuclear exit corresponded to an average of forty-four years, adding only four extra years. Of course, if one took as a baseline the 2002 agreement, which involved shutting down plants after an average of only thirty-two years, the new deal was more acceptable for the operators. Even allowing for the special taxes – theoretically non-existent in the case of the 2002 agreement, €30 billion with the new deal – it was more attractive.

The Fukushima Daiichi disaster upset this arrangement. The extension, which Parliament had just approved, was cancelled, and the timetable for phasing out nuclear power that had been negotiated ten years earlier was reinstated. All this happened very quickly. Three days after the disaster a moratorium on the extension of the operating life of reactors was decreed. The next day, it was decided immediately to shut down seven of the oldest reactors for three months. Plans to restart another reactor (Krümmel) were shelved. A week after Fukushima Daiichi, Chancellor Angela Merkel set up an Ethics Committee for a Safe Energy Supply, tasked with reassessing nuclear risk. At the end of May the Committee recommended phasing out nuclear power over the next decade. In August Parliament approved yet another amendment to the Atomic Energy Act.

It reinstated the shutdown timetable from the 2002 plan for the nine plants still operating and indefinitely extended the moratorium on the eight others. This was a serious blow for the utilities, taking them back to square one but with the additional burden of the special tax on fuel. They filed a complaint with the Constitutional Court and sued the Federal Government for damages, demanding several tens of billions of euros in compensation.

Why did Germany choose such a hasty nuclear exit? Foreign observers were stunned by the speed of this move. In a country committed to consensus-based politics decision-making is reputedly slow. Moreover, Mrs Merkel is not one to change her mind easily. The political context influenced the process. The Fukushima Daiichi accident occurred in the middle of an election campaign, with three regional elections set for late March in Germany. The CDU was determined not to lose Baden-Württemberg, which it had governed for the previous sixty-two years. By announcing a moratorium just a few days after the nuclear disaster, party leaders hoped they might contain the rising tide of Green voters. It certainly did some good, but not enough to prevent a Green–SPD coalition winning a narrow majority and electing a Green President to head the regional assembly. The CDU's share of the poll dropped by 5 per cent, whereas the Greens gained 12 per cent, compared with the previous election. Without the moratorium the swing would probably have been even greater. Another election was held in Bremen in May 2011, returning the incumbent SPD–Green majority to power. Here the Greens finished in second place, polling more votes than the CDU.

The cost of fast-tracking the nuclear phase-out also came as a shock abroad. In economic terms there is nothing to be gained from a swift shutdown, rather than a more gradual process. But the Germans, who habitually avoid unnecessary expense, did just the opposite. Early closure of safe, fully operational nuclear reactors represented a dead loss for the operator: the power no longer generated had to be replaced by drawing on other, more expensive sources.[5] The price of electricity for consumers went up, leading to unfavourable macro-economic impacts. Keppler, cited above, estimated the excess cost of replacing 20.5 GW of phased-out nuclear capacity with alternative sources at €45 billion, equivalent to an increase of €25 per MWh. The purpose of this estimate was to measure precisely the difference in cost between the two exit scenarios, before and after Fukushima Daiichi. In the first case generating 1,800 TWh would have cost €30 billion (see above). In the second case the author estimated that it would cost about €75 billion.[6] Other microeconomic studies of the cost of fast-tracking the shutdown of reactors have yielded comparable results, amounting to several tens of billions of euros.[7]

The economic loss entailed in hastening nuclear exit underlines the fact that the motives for the German decision were not economic. It was the Ethics Committee which recommended taking the shortest route. Chaired by Klaus Töpfer, a former Environment Minister, the committee achieved a consensus in a couple of months: nuclear power should be phased out as soon as possible. Its report cites 'the three pillars of sustainability: an intact environment, social justice and healthy economic strength', noting that the 'eternal burden' of nuclear-waste pollution runs counter to these goals. The Committee found that Fukushima Daiichi had changed public awareness of risk. Firstly, the fact that a major accident had occurred in a technically advanced country such as Japan undermined the conviction that a similar event could not happen in Germany. Secondly, this previously inconceivable disaster had revealed the inadequacy of probabilistic risk assessments. Lastly, the Committee emphasized that the damages could not be assessed, even approximately, before an accident, or even afterwards. Several weeks after the meltdown of the reactors at Fukushima Daiichi, there was still considerable uncertainty as to the final extent of pollution and its effects. None of the hazards were under control. It was not even possible to circumscribe a worst-case scenario. So there was no way of comparing the risks associated with nuclear power with those of other energy sources. Yet there were alternative means of generating electricity, in particular renewables, which were not a danger for humans or the environment. They should consequently be deployed as soon as possible in the place of nuclear power, within a decade according to the authors of the report. This brief summary outlines the arguments set forth by the Ethics Committee. We may note in passing that its diagnosis of the Japanese disaster was mistaken. The accident at Fukushima Daiichi could have been foreseen; it was not a 'black swan', as risk specialists put it. Furthermore, the real cause of the accident was an institutional breakdown, due to industry's capture of the regulatory authorities (see Chapter 8). Being technologically advanced, or not, had no bearing on the matter.

What prompted the decision to make the transition over a decade, rather than five or fifteen years? The report offers no explanation, simply suggesting that a shorter period, though ideally desirable, would jeopardize German competitiveness. No evidence was cited to substantiate the claim that ten years would be sufficient to avoid this risk. The ten-year timeframe was probably taken from the previous exit plan, which stipulated that the last power plant should be shut down in 2022. The same milestone was adopted without further calculation or debate. Whether it reflects lack of thought or political determination, the deadline has now been signed into law and Germany must lose no time in implementing its *Energiewende* (energy transition).

We lack sufficient historical hindsight fully to appreciate the consequences of speeding up transition. Apart from the dead loss discussed above and the compensation which the Federal Government – and consequently the taxpayer – may have to pay to the utilities, the change of timetable will probably have a negative impact on employment, inflation and economic growth. Such impacts are hard to assess, for all we can see at present are effects such as job cuts at nuclear power companies, higher electricity prices for households and a surge in investment in other energy sources.

They are difficult to untangle from the effects of the financial crisis, which has led to a drop in demand for energy, and those of the shift to renewables which started well before the decision to speed up nuclear exit was announced. Moreover, the impact of price shocks and investment bubbles must be seen in a long-term perspective, which may mean they have the opposite effect: an immediate rise in the number of jobs may in fact lead to long-term losses.

We cannot estimate the scale of the macroeconomic cost of accelerated transition, but it will probably be negative. It is hard to see any tangible economic benefit from such haste. In terms of labour, we shall see more rapid destruction of jobs in the nuclear industry, with less scope for reconversion than with a more gradual exit timetable, because training takes time. The renewable energy industry should benefit from the sudden increase in demand, but the inertia caused by training will also come into play here, preventing firms from taking full advantage of the situation. As for infrastructure, the massive investment in the power grid which will be needed is a major obstacle for transition. High-voltage power lines, thousands of kilometres long, will have to be built across Germany, in order to connect the wind farms in the north to major industrial centres in the south, where two-thirds of nuclear capacity is currently located. Here again there is considerable inertia. It takes years to complete power transmission infrastructure projects, due to the powerful local opposition they encounter. The plan for a gradual transition had already run into problems in this respect; the decision to speed up the process will only make things worse.

The only hope of any benefit depends on a sudden change of heart. Speeding up the nuclear phase-out, by accentuating the challenge posed by the energy transition, could galvanize the German people, stirring up its enthusiasm; greater collective effort and higher productivity could make the country more competitive in all the trades and industrial sectors involved in next-generation energy technology. The report by the Ethics Committee suggests a scenario of this sort. It is certainly the only one which would reconcile economic interest with the decision to fast-track nuclear exit. But such hopes are faint, perhaps completely vain. In economic terms, speeding up a transition process leaves no option but to make greater use of existing technology, even if it has to be imported, while investing less in research and development to improve future competitiveness. Since 2011 the change in plan seems, above all, to have played into the hands of coal and lignite, which also benefit from lower prices on foreign markets and on the EU Emission Trading Scheme.

In conclusion, on the basis of the German case we may suggest a scheme for explaining the decision to phase out nuclear power, and why the process was speeded up. It is based on two conditions: a political party which makes phasing out this technology a central plank of its platform; and government intervention on risk led by perceived probabilities, not expert calculations (see Chapter 5). Let us imagine then that the entire electorate is spread along a straight line of finite length, with at one end the person most hostile to nuclear power, who advocates the immediate shutdown of all reactors, and at the other the person most in favour of nuclear power, who would endorse the construction of dozens of new reactors. Moving in from the two extremities, towards the median voter – leaving the same number of people on either side – the views will become increasingly moderate. To be elected, the candidate must determine the median voter's preferences, in order to target that person and gain his or her support. If this can be achieved the candidate takes half the poll plus one vote, thus winning a majority.

Obviously an election is much more complex, with voters expressing a view on a large number of different topics such as living standards, jobs and education. Furthermore, there are alliances between parties specializing in various segments of the electorate. But this simple model taken from the theory of political marketing is sufficient for a basic understanding. If nuclear power ranks as a key issue and there has been a shift in public opinion, following a nuclear accident for instance, the median voter will view this technology less favourably. Unless the candidate changes his or her platform, votes will be lost with the risk of election defeat. A choice must be made between personal conviction, prompting the candidate to advocate keeping nuclear power, and gradual phase-out, if the latter option corresponds to the results of the expert appraisal; economic calculation; and his interest in winning the election by keeping step with the electorate's changing perception. On the other hand, if anti-nuclear feeling ebbed, a Green candidate would have to choose between keeping faith with party militants and combating nuclear power, and the risk of losing votes.

In France early plant closure and nuclear cutbacks

Unlike Germany, France has not decided to phase out nuclear power. But it plans to close the Fessenheim nuclear power plant, in Alsace, ahead of schedule. It has also made a commitment to reduce this technology's share in its future energy mix. Underpinning these decisions we find the same factors as in Germany: a party built around combating nuclear power; a more acute perception of nuclear risk in the aftermath of the Fukushima Daiichi disaster; electoral competition; and political alliances which make allowance for risks as perceived by the general public, not as calculated by experts. Just as in Germany, we shall see that decisions on targets and the time schedule have been based mainly on approximation, without paying much attention to economic factors.

The Fessenheim plant, located close to Germany and Switzerland – west of Freiburg, north of Basel – has been a bone of contention ever since it was built. Its two reactors were connected to the grid in April and October 1977. Due to its position it is subject to specific safety measures. The seismic risk, though low, is higher than average due to the proximity of a fault line in the Rhine plain. The plant must also be able to withstand flooding, in the event of a break in the dyke on the Grand Canal d'Alsace. Lastly, it is built on top of a large aquifer; contamination of this source of freshwater would be a major disaster. In July 2011 France's Autorité de Sûreté Nucléaire reported favourably on plans for Fessenheim's number 1 reactor to continue operating for a further ten years. The decision was conditional on work estimated at several tens of millions of euros being carried out, most importantly measures to consolidate the con-crete slab below the reactor in order to limit the risk of polluting the aquifer. The second, similar reactor had also qualified for an exten-sion, subject to comparable requirements for improved safety. In short, the regulator concluded that, subject to the prescribed work being carried out, in compliance with the law, the risks would be 'adequately' limited (see Chapter 9).

Does the French President have a different opinion? Opening an environmental conference on 14 September 2012, Mr Hollande announced that the Fessenheim plant would close in 2016.[8] Justify-ing this decision, he cited its age – it is indeed France's oldest nuclear power plant – and position in a seismically active area, subject to flooding.[9] At first sight, there is little one can say: the democrat-ically elected government supervises the independent regulator in the exercise of its mission. The former is empowered to intervene if it considers that safety targets are not being reached, or because the regulator has wrongly interpreted, or opted not to apply, the necessary measures. There is nothing surprising about policy-makers exercising their power over safety on national territory and setting stricter safety requirements to make allowance, for example, for new data.

Unfortunately this explanation does not add up. Firstly, however counter-intuitive this may seem, age is not a very useful criterion for determining how dangerous reactors are. Think for a second and you will soon see why. Contrary forces compensate for the dual effect of wear and technological obsolescence on the safety of old reactors. Due to their age, they are the focus of greater attention on the part of operators and safety authorities. Frequent, thorough inspections are carried out. In France, for example, the thirty-year inspection, prior to a possible extension of its operating life, involves a complete overhaul. Furthermore, the older a reactor is, the more new parts and equipment it boasts, for instance the new steam generators EDF has fitted to its oldest reactors. Above all, the regime implemented by the safety authority is not a two-tier process, with lower requirements for old reactors and much higher standards demanded of their more recent fellows. All the reactors, young and old, are subject to the same rules, the same level of safety with regard to maintenance and operation. It is consequently misleading to assert categorically that the oldest reactors are not as safe (see box).

Secondly, the French President's decision has not been endorsed by any new study or review of existing data by his advisors, the government, the administration or even an ad hoc group of experts. No technical input on the risks entailed by reactors informed the choice made by Mr Hollande. He was no better informed as a presidential candidate, when retiring Fessenheim featured among his campaign commitments. In fact closure of the plant is entirely due to a political compromise. The French Socialist party (PS) is a long-standing ally of the Green party (EELV), which has opposed nuclear power since its inception. Six months before the presidential election in 2012 an agreement was signed by the two parties. It included Fessenheim's immediate closure and a cut in nuclear power's share of the energy mix, bringing it down to 50 per cent by 2025. At the same time agreement was reached in preparation for the parliamentary election, following the presidential poll. It allocated about sixty constituencies to the Greens with no opposing Socialist candidate in the first round, in order to strengthen their local powerbase. Agreement on their political platform also opened the way for Green support for the Socialist candidate in the second round of the presidential contest. On the campaign trail, a few months later, Hollande endorsed the target of a 50 per cent nuclear share in the energy mix. But he

Age is a misleading criterion for determining how dangerous reactors are

'Start by shutting down the old nuclear plants, as they're the most dangerous' would appear to be a slogan rooted in common sense. The older a reactor, the more worn-out its parts; they must consequently be more fragile, making the reactor more accident-prone. QED. Furthermore the oldest reactors were built longer ago, at a time when safety standards were less strict than nowadays and safety technology more rudimentary. Unfortunately, the facts do not confirm this intuitive reasoning.

A simple method involves checking whether there is a relation between the age of reactors and the number of times an emergency shutdown is caused by a human or material failure jeopardizing safety. Unplanned reactor shutdowns, not connected with scheduled maintenance work, refuelling or inspections, are a widely used safety performance indicator. It – the Unplanned Unavailability Factor, as it is technically known – is listed in the International Atomic Energy Agency database, which is easily accessible online. We used it to analyse the 143 reactors in the European fleet, in order to work on a larger number of observations than for just the French fleet.[10] This method shows that reactors do, on average, suffer more technical problems giving rise to unplanned shutdowns between the age of 30 and 40 years – 16 per cent more to be exact. But if we compare this age group with the performance of reactors in the first years of their operating life, the balance tips in favour of the oldest plants. More technical problems occur during the first years of operation. This may come as a surprise, but it reflects the difficulties encountered on reactors while they are being commissioned and during the first few years of operation. Care should also be taken with reasoning based on an average. There are few old reactors. Only two reactors in Europe are more than 40 years old: Oldbury 1 and 2 in the UK. As a result, the safety-indicator average is based on too small a number, reducing its statistical value. With this exercise there is no way of knowing whether the curve plotting safety against age flattens out after the first five years, or whether great age translates into declining safety. Indeed, there is no statistical evidence against the hypothesis that safety actually improves with age.

A more complicated method, based on data which though available to the general public takes a long time to obtain, involves looking for a correlation between the age of reactors, their operating characteristics and the number of incidents (level 1 or 2 on the INES scale: see introduction to Part II). The number is about ten per reactor per year. Here the results are more conclusive. The first observation is that incidents occur most frequently during reactor shutdown. There are two reasons: it is easier to observe failures, a much larger part of the reactor being accessible to inspectors; and work is mainly carried out during reactor shutdown, with intervention by machines or humans, which in turn entails a higher risk of incidents. Consequently, if the aim is to analyse the number of incidents on two nuclear reactors, one cannot compare a unit which has been shut down for some while for refuelling or a ten-year inspection with one which has been operating non-stop. After correcting this bias, we found that the oldest reactors suffered fewer incidents than the more recent ones. Those familiar with the EDF fleet will not be surprised. The fleet consists of various reactor models, known as *paliers*. Reactors belonging to the first *paliers* are characterized, on average, by a lower number of incidents than those in the last group.

To distinguish the age effect from the 'reactor model' effect, we must compare reactors in the same *palier*, depending on whether they were built first or last. Statistical processing shows that there are fewer incidents on the oldest reactors in any one *palier*. This finding may reflect a learning effect. The first unit in a series certainly displays more defects than the following one, due to the management and running of construction; commissioning is fraught by teething problems. Similarly there is more trouble on the second unit than the third. Only four reactors belonging to the N4 *palier* were actually built, which partly explains why this model, despite being the most recent and the most technologically advanced, has also notched up an above-average number of safety incidents. So if the construction date were to be taken as the only criterion for retiring a reactor, attention should focus on Civaux and Chooz, France's most recent operational reactors! This quip should serve to underline how misleading it is only to use age as a basis for ranking reactors, deciding in which order they should be retired, and reducing the share of nuclear power in a nation's energy mix.

It is consequently inaccurate to state categorically that the oldest reactors are not as safe.

only made a firm commitment to close one nuclear power plant – Fessenheim – during his first term of office. So his statement in the environmental conference in September 2012 merely confirmed an earlier decision.

Clearly a concern for political and electoral balance prevailed. The PS-EELV agreement is a compromise between a party which wants to keep nuclear power and another which advocates its rapid phasing-out. At first sight agreement seems impossible. In fact by adding an adjective both sides could accept the accord, for it promised 'la sortie du tout nucléaire', an end to [the] all-nuclear [energy mix]. France's nuclear-electricity fleet currently covers almost all of semi-base and baseload demand, amounting to three-quarters of the nation's electricity consumption. Of all the large countries which developed nuclear power, France is the only one where this technology is so predominant. Expressed in figures, ending the all-nuclear energy mix means halving the share of electricity generated by nuclear power plants. But cutting back its share of the mix from 75 to 50 per cent by 2025 is little more than a game with round numbers which are easy to remember and communicate. No technical factors underpinned this choice, nor yet an age limit requiring the closure of all reactors more than 30 or 40 years old.[11] The 2025 deadline echoes the 25 per cent difference between three-quarters and a half![12]

In terms of electoral balance Hollande seems to have made the right choice, winning the Socialist primary and then the presidential election. Let us return to the median voter model, which posits that in order to be elected a candidate must guess the preference of this hypothetical voter. Countering his main adversary in the primary, Martine Aubry, Hollande refused to support completely phasing out nuclear power, even in the long term. The number of Green supporters this stance lost him was no doubt fewer than the number of Socialist voters that he gained from it, the latter taking a much more moderate view of the role of nuclear power. Subsequently, in the presidential campaign, Hollande came up against Nicolas Sarkozy, who was in favour of an 'almost all' nuclear energy mix and criticized plans to close Fessenheim. Here again, Hollande was probably closer to the preferences of the median voter.

So, if any calculations preceded the decision to close Fessenheim, they focused on vote projections, not nuclear safety.

Nor did the calculations focus on projected costs. Debate on how to assess the economic cost of closing Fessenheim only started once the decision had been reiterated.[13] Newspapers asserted that several billions would go up in smoke.[14] The plant's early retirement would entail particularly damaging asset destruction for the operator: large components, such as the steam generators, have recently been replaced. Moreover, as we mentioned above, ASN demanded additional work costing several tens of millions of euros as a condition for issuing a licence for another ten years' operation. All these investments may be considered a dead loss and EDF might demand compensation. The fact that the company is publicly owned does not necessarily make a difference. Private minority shareholders are unlikely to allow themselves to be cheated. In addition, Swiss and German utilities hold special production rights on almost a third of the output from the two reactors. They will probably expect compensation, which might help EDF press its case. In terms of the general interest, early retirement of Fessenheim is not an ideal solution. It entails a microeconomic loss which depends, as we saw previously with the German plants, on a whole series of assumptions, such as electricity prices in the future, the cost of alternative resources, investment in further refurbishment, the level of the load factor and the 'normal' operating life of nuclear power plants. This loss could amount to several billions or even more.[15]

I wish to make it clear that I see no problem with policy-makers opting to prematurely retire nuclear power plants, even if their motives are exclusively electoral or driven by a political alliance. That is how democracy works. My concern is that at no point was the debate properly informed, documented or debated in technical and economic terms. Decisions were taken on the early retirement of reactors, despite their having received a clean bill of health from the safety authority and with total disregard for the consequences, other than shifts in voting patterns and the balance within and between political parties. It is quite possible that making allowance for these technical and economical factors would not have made any difference to the final outcome, but at least the political decision would have been taken with full knowledge of the facts and consequences.

In conclusion, the issue of phasing out nuclear power needs to be uncoupled from the question of the length of a nuclear fleet's operating life. This separates the decision not to build any more nuclear reactors from the other one regarding the early or late retirement of existing plants. Deciding to keep nuclear power as part of the nuclear mix is a major gamble. As we have seen in preceding chapters, the future competitive advantage of nuclear power is uncertain, much like the frequency and scale of accidents and the effectiveness of safety regulation. The decision to extend the life of existing reactors once the safety authority has given the green light is in no way comparable. We have a clear idea of how much it costs to generate electricity using existing nuclear power plants, and each plant has been examined in painstaking detail. When policy-makers decide in favour of fast-track rather than gradual exit, they are not settling an uncertain wager but engaging in massive asset destruction contrary to the general interest.

TWELVE

Supranational governance

Learning from Europe

Let us step back now from domestic politics to look at international nuclear governance. We shall start by examining cooperation to prevent nuclear accidents, with a review of work in Europe. In this respect the European Union is a remarkable test-bench: the political and economic integration of Member States is far-reaching and long established; cooperation on safety operates within the framework of supranational bodies such as the European Commission and Parliament; there is even a specific treaty, which set up the European Atomic Energy Community. Moreover, the EU possesses an impressive nuclear fleet, almost a third of global capacity, occupying a relatively small space, divided by national borders: one in four nuclear power plants is located less than 30 kilometres from another Member State. A major accident is therefore likely to affect the population of several countries at the same time. Lastly, almost all of Europe's centres of electricity consumption and production are connected by a power grid. Shutting down power plants in one country impacts on the others; consumers in nuclear-free nations are partly supplied by nuclear-generated electricity. In short, with this level of political and energy interdependence, Europe is an ideal place to observe supranational nuclear governance, its advantages and limitations.

Why is the national level not sufficient?

The national level is not sufficient, quite simply because radioactive clouds do not stop at borders, and nor do electrons. Chernobyl made the transnational nature of damage caused by a nuclear accident painfully clear to Europeans. Starting from Ukraine, the radioactive pollution mainly contaminated neighbouring Belarus. Driven by southeasterly winds, material from the reactor core also soon reached Scandinavian countries. Poland, Germany, France and the United Kingdom were also affected. The pollution had no impact on public health in the EU but caused serious concern, fuelling a lively controversy between the authorities and environmental groups.[1] As for electrons, the only border they encounter is the one formed by the power grid. The European grid interconnects all Member States,[2] reaching from Finland to Greece, from Portugal to Poland. More precisely, it is the electrical load which does not encounter any borders, as electrons only travel very slowly. It is a bit like water in a garden hose, which immediately spills out of the end when you open the tap but bears no relation to the liquid entering the other end of the main. It is the pressure which is transmitted so quickly, not the water.

The concept of a collective – or public – good casts light on the problem posed by permeable borders. As far as economic theory is concerned, it is at the root of the need for international governance. Public goods are collectively consumed products or services: they are accessible to all and each user consumes the same good. In other words, it is impossible to exclude users, and consumption by one user does not reduce availability for others. Street lighting in towns is a simple example often cited in the literature on such goods. It is there for everyone – residents, passers-by and even thieves who would probably prefer the cloak of obscurity. None of them deprive others of light by consuming it. These characteristics justify public intervention in supply of these goods, in particular to provide funding and determine both the quantity and quality available for all users.

Protecting the population against nuclear accidents counts as a collective good. Everyone benefits from this protection and enjoys, for better or worse, the same level of quality, which they may consider excessive or inadequate. Compared with street lighting, this service is more abstract, particularly as it is universal, not local, in its coverage. So it is more difficult to grasp its collective dimension. It is nevertheless of prime importance, the same problem arising as for street lighting with the need to take everyone's preferences into account, while ultimately imposing a uniform standard. Some people, because they live close to a power plant or have a heightened perception of risk, may demand a higher level of protection; others would happily make do with less. Were this an 'ordinary' good, it would not be a problem. The market supplies apples of various sizes and colours, and shoppers are free to choose whatever suits their taste. Not everyone is obliged to accept the same product.

To some extent local authorities and national governments can cope with such divergent preferences regarding collective goods. They can base their decisions on the institutions and rules which govern local and national democracy. But what is to be done when a collective good concerns several foreign jurisdictions? There is no alternative but to set up mechanisms of international governance. In the absence of common elections or rules, each state will decide on its own. On one side of the border residents might, for example, benefit from safety targets for nuclear installations twice as strict as the standards in force on the other side. Similarly, in the event of an accident, with liability regimes varying from one state to the next, people living on either side of the border would not receive the same compensation. Moreover, without common rules, if damages exceed the upper limit on liability, taxpayers in the country least affected will not contribute to compensating their neighbours in the most severely affected country.

Without supranational governance, tension is potentially highest between neighbouring countries which have adopted opposite courses of action on nuclear power. It is further exacerbated when their electrical systems are interconnected, as is the case in Europe.

The security of the power transmission network, balancing input and output, is a collective good in itself. The Germans and Italians, both now opposed to nuclear power, enjoy the same quality of service – in terms of voltage and security of supply – as the French. The collective dimension of the network is more clearly apparent in the compulsory nature of consumption which characterizes public goods. Just as thieves would gladly dispense with street lighting, those opposed to nuclear power would rather not be supplied by reactors in their own or neighbouring countries. However, this is impossible, unless they refuse to connect their dwelling to the power line. Europe's interconnected network means that consumers cannot forgo nuclear power. Short of disconnecting their homes, anti-nuclear campaigners determined not to use this energy source have no option but to leave the EU.[3] The same applies to militant nuclear advocates opposed to renewable energy sources: there is no escaping green electricity.

How, at a practical level, does the EU go about reducing such tension? With regard to its success achieving a relatively high level of safety, it may serve as an example; on the other hand, when it comes to rules on liability, it is in no position to lecture other countries. We shall see in detail how and why this is the case.

European safety standards

Surprising as it may seem, there is no economic reason why all EU Member States should apply the same safety standards. In other words, there is nothing odd about a reactor being retired in one country after fifty years' service, whereas a unit registering exactly the same safety performance could be authorized to operate for a further ten years in another country. European safety standards need to be harmonized, but not equalized. This is due to the variation in costs and benefits of nuclear energy, depending on the population and where they reside.

Either they live in the immediate proximity of the nuclear power plant, or in a much larger surrounding area. Damage in the event of an accident mainly concerns local residents. The latter also enjoy a share in the benefits, in the form of jobs and local taxes. From an economic standpoint the safety target set for the plant must make allowance for local interests. These may vary a great deal from one region to the next. Some local authorities are very keen to keep nuclear power, others would rather it was banned. Looking at the bigger picture, damage may affect a much larger area and even remote residents may benefit from nuclear power, in particular with regard to electricity prices. Safety targets – and the standards required to achieve them – must consequently make allowance for the preferences of both local residents and people living well beyond the immediate proximity of the plant. As ever, a balance must be struck.

We may now apply the same local–global dichotomy to the separation between Member States and the EU. This is not a misleading over-simplification, because many EU countries are small and a large number of reactors are located close to an intra-Community border. Furthermore, Member States display widely divergent attitudes to nuclear power. An average of 35 per cent of EU citizens think the advantages of nuclear power counterbalance its risks, but the share rises to 59 per cent in the Czech Republic and plunges to 24 per cent in neighbouring Austria.[4] It is consequently impossible to set the same safety goals for the whole of the EU, in line with the highest, lowest or even median level. On the other hand, no country can behave as if the rest of the Community did not exist. In particular, low safety goals, which one Member State might accept, must not be possible if its immediate neighbours set higher targets. In short, neither the national nor the supranational safety level should be unilaterally imposed.

Europe seems to have found a satisfactory way of achieving a local–global balance in this respect (see box). Obviously, given the

Europe's successful balancing act

The Commission succeeded in reconciling the Czech and Austrian positions on starting up the nuclear power plant at Temelin. The village is located less than 60 kilometres from the border with Bavaria and Upper Austria. In 1986 work started here on two reactors of Russian design, but things did not go smoothly. The original command and control system – the reactor's nervous system – proved defective and had to be replaced. At the end of the 1990s Austria opposed commissioning of the plant, on the grounds of inadequate safety. The Czech Republic, which had applied to join the EU, said it was prepared to continue upgrading the reactors to meet the strictest safety standards. Bilateral negotiations between the two countries ran into stalemate and the Commission stepped in to act as a mediator.[5] In the early 2000s the two parties signed an agreement which entitled Austria to monitor safety at the Temelin plant, in particular regarding compliance with the new standards the Czech government had promised to enforce. In those days there was no relevant EU directive. Had it existed, the previous agreement and the arbitration process carried out by the Commission would not have been necessary. On joining the EU the Czech Republic would have been required to raise the level of safety at Temelin to comply with the directive, and Austria, in the event of non-compliance, would have been able to take the matter to the Commission and the European Court of Justice. On the other hand, had the Czech Republic not wanted to join the EU it could have exercised its sovereign right to decide the appropriate level of safety at its plant. So, despite pressure from Austria, Temelin did not close, and thanks to the Czech Republic's determination to join the EU, its safety was substantially upgraded prior to commissioning. Europe did its job.

It was equally effective in imposing the shutdown of eight first-generation Soviet reactors in Bulgaria, Slovakia and Lithuania. It would have been impossible, without exorbitant expenditure, to upgrade these reactors to meet prevailing European standards.[6] The EU made their closure a condition for allowing the three countries to join the Community. To substantiate its case it drew on the expertise of the heads of national safety authorities, who belong to the Western European Regulators Association. In so doing, it succeeded where international cooperation had previously failed. When the Soviet bloc collapsed, the Group of Seven countries set up a programme to improve reactor safety in Central and Eastern Europe. But it was never really implemented. It only led to one closure: reactor number 3 at Chernobyl. Reactor number 2, at the Metsamor nuclear power plant in Armenia, is one of the most dangerous in the world but it is still running.

difficulties in setting targets and criteria for assessing safety performance, the balance does not take the form of quantitative risk thresholds, more a set of rules and standards. The EU requires for instance that safety in each Member State should be regulated by an independent authority. More broadly, all the standards recommended by the International Atomic Energy Agency are binding throughout the EU. They are mandatory and non-compliance is sanctioned. This constraint is enshrined in the European Directive, of 25 June 2009, 'establishing a Community framework for the nuclear safety of nuclear installations'. As with most European legislation, drafting this directive was a long, difficult process, spread over several years and involving many versions. Member States disagreed over its necessity and aims; the Commission advocated a more federal project than the Council.[7] But the result is there for all to see, the first binding supranational legal framework ever to apply to nuclear safety.

Europe's patchwork of liability

European Union citizens do not all enjoy the same compensation rights in the event of a major nuclear accident. The amount varies depending on the country in which the plant is located. This discrimination is exacerbated by the many discrepancies from one state to the next regarding the legal definition of damages, the time limit for filing claims and their subsequent investigation, the rules prioritizing the allocation of funds, and so on. As a result, if an accident happens in a power plant close to the border between two Member States, residents will not receive the same compensation, depending on which side they live. Exaggerating slightly, there are as many civil liability regimes for nuclear damage as there are Member States. Yet, in a broader perspective, international nuclear law should bring about a certain uniformity. There are only two Conventions – one signed in Paris, the other in Vienna – to which countries may be a party, and the Euratom Treaty provides a basis for joint legislation on liability. Unfortunately, in practice changes and revisions to the two conventions have created an impenetrable legal jungle, and Euratom is, to all intents and purposes, still an empty shell or almost (see boxes).

There is nothing inevitable about the patchwork of liability which blankets Europe. A legal framework exists, in particular in the Euratom Treaty, within which Community legislation on liability and insurance could be established. The Commission plans to table a draft directive on the matter in 2015. Member States hostile to nuclear power will probably press for very high levels of liability and insurance coverage, whereas advocates of further nuclear growth will certainly oppose such measures. A compromise is quite possible, even if coexistence between countries for and against nuclear is increasingly fraught.

The Paris and Vienna Conventions

The Paris Convention of 1960 on Nuclear Third-Party Liability was adopted under the auspices of the Organisation for Economic Cooperation and Development, and its Nuclear Energy Agency. The Vienna Convention, which is slightly more recent, was the work of the IAEA. Each of these liability regimes has established its own rules, capping compensation, determining the scope of damage covered and investigating complaints. So no country can ratify both conventions. For historical reasons, the first nations to join the European Community signed up to the Paris Convention, whereas more recent Member States such as Bulgaria and Romania, and all former eastern-bloc countries, subscribed to the Vienna Convention. This initial separation was followed by a multitude of other divisions. An additional Brussels Convention, already amended once, supplemented its Paris counterpart, which has itself been amended twice. The Vienna Convention has been revised once. But signatory countries have not necessarily kept pace with these changes. Some have stuck to the original versions, others have signed the latest versions, but not ratified the texts. Similarly some countries have signed or ratified a protocol bridging the gap between the two conventions, others have not. The protocol establishes mutual recognition between the two international regimes: victims in a third country will be compensated in line with the regime in force in the country where the accident occurred. To complicate matters further, a third convention was drawn up in 1997. It commits countries – whether they are bound by the Vienna or Paris–Brussels regime – to pay additional compensation to victims. Only three EU countries have signed it. Lastly, any Member State is at liberty to set ceilings and levels of liability higher than those established in the various conventions. All in all, these disparities make for substantial differences between individual countries in the EU. Take for example three neighbours: in France the upper limit on EDF's liability is about €100 million, to which the state undertakes to add the same amount; in Belgium the ceiling for GDF-Suez is €300 million, but with no commitment by the state; in Germany there is no limit to the liability of operators, with a state commitment amounting to €2.5 billion.

Euratom, a pointless treaty?

In 1957 two treaties were signed in Rome. One, as we all know, established the European Economic Community. It brought into existence the Common Market, evolving after a series of revisions into the European Union as we know it today. The second treaty, now largely forgotten, established the European Atomic Energy Community. It aimed to encourage and assist the development of joint nuclear activities. But Euratom, as it is known, made little contribution to European integration and is still a largely empty shell.

Of the two Communities, Euratom seemed at first sight the more promising. Jean Monnet, one of the prime movers behind European integration and an instigator of this treaty, thought it was more likely to succeed, due to its focus on a specific sector. Nuclear power followed on from coal and steel in the gradual advance towards economic integration. Once its benefits had been demonstrated in a particular sector, it would be easier to overcome resistance in other sectors. Pro-Europeans all subscribed to this belief. In contrast, the customs union affected all industrial activities and could be construed as impinging on national sovereignty. Euratom was expected to be all the more effective as nuclear power was a brand-new technology, purportedly without deep-rooted national interests. The benefits of nuclear integration were perfectly obvious: the Six were individually too small to cope with the massive investment required to develop this energy source; they all faced rising demand for energy and were fully aware of their dependence. It should be borne in mind that in the late 1950s civilian nuclear power was seen as the solution to the lack of cheap, abundant energy. The preamble to the Treaty asserted that 'nuclear energy represents an essential resource for the development [. . .] of industry'. The aim was 'to create the conditions necessary for the development of a powerful nuclear industry which will provide extensive energy resources, lead to the modernization of technical processes and contribute, through its many other applications, to the prosperity of their peoples'. Germany was strongly in favour of the customs union, but France less so. On the other hand, it advocated nuclear integration. So to win over both parties it was decided to join the two projects.

Euratom was based on mistaken assumptions and never developed. Nuclear power was not brand new. Some states, including France, had already taken the lead, whereas others, such as Germany, reckoned their industry could catch up, particularly with American help. There was no sense of an equal footing, and there were already powerful national interests, both industrial and diplomatic. It proved hard to achieve the smooth progress posited by the advocates of an atomic confederation. Civilian nuclear power, much like its military cousin, had become a national affair, a field in which to assert nationalist ambitions. Unlike the Common Market, negotiations as part of Euratom failed to contain the rival interests of Member States through trade-offs between sectors.[8] Furthermore, the energy environment had changed. The blockade of the Suez Canal in 1956 had prompted fears of lasting oil shortages and high prices, but these were soon allayed, with oil prices dropping again.

The missions set forth in the treaty included establishing joint companies, to develop a European nuclear industry; securing a centralized supply of uranium ore and nuclear fuel; harmonizing rules on liability; and facilitating insurance contracts. But in practical terms these, and other objectives, came to little, due to the lack of large-scale concrete undertakings. Indeed, there was even talk of disbanding Euratom altogether. However, the treaty has survived, with its original aims. This other Community is still a legal person, separate from the EU, though they share various institutions such as the Commission and the Court of Justice.

Euratom has nevertheless progressed in some areas, particularly research, public health and safety. It funds a joint research centre and has engaged in an ambitious project to develop nuclear fusion, with the construction of an international experimental 500 MW reactor, known as ITER. It has also established common standards to combat ionizing radiation, particularly to protect people exposed at work (staff at nuclear power plants, radiologists, among others). It contributes to efforts to contain proliferation and, thanks to its regional reach, carries more weight than individual Member States. Lastly, with regard to safety, Euratom was behind the 2009 Directive on the safety of nuclear installations. It also set conditions for former eastern-bloc countries joining the EU, requiring them to upgrade safety on existing nuclear power plants. Ironically, the treaty made no provision for this particular advance. None of its 294 articles, despite all the detail, make any explicit reference to the Community's competence over the safety of ionizing-radiation sources, either to establish standards or to monitor compliance. A ruling by the Court of Justice was needed to give a broad interpretation of Euratom's initial competence for protecting public health, extending its remit from setting standards on the admissible effects of ionizing radiation to include equipment likely to cause radiation.

In view of its initial ambitions the Euratom Treaty has not achieved a great deal. But compared with the vacuum its absence would have left, it has not been entirely useless.

Coexistence fraught by conflicting views on nuclear power

Once perceived as a force for European integration, nuclear power has become a source of discord between Member States. They all share the same network, but some are building new reactors (Finland, France) or plan to do so (UK, Czech Republic), whereas others have outlawed the technology (Austria) or decided to phase it out of their energy mix (Germany, Belgium). Tension between the two sides was palpable after the Fukushima Daüchi accident, when stress tests were carried out on the European fleet. The nuclear divide is preventing the EU from framing a joint energy policy.

In Europe, just as elsewhere, the disaster in Japan prompted national governments and regulators to review the safety of nuclear installations. With the financial crisis still looming large in people's minds, the term 'stress test', originally hatched to assess the resilience of banks, was recycled to assess the response of nuclear power plants to various hazards, in particular flooding and earthquakes. Unlike elsewhere, the tests were coordinated between neighbouring countries under the aegis of the European Commission and the European Nuclear Safety Regulation Group (Ensreg), which advises on safety.[9] This group brings together heads of administrative bodies or independent nuclear safety authorities in all Member States.

Coordinating the tests caused some tension. During the weeks following the accident at Fukushima Daiichi the European Energy Commissioner Günther Oettinger adopted an extreme position. Referring to an 'apocalypse', he claimed that some reactors in Europe did not meet the standards set by the Directive.[10] He asked for the stress tests to be extended to include terror risks, such as the possibility of an airliner being hijacked and targeted at a nuclear power plant. Most national regulators dismissed this idea. The Council of Ministers had not given the Commission a mandate to assess such extreme situations, quite unconnected with the causes of the Japanese accident. The head of France's Autorité de Sûreté Nucléaire, André-Claude Lacoste, suggested that this move by the Commission reflected its determination to shift the balance of power,[11] calling into question the existing national and supranational distribution of competence and power, laboriously hammered out during negotiations for the 2009 Directive. Ultimately, a compromise was reached. Ensreg would check certain issues at the interface between safety and security, such as falling planes, and an ad hoc group would be set up to address the security threat posed by acts of terrorism.

Another skirmish followed when the Commission presented the results of the stress tests. In a communication to the Council of Ministers and Parliament, it returned to the Ensreg results published six months earlier.[12] The summary report by the regulators concluded that given the level of safety there was no need to shut down any reactors. It also proposed a series of recommendations designed to increase reactor resilience in extreme situations. The detailed reports highlighted the shortcomings which needed to be corrected for individual countries and plants. But the summary of Ensreg results which the Commission included in its communication was much more alarmist. It criticized France, where allegedly only three installations made allowance for seismic risks. It also addressed seven recommendations for improvements to France, and only two to Germany. In a press release the ASN regretted 'the working methodology used by the Commission for drawing its conclusions' which 'ignore some important recommendations of the stress-tests final report'.[13] Lacoste subsequently explained that this statement was a much toned-down version of what he really thought. He accused Oettinger of intervening unduly in the stress-test process, of using Ensreg, and sapping national regulators' confidence in the Commission, which would make future cooperation between the two echelons more difficult.[14] In referring to national regulators, Lacoste meant active and experienced regulators. It should be remembered that he instigated the Western European Nuclear Regulators Association. Unlike Ensreg, Wenra only brings together the authorities of countries which possess nuclear power plants. States such as Ireland or Austria, which condemn nuclear power and have no experience in its supervision, are not represented. At Ensreg each country can vote and have its say, advocating safety requirements so strict as to be unattainable. The two organizations are emblematic of Europe's divisions over energy, with on the one hand the EU's twenty-eight Member States and on the other its fifteen nuclear-power countries. The Commission seeks to reconcile the interests of all parties, but the balance varies over time. The nuclear states – Wenra members – gained ground in the 2000s with the arrival of former eastern-bloc countries, most of which were open to this technology. But Germany's sudden determination to phase out nuclear power quickly was a blow, as was Italy's decision to shelve construction plans.

The nuclear divide is an insurmountable obstacle in the path of a common energy policy. It limits the effectiveness of EU policies to combat climate change, and establish a single gas and electricity market. A common energy policy, as advocated by Jacques Delors, former President of the European Commission,[15] would require Member States to give up, or at least share, sovereignty over their energy mix. But as long as the nuclear divide persists, a transfer of this sort is out of the question. It is comparable to the problem posed by the euro single currency. The euro crisis confirmed the views of theoretical economists who demonstrated that a single currency was not viable without coordinated or common macroeconomic, budgetary and fiscal policies. The Member States which make up the Eurozone do not all hold the same views on inflation, unemployment or growth; in the absence of coordinated budgets and economic targets, conflicting national strategies prevail, undermining trust in the currency and its overall resilience. In a similar way, a common energy policy cannot be viable without close coordination of decisions on the energy mix.

The Treaty of Rome, which established the EEC, left major decisions on energy policy in the hands of Member States. The exploitation of energy resources (the conditions of access and rate of extraction, for example), the choice of energy sources (in the case of electricity the mix between coal, uranium, gas, biomass, wind, water and so on), and the modalities of energy procurement (in particular its geographical origin) fell within their exclusive remit. The most recent update, the Lisbon Treaty, reiterated this national prerogative. But, for the first time, a specific article was devoted to European policy on energy. It is reproduced in the box here, almost in its entirety, there being no better way of summarizing it or high-lighting the tension between the national and supranational levels.

A country's choice to include nuclear power in its energy mix, or not, is certainly the most crucial decision for its EU neighbours. As we explained above, neither radioactive clouds nor electrons stop at borders between Member States. Furthermore, as individual EU countries display highly contrasting preferences, borders may separate – as with Austria and the Czech Republic – a Member State fiercely opposed to nuclear power from a keen advocate of the technology. Under the circumstances, it is hard to see supranational rules being framed which would require one state to phase out nuclear power, or on the other hand oblige another to adopt it. There is no likelihood of a unanimous vote on such a motion. However, setting aside nuclear power, national energy mixes in the EU are gradually converging. The overall trend suggests that coal is on the way out, whereas renewable energy sources are gaining ground. With increasing similarity in the mix among Member States, national sovereignty with regard to its make-up should be less of an obstacle for engaging and developing a common energy policy. As nuclear power exists, and is here to stay for a long time, it makes convergence impossible,

Article 194 of the Treaty on the Functioning of the European Union

1. In the context of the establishment and functioning of the internal market and with regard for the need to preserve and improve the environment, Union policy on energy shall aim, in a spirit of solidarity between Member States, to:
   (a) ensure the functioning of the energy market;
   (b) ensure security of energy supply in the Union;
   (c) promote energy efficiency and energy saving and the development of new and renewable forms of energy; and
   (d) promote the interconnection of energy networks.
2. Without prejudice to the application of other provisions of the Treaties, the European Parliament and the Council, acting in accordance with the ordinary legislative procedure, shall establish the measures necessary to achieve the objectives in paragraph 1. Such measures shall be adopted after consultation of the Economic and Social Committee and the Committee of the Regions.

   Such measures shall not affect a Member State's right to determine the conditions for exploiting its energy resources, its choice between different energy sources and the general structure of its energy supply [. . .].

The four goals cited in Article 194 endorse previous decisions by the European Council, Commission and Parliament. The decision to set up a large internal market for gas and electricity goes back to the late 1990s. Its aim was to open these sectors to competition and reduce barriers inside the Community, particularly regulatory obstacles to energy trade. Since then a great deal of legislation has been introduced, in the form of directives and regulations. The market is nearing completion. But to be a real success it must develop infrastructures connecting Member States for gas and electricity transmission. Progress has been made build-ing interconnections, but much remains to be done. The goal for energy efficiency and renewables also corresponds to earlier com-mitments, which have been calculated precisely and established as mandatory targets for 2020. As for the security of supply, this above all concerns the gas imports on which Europe is depen-dent. This goal became a priority following the stoppage, during two successive winters in the late 2000s, of gas deliveries between Russia and Ukraine. The interruption in supply had a knock-on effect on several Member States. Hundreds of thousands of people in Bulgaria, Hungary and Poland were left without heating. The EU struggled to cope, hampered by poorly coordinated action by individual countries, non-existent exchange of information and the lack of a single spokesperson to deal with its Russian and Ukrainian neighbours.

The list of goals set forth in the Treaty is now closed, so new objectives can only be added if all the Member States agree. A unanimous vote is also required for measures to achieve the four targets. The end of Article 194 emphasizes that these mea-sures must not impinge on Member States' right to exercise the sovereignty they have enjoyed since the Rome Treaty, that right being backed by a veto.

The spirit of solidarity invoked at the beginning of Article 194 offers the only opening for closer cooperation between EU countries. But the instruments, outlines and extent of this spirit remain vague.[16] Solidarity tends to affect relations with the out-side world. Even in this respect it is of limited value. The EU as a whole was unable to agree on the routes to be taken by pipelines transporting gas from Russia and competing countries on its bor-ders. Member States funded rival projects displaying a complete lack of organization, going so far as to short-circuit one another's schemes. Germany, for instance, gave preference to a pipeline along the Baltic seabed, rather than an intra-European land route via Poland.

With regard to EU energy policy, whether it concerns the single market, energy efficiency or development of renewables, the spirit of solidarity is even hazier. Does it involve compensatory measures in favour of countries such as Poland, where decarbonizing electricity generation is particularly costly for geographical or historical reasons? With regard to the choice of conventional means of generating electricity, does the spirit of solidarity require countries to announce their decisions in advance and coordinate their application in order to limit the resulting disruption in other Member States? Germany has decided to phase out nuclear power by 2022. It did so without consulting any of its partners. France is thinking about halving this technology's share in its energy mix by 2025. It has not discussed the matter with its neighbours either. It seems therefore that the solidarity cited in Article 194, already in force before these decisions, does not require national decisions on the energy mix to be coordinated nor yet information to be exchanged. Perhaps one day the solidarity proclaimed by Article 194 will exert leverage on a common energy policy, but for the time being there is no sign of any shift in that direction.

ruling out a European Energy Community. This divide has become all the more impossible to bridge since France and Germany have adopted different stances on the issue. So the team formed by the two countries, acting as a driving force for their partners in other fields, will not work for energy.

We should point out in passing that national sovereignty over the energy mix limits the effectiveness of two key policies: measures to combat global warming and the development of the internal market. Take, for instance, the case of renewables. To achieve the target of a 20 per cent share by 2020, it is 'every man for himself', with no overall organization. Germany is well ahead of Spain in terms of solar installed capacity, despite enjoying fewer hours of sunlight. Spain itself is far ahead of the UK for wind power, despite being less windy. In other words, installations are decided by national policy – in practice in the places where the subsidies for their development are highest – not according to resource availability. This makes the 2020 target, for the whole of the EU, all the more costly to achieve. Regarding the internal gas and electricity market, the effectiveness of European policy is undermined by the industrial nationalism which drives sovereignty over the energy mix. To achieve energy equilibrium, a country needs equipment and generating companies which are pursuing that goal. With certain energy sources being subsidized – by consumers or taxpayers – government and policymakers are tempted to offer local jobs in exchange. A national mix often goes hand-in-hand with national industry. Stiffer competition in the Community gas and electricity markets does not necessarily suit some Member States – certainly as long as they lack a national champion capable of taking a share of neighbouring markets. The setting up of a single gas and electricity market consequently has been and still is hindered by the creation and consolidation of national energy industries.

In short, the nuclear issue makes it impossible for the EU to transfer sovereignty over the energy mix to the supranational level, which in turn rules out a common energy policy. Yet the lack of such a policy jeopardizes policies to consolidate the internal market and to combat global warming. Nuclear power is the root of the problem holding up a European Energy Community and it is hard to see how a solution may be found.

Reaching the end of this tour of Europe, what may we conclude about international nuclear governance? It seems fair to say that the EU has achieved a degree of cooperation between states on nuclear safety which it would be difficult to surpass. It certainly represents the upper limit of what the IAEA might one day achieve in terms of cooperation. The EU's legal framework provides precisely what the IAEA lacks, namely the authority necessary to make its safety standards and recommendations binding. The European Commission can enforce the requirements of the 2009 Directive approved by Member States, sanctioning those which fail to comply. It can impose fines and refer cases to the European Court of Justice. The only form of coercion available to the IAEA is peer pressure. If, for instance, an exceptional event occurred – a disaster causing a shock sufficient to galvanize all the countries defending this technology – and more extensive powers for monitoring safety were invested in the Agency, it would still not be able to do any better than the Commission. The latter body succeeded in having some hazardous reactors shut down, but only because it could play on the determination of the relevant countries to gain EU membership. In the aftermath of the Fukushima Daiichi disaster, had the result of a stress test been sufficiently bad to justify a plant being closed, the Commission would not have been empowered to take the decision on its own. The decision to commission or shut down a nuclear power plant is still within the remit of national governments. This sovereign power limits the scope of European nuclear governance, but it shows little sign of waning.

THIRTEEN

International governance to
combat proliferation

Politics and trade

The proliferation of nuclear weapons is a collective security issue, but microeconomics does not throw much light on efforts to manage this particular global public good, and the associated pitfalls. Political analysis and the application of game theory seem more helpful for understanding rivalry between states and their various strategies. Much has been written on global politics and strategy, and more specifically on the arms race between the Soviet Union and the United States, followed by de-escalation. We shall consequently not address the rising number of warheads deployed by nuclear powers, referred to as vertical proliferation. Its only connection with the economics of nuclear power is historical.

On the other hand, horizontal proliferation – the acquisition of nuclear weapons by countries not previously armed – is linked to the development of this energy. We have already cited the example of Pakistan, which has used civilian nuclear power as cover. We have also noted the utopian attitude of advocates of the Atoms for Peace doctrine, who believed that help with developing nuclear power could contribute to preventing widespread nuclear armament. This form of proliferation, by the gradual spread of nuclearized territory all over the planet, is linked to trade. The larger the number of new countries adopting nuclear power, the greater the risk of proliferation. The vast majority of the countries which currently own nuclear power plants have certainly refrained from developing military applications, but there is no technical obstacle to them doing so in the future. They already have the fissile materials, and the necessary scientific and engineering skills. Japan, Brazil or indeed South Korea could very rapidly become nuclear powers. Nations on the verge of deploying nuclear power, such as Turkey or the United Arab Emirates, could start by abstaining, then change their minds. It is also interesting to note that many of today's aspiring nuclear-power nations display features which justify fears of further proliferation. Compared with the countries already exploiting this technology, they are, on average, characterized by more widespread corruption and greater political instability, weaker democratic institutions, higher crime rates and more frequent terrorist attacks.[1] All these factors potentially increase the risk of nuclear power being diverted for military ends.

Stronger international governance is needed to contain the growing risk of proliferation. This is the purpose of the Treaty on the Non-Proliferation of Nuclear Weapons and the mission of the International Atomic Energy Agency. It is also the purpose of export controls over sensitive technologies, and the mission of a little known, but effective organization, the Nuclear Suppliers Group.

The IAEA and the NPT: strengths and weaknesses

The International Atomic Energy Agency (IAEA) is one of many agencies established by the United Nations, much like the World Health Organization or the International Civil Aviation Organization. It was launched in 1957, largely inspired by the ideas proclaimed by President Eisenhower in his Atoms for Peace speech. It was consequently tasked with promoting the development of nuclear power worldwide and ensuring it was not diverted for military purposes. The Agency subsequently played an increasingly important part in nuclear safety, framing standards and guidelines. Its mission as an atomic police force was substantially reinforced with the signature of the Non-Proliferation Treaty (NPT), which came into force in 1970.[2] It was tasked with establishing supervisory measures to prevent nuclear technology being diverted. All the parties to the NPT were encouraged to accept technical safeguards applied by the IAEA.[3] The Treaty was initially ratified by 70 states. They now number 159, more than four-fifths of UN membership.

The best-known countries that have never signed up to the Treaty are the ones who acquired nuclear weapons after 1 January 1967: India, Pakistan and Israel. In the jargon of proliferation experts they are the 'non-NPT states', as opposed to the authorized nuclear-weapon states – France, the United States, the United Kingdom, China and Russia – which developed nuclear weapons before 1967. These five states have made a commitment not to help other countries to acquire nuclear weapons and to 'undertake effective measures in the direction of nuclear disarmament'. This obligation goes hand-in-hand with that placed on the other signatories never to receive, manufacture or acquire nuclear weapons. It is the source of considerable tension because the authorized nuclear-weapon states consider that the requirements of the Treaty regarding disarmament only constitute a limited constraint. It simply states that they must 'pursue negotiations in good faith on [. . .] a treaty on general and complete disarmament'. Most other signatories dispute this interpretation, demanding the destruction of the 20,000 or so nuclear warheads the 'big five' have accumulated. In the words of the former head of the IAEA, Mohamed el-Baradei, it is like 'some who have . . . continued to dangle a cigarette from their mouth and tell everybody else not to smoke'.[4]

Over and above disarmament and proliferation the Treaty encourages the spread of nuclear power through scientific cooperation and technology transfer. It restates the terms of the deal outlined by Eisenhower and set forth in the IAEA statute, granting access to civilian technologies in exchange for giving up military aims.

At first sight the Non-Proliferation Treaty and the IAEA are totally ineffective. This system obviously does not prevent non-signatories from acquiring nuclear weapons, as was the case with India; but above all it does not prevent signatories from attaining the threshold for producing nuclear weapons, while remaining a party to the Treaty: Iran attempted to do just this before international sanctions finally dissuaded it; North Korea simply withdrew.[5] But such a categorical judgement would be out of place, because a system's effectiveness cannot be assessed on a binary basis. Rules and organizations are necessarily imperfect and neither the Agency nor the Treaty are an exception. So the question is rather how effective they are. To find out, we need to make allowances for their failures and successes – some countries such as South Africa having shelved their nuclear weapons programme. We also need to consider what might have happened in the absence of this system, or if a different one had existed. But to judge by the literature, the jury is still out on the matter of feeble or strong effectiveness. In the view of some authors,[6] the Treaty – and the various forms of pressure it can exert – has done little to prevent proliferation. Non-proliferation is primarily the result of the determination and capacity of individual states. Some countries which could have produced nuclear weapons decided against the idea, typically Germany and Japan. Others, such as Egypt or Iraq, wanted to become nuclear powers but were unable to do so. Lastly, a small number took the decision and ultimately succeeded in producing weapons, witness North Korea. But other analysts contend that the Agency and Treaty definitely curbed proliferation of nuclear weapons, the last two countries cited above being particular cases.

Be that as it may, we must underline two shortcomings in efforts to stop proliferation. The first is the IAEA's lack of resources, both in terms of its budget allocation and the tools at its disposal for intervention. The Agency's budget has remained low and for a long time its interventions consisted merely of limited checks on installations, subject to the authorization of the host country. This left very little scope for inspecting and more importantly detecting diversion of civilian technology. The second relates to the linkage between non-proliferation and the promotion of nuclear power. Scientific cooperation has turned out to be the main vector for proliferation. To develop nuclear weapons, it is not even necessary to possess nuclear power plants; a research reactor is quite sufficient.[7] The IAEA and the NPT have greatly contributed to disseminating them all over the world. In this respect the deal set out by Atoms for Peace was an illusion.

Relations between international nuclear trade and global efforts to combat proliferation are complicated. There would certainly be less proliferation if there was no trade, but there would also be less nuclear trade with no international governance combating proliferation. We shall now look at how markets, politics and governance are entangled.

Nuclear trade

International trade in nuclear goods is a small market. This may seem surprising, as public attention often focuses on large contracts for the sale of power plants costing tens of billions of euros. Understandably, the news that the South Korean consortium led by the Korea Electric Power Corporation had won the $20 billion tender to build four reactors in the United Arab Emirates made a powerful impression. But the payments for such contracts are spread out over about ten years – the time it takes to build the plant – and, above all, there are very few large contracts of this nature. In 2000–10 the global export market amounted to orders for two new reactors a year, some awarded following a call for tenders, others by mutual agreement. Furthermore, a nuclear power plant is a complex assembly comprising a pressure vessel, steam generators, piping and a control room, associated with equipment for generating electricity with steam. As with any thermal power plant, it is necessary to install turbines, alternators, capacitors and such. The nuclear island – the specifically nuclear part of a plant – accounts for roughly half its cost, with the conventional part making up the rest. Thus reduced to its essentials, the global reactor market is worth less than €5 billion a year.

However, to this relatively low figure for annual sales of new reactors must be added trade in uranium, fuel, maintenance services, spare parts, reprocessing of spent fuel and waste management. These specifically nuclear up- and downstream activities multiply by three the value of the world market. For integrated companies, such as Areva or Rosatom, which cover the whole cycle, business connected to building new reactors represents, at the most, only one-fifth of total revenue. Upstream and downstream activities are crucial for such companies, for they are recurrent and profitable. They are less erratic than orders for new equipment, less subject to intense competition. The operators and owners of nuclear power plants are to a large extent tied by their inputs to the company which built the reactor. For reasons of compatibility, know-how and technical information, the vendor has a competitive advantage over other suppliers of enriched fuel, spare parts and maintenance services. It enjoys market power, allowing it to increase prices and thus profits. Industrial economists who focus on markets for complementary goods (printers and ink cartridges, razors and blades, coffee machines and pods) are familiar with this mechanism. The first item is sold at cost price, or perhaps even subsidized, but the supplier makes up the initial loss on sales of recurring products.[8]

The US dominated the international market for many years. Until the mid-1970s three-quarters of the plants built elsewhere were either built by US firms or under licence.[9] But this dominant position subsequently crumbled. Its share has dropped to less than a quarter of all the reactors built in the past twenty years. By value, the US accounts for less than 10 per cent of global exports of nuclear equipment (reactors, large components and small parts), and about 10 per cent of materials (natural uranium and plutonium).[10] Indeed, it has become a net importer, amounting to $15 billion a year.[11] Meanwhile Canada, Russia and France have increased their market share. The first two export their proprietary reactor technology; France too,[12] though its technology was originally derived from US imports. South Korea recently joined the nuclear exporters' club, taking a similar route to achieve technological independence gradually. Japan is poised to do likewise. Its nuclear engineering companies have responded to calls to tender by new entrants such as Turkey and Vietnam. Former General Electric and Westinghouse licensees, they have gone further than their French and Korean counterparts, purchasing the nuclear assets of the two US companies.[13]

The decline in US nuclear sales abroad is not due to the arrival of more powerful competitors, rather to the collapse of domestic demand. From the mid-1970s to the end of the 2000s not a single contract was signed for a new nuclear power plant in the US. Engineering firms have had to weather more than thirty years without any domestic demand, preceded by years of uncertain profits sapped by the vicissitudes of regulatory pressure (see Chapter 9), with a major accident in 1979 (Three Mile Island) to crown it all. Enough to floor any industrial operation. The decline at home led to a massive loss of industrial capacity and skills in enrichment, the manufacture of large forged parts and construction engineering. On the other hand, reactor R&D and design has survived and is still of first-class quality. The first new reactors to be built on US soil in the 2010s are Westinghouse AP1000s. In 2006 China ordered four of these innovative next-generation reactors. General Electric has developed advanced boiling-water reactors too. So the US still features in new nuclear and the international market thanks to innovation and technology transfer. Westinghouse now sells brainpower rather than equipment. It is still earning money thanks to licence fees. For example, it received its share of fees on the construction of the four Kepco reactors in the UAE. The export version of this reactor still contains parts which belong to Westinghouse, including the software which controls the nuclear chain reaction in the reactor core. In short, the nuclear industry still operating in the US no longer comprises many factories and is partly controlled by Japanese firms, but it is still alive and profitable.

In general, the state of a nuclear engineering firm's domestic market and its export potential are very closely connected. Just as with the US, it is difficult to enjoy a significant share of the export market, without at the same time building nuclear power plants at home. The industrial fabric is not responsive enough, highly trained staff are not available in sufficient numbers and the technical skills are lacking. Oddly enough, when a domestic market is enjoying powerful growth, there is also less scope for exports: all efforts are focused on success on the home front, meeting deadlines, coordinating production and construction. China is a good example of this point. It is currently building twenty-eight reactors at various places in the People's Republic. Bearing in mind that the manufacture of heavy engineering parts is scheduled several years ahead of the construction project, winning foreign contracts would mean reallocating manufacturing output originally intended for the home market. This would slow down the national programme and delay the projected supply of additional electricity. So the ideal situation for exports is somewhere between non-existent and booming domestic demand. This is the case in Russia, which has exported the largest number of reactors in the past fifteen years. Unlike the US, work building new capacity never stopped, though new orders were temporarily shelved in the aftermath of Chernobyl and the collapse of the Soviet Union. Exports to Iran, China and India helped compensate for the momentary drop in demand at home. Ten new reactors are at present being built in the Russian Federation, and since the end of the 2000s additional contracts have been signed with India and China, but also Turkey and Vietnam. Another case in point is South Korea. Much as in many other sectors this country has succeeded in developing a top-grade national nuclear industry in a very short time. Initially output catered exclusively for the domestic market, building a fleet of reactors which now numbers twenty-three and supplies a third of the country's electricity. The aim is to reach 60 per cent by 2030. There is little likelihood of the fleet growing any more. South Korea is a small island, in electrical terms, with no scope for selling surplus output to either its neighbour in the north, or Japan. So without exports there is no room for South Korea's nuclear engineering industry to expand further. Just as it has done in shipbuilding, car manufacture or consumer electronics, it must export or die. It scored its first success with the UAE and it very much hopes others will follow soon.

Which model: the armament industry, or oil and gas supplies and services?

The nuclear industry is very similar to defence procurement in many respects, but in the future it could resemble oil and gas supplies and services. In addition to the reasons cited above, the international nuclear market is small because individual states keep their orders for national industry, just as for arms. They give priority to technology that is either indigenous (Canada, Russia) or was originally licensed but has subsequently been developed locally (France, South Korea). In the immediate future, it is hard to imagine Russian or South Korean utilities issuing an international call to tender for the construction of a nuclear power plant on their home ground. China today and India tomorrow – if the latter launches an ambitious construction programme – also rely primarily on national firms and their own reactor models. The international market is thus restricted to the delivery of the first plants to be built by one of the main new entrants – in other words, countries which will subsequently develop their own fleet – and to supplies to countries which will never possess more than a few units. In both cases, a certain proportion of local content is one of the factors determining the outcome of a tender. The market is more open for large engineering components. EDF recently purchased forty-five steam generators, worth an estimated €1.5 billion, to refurbish its plants, entrusting a quarter of the order to Westinghouse and the rest to its traditional French supplier Areva. As there is only limited global capacity for producing the pressure vessels fitted to the largest reactors, two of China's AP1000s are fitted with boilers manufactured by Doosan,[14] of South Korea, whereas the French EPRs being built in France, Finland and China will use pressure vessels made by Japan Steel Works.

Another feature reminiscent of the arms industry is the active involvement of government in export contracts. Ministers and even heads of state intervene at a diplomatic level, but also meddle in finance, strategy and even organization. The UAE tender is emblematic in this respect. By 2009 two national consortiums remained in the running for the contract to build the Barakah nuclear power plant. One, led by Kepco, brought together Doosan for the steam-supply system, Hyundai for civil engineering, Korea Hydro and Nuclear Power for system engineering and Korea Power Engineering for design. The rival team, led by Areva, consisted of the utility GDF-Suez, turbine manufacturer Alstom, oil company Total and civil engineering specialist Vinci. Each consortium enjoyed the political and diplomatic backing of their respective head of state. Mr Sarkozy and Mr Lee Myung Bak visited Abu Dhabi several times to persuade UAE President Sheikh Khalifa bin Zayed al-Nahyan to choose their champion. To clinch the deal they offered financing facilities to the buyer, a move that seems almost laughable given the UAE's ample liquidity. The Import-Export Bank of Korea subsequently took out an international loan to fund half the project, no doubt borrowing at a higher rate than UAE banks would have obtained. The two political leaders very probably offered additional sweeteners. It is commonplace for large nuclear contracts to be associated with offers of military assistance, arms sales or infrastructure development projects, but such information is seldom made public. Regarding the Korean bid, the only detail which leaked to the press was that a battalion had been promised by Seoul to train Emirati armed forces.[15] More surprisingly, heads of state may even become involved in details of organization. In the run-up to the final decision Mr Sarkozy intervened to bring EDF into the French consortium, alongside Areva and GDF-Suez. On the Korean side, Mr Lee behaved like a commander-in-chief hectoring and encouraging his troops.[16] He intervened repeatedly in the preparatory stages of the project and negotiations to seal the contract.

State involvement at the highest level in nuclear export contracts results in companies rallying round the flag. Consortiums are national. Unlike major gas and oil infrastructure projects, they do not field companies from all over the world, which choose to make a joint bid for a tender on the basis of their respective affinities and complementary assets. This inevitably means nuclear consortiums are less competitive. Despite being less effective in terms of costs or know-how, a civil engineering firm or own-equipment manufacturer may nevertheless be co-opted because, like the other members of the team, it is French, South Korean, Japanese or Russian. State intervention is not necessarily an advantage for the vendors either. It forces them to reduce their margin, sometimes excessively. As a large nuclear contract attracts considerable media attention, any head of state is very keen it should be awarded to his or her country, in the hope of basking in the glory of successful national firms, particularly as an election campaign approaches. To clinch the deal a head of state may push the national consortium to offer the buyer more favourable terms and prices. It is particularly easy to exert such pressure when, as is often the case, nuclear companies are wholly or partly state-owned. The shareholder in person orders senior management to make do with a pitiful margin, or even to sell at a loss. The winner of a tender is often the biggest loser!

So on the one hand, the consortium needs the diplomatic, financial and strategic support of its state apparatus, but on the other hand, this may come at a high price. When it comes to political intervention, Russia leads the pack (see box).

Russia: exports under Kremlin's control

Civilian nuclear exports are a priority for this country. Like most gas and oil exporting countries, it has very little industry which can compete on the export market. It must rely on raw materials. There is no manufacturing sector but arms which can compete in global markets with top international firms. The only exception is nuclear power. In this field Russia possesses considerable scientific and technical skills, a range of recently designed, powerful reactor models and dense industrial fabric. Russian leaders see the export of nuclear technology as a matter of national pride and a source of great prestige. Above all, it helps to achieve their diplomatic and strategic goals. The Russian reactors sold abroad are pieces on a global chessboard. In 1995 Russia carried on the job started by Siemens, building a reactor at Bushehr in Iran, on the shore of the Persian Gulf. After a whole series of setbacks, it was finally connected to the grid in 2013. The Russians lost a great deal of money on this scheme. In the same part of the world they won a contract with Turkey in the late 2000s for the construction of four reactors. Moscow is funding the whole project, drawing to a large extent, if not wholly, on the federal budget.[17] This subsidy is understandable when seen in the larger context of Russian gas interests. Turkey agreed to allow the projected South Stream gas pipeline to run through its territorial waters. In so doing it changed sides, withdrawing its earlier support from the rival Nabucco project, backed by the European Union. The sale of Russian reactors to Vietnam at the end of the 2010s was also sweetened by advantageous financial terms, this time in the form of export credits. Vietnam has long been a Russian ally in southeast Asia, particularly on the military front. For nuclear vendors from France, Japan or South Korea, Russia is a particularly tough competitor, the authorities being prepared to invest massively to facilitate reactor exports. Thanks to its gas rent, Russia's pockets are well lined. French, Japanese and South Korean heads of state are keen to help their nuclear companies win large contracts abroad, but they do not enjoy the same latitude as Vladimir Putin, nor are their arms so heavily laden with gifts.

State intervention obviously plays a key role in importing countries. Reactor vendors have two customers: the utility which will be operating the nuclear power plant, and the state. It is often more important to win over the latter, particularly if it is the former's only shareholder. The political dimension which dominates the importer's choice of a reactor vendor is manifest in bilateral agreements. For example, China and Vietnam did not organize an open call for tenders prior to choosing the plants they purchased from Rosatom in the late 2000s. An opaque selection process enables government to exercise its political and strategic preferences more freely and obtain often unavowable forms of compensation. Allowing an electric utility to organize an international call for tenders substantially reduces government's discretionary powers. However, in some cases the transparency and competitive openness of the tendering process is merely a front. What really counts is not the score awarded by the expert committee which analyses the bids, but the opinion of government. It may choose the losing party. Or the loser may be brought back into the running for equally political reasons. China opted to base its first four third-generation reactors on Westinghouse's AP1000, not Areva's EPR. But it nevertheless ordered two EPRs from the firm shortly afterwards.

Taking the oil and gas supplies and service industry as its model would make the nuclear industry truly international. This industry comprises the firms which supply the infrastructure for oil and gas exploration and production. It is cited here as an example of the engineering, procurement and construction industry, commonly known as EPC. It covers the whole supply chain that contributes to delivery of an oil rig or refinery, but in a broader context refers to any major industrial installation. So it can equally well apply to nuclear power plant construction projects, which involve drawing up an overall plan, adapting to a given site, purchasing hundreds of thousands of parts and the corresponding services to implement the project, and of course its overall completion. Who does what in this huge puzzle depends on the specific contracts, customers and suppliers. Some buyers just want to take possession of a turnkey project. In this case, either it will be delivered by a single contractor, as is the case with the plant supplied by Areva at Olkiluoto in Finland, or it will be the work of a consortium comprising various contractors, as with the Barakah plant in the UAE. Other buyers want separate contracts for the various parts of the job, for instance making a distinction between the nuclear island and the conventional generating units. In this case the customer must take charge of, or delegate to a design office, the coordination of the various contractors and their respective work packages. The utility may also opt to draw up a large number of supply contracts, acting as its own architect and engineer, as EDF has done at Flamanville, France. Or alternatively it may hire an outside service provider.

The diversity of approaches to project management is no different in oil engineering, procurement and construction. Firms such as Technip, Halliburton or Schlumberger organize themselves in much the same way, depending on the circumstances and the demands of the oil companies for which they are working. What is strikingly different in the nuclear industry is the uniformity of the national colours flown by individual companies making up a consortium, and most of their main customers. Russian firms work primarily for Russian utilities; the same is true in Japan; and so on, and so forth. Basically, the nuclear industry is not a global industry selling to customers all over the world, working with similarly diverse partners and suppliers. In oil engineering, procurement and construction, issues related to national politics are only apparent on the demand side, as the world's largest oil companies are publicly owned, from Saudi Arabia to Venezuela, through Norway and Russia.

So could the supply side of the nuclear industry become a multinational undertaking? Could the various companies open up to foreign, private capital, form alliances which disregard their nationality, and cast off the yoke of domestic politics? Or in other words, could the nuclear industry take its cue from oil engineering, procurement and construction, rather than mimicking defence procurement? Two examples (see box) suggest this may be possible.

But one swallow does not make a summer. These alliances, between US and South Korean, or French and Japanese companies, are not the first signs of a shift towards multinational consortiums exporting nuclear power plants. At least not in the immediate future. A change of this nature is not on the cards, for it would have to satisfy several improbable conditions. The national character of most bids is due to the diplomatic and geopolitical stakes for nuclear power. We have seen how government meddles in these contracts, on both sides of the bargaining table. If only with respect to the risk of proliferation the stakes will remain just as high. For nuclear companies keen to export their technology, collaboration with government – and the collective game they must consequently play – is all the more critical, given that the firms are dependent on domestic orders. It would make no sense to take the risk of undermining their position at home in exchange for a few sales abroad, as part of multinational consortiums disapproved of by government. Only companies confronted with a moribund domestic market have sufficient latitude to break loose. Substantial growth of the international market, driven by widespread adoption of nuclear power or the opening up of protected home markets, would certainly encourage the formation of multinational consortiums. But hopes of a nuclear renaissance are fading and the main domestic markets, in China, Russia and even South Korea, are closed. As long as the export market for nuclear power plants remains so restricted, there is little likelihood of the industry developing in the same way as its oil counterpart.

Korean–US alliance in the UAE, Franco-Japanese partnership in Turkey

The consortium which won the UAE tender was not exclusively South Korean. Westinghouse, headquartered in Pittsburgh, PA, is part of the team, supplying parts, technical and engineering services, and licensing its intellectual property. Toshiba, which holds a majority share in the US firm, is also involved. The contract does not explain its role, but it will be supplying equipment as a subcontractor for Doosan. The South Korean companies did not have much option but to accept the presence of these two partners. As they are not yet fully independent regarding technology, they needed Westinghouse's agreement. But in turn the latter needed to be authorized by both the US Administration, which controls exports of nuclear equipment, and by its Japanese shareholder. Without the agreement of these two parties, South Korea stood no chance of honouring an export contract. But the US and Toshiba used this bargaining power to their economic advantage. Over and above such legal considerations, US involvement also brought the South Korean bid a valuable political endorsement to counter the French offer. Indeed, the project to build the nuclear power plant started life as a mutual agreement between France and the UAE. The latter's decision to issue an international call for tenders came as a surprise, marking the beginning of the end for the French consortium led by Areva. The US purportedly had a hand in this volte-face.[18] It was bound to take an interest in a nuclear project in the Gulf, opposite Iran. The US has a very strong presence in the UAE, with about 2,000 military and 30,000 residents, some of whom hold key positions in civilian nuclear power.[19] The tender reshuffled the cards and brought General Electric into the game, through its joint venture with Hitachi, GE Hitachi Nuclear Energy. Washington would no doubt have preferred General Electric to have been awarded the contract, but it soon emerged that its bid was more expensive than the others, at which point US support switched to the Korean option.

The order, which has yet to be finalized by Turkey at time of writing, is for a medium-sized Atmea reactor, designed by Areva and Mitsubishi Heavy Industries. The consortium is led by the Japanese firm and also comprises Itochu, a Japanese fuel supplier, and the French energy company GDF-Suez. The latter, which operates Belgium's nuclear fleet and boasts a highly qualified team of nuclear engineers, took an early interest in the new reactor. Acting as both architect and engineer, it hoped to build and operate one in France, but it ran into opposition from the government and trade unions at EDF. As well as being a potential buyer, it has also positioned itself as a partner in future consortiums, when the customer wants plant operation to be entrusted to an experienced nuclear generating company, at least for the first few years. GDF-Suez has taken on this role for the Turkish project. Japan has several companies with experience in this field, but never overseas. Furthermore, their financial situation has been very challenging since the Fukushima Daiichi accident, not to mention the stain on their reputation. Parliamentary inquiries have shown that Tokyo Electric Power was not the only Japanese operator to cut corners on safety in the past. The bid for the project in Turkey was, however, largely Japanese, not Franco-Japanese as the French media rather hastily claimed. Indeed, the agreement was sealed by the President Tayyip Erdogan and Prime Minister Shinzo Abe, with no French representatives to be seen. This project is nevertheless much closer to oil engineering, procurement and construction than its UAE counterpart, the political dimension having played a much smaller part on both sides of the deal. All the firms in the consortium are privately owned[20] and the two-nation alliance is the result of a strategy based on industrial cooperation on a new reactor model, not some legal obligation.

Finally, a change of paradigm of this sort would require massive industrial reorganization. The global nuclear industry is still dominated by vertically integrated companies, spanning the entire cycle, such as Areva, Rosatom, China Nuclear Power and even Korea Electric Power.[21] Furthermore, these companies are wholly or partly under state control. It seems unlikely that a subsidiary specializing in fuel preparation, reactor design, engineering or operation would go it alone and join a consortium. Such a move would mean joining forces with foreign competitors of its fellow subsidiaries. Why should the mother company's management and shareholders encourage behaviour of this sort? You can count the potential candidates for creating international consortiums on the fingers of one hand. They are all private companies, with limited vertical integration and an almost non-existent home market: General Electric and Westinghouse in the US, GDF-Suez, a company with international interests and the incumbent operator of Belgium's nuclear fleet, and maybe one or two Japanese firms.

Export controls

Controls over the export of nuclear material, equipment and technology are primarily the preserve of international cooperation. That is not to say that individual countries do not enforce their own policies, but being uncoordinated they are inevitably less effective. Countries introducing strict legislation are likely to see their industry ousted from international contracts, in favour of companies subject to fewer constraints at home. Buyers prefer to deal with the latter to avoid waiting too long, cumbersome obligations regarding enrichment and reprocessing, or indeed bans on re-exports. Without international governance the threat of losing a contract reduces national policies to the lowest common denominator. 'If our industry isn't chosen, the job will go to another, less law-abiding country', some might argue. 'All in all, it would be better if our industry wins the contract;

The US control on exports

The US is an excellent example of how national policy works in this area. As long as US firms had few competitors, it was relatively easy to apply effective export controls, only one country really being involved. Things are very different now. Of all the nuclear countries exporting materials or technology, the US has so far been the one most concerned about the risk of proliferation. Witness, as a by-product, the voluminous output of US academics on this topic. Dozens of researchers have specialized in the field, exploring it in the light of games theory, law or political science. US policy on nuclear export controls is the strictest, and by consequence it places the greatest constraints on its industry.[22] Companies can only sell goods abroad if the importing country has signed a nuclear cooperation agreement with Washington. So-called 123 Agreements (a reference to Section 123 of the US Atomic Energy Act which requires their use) place various obligations on signatories. The agreement negotiated with the UAE – commonly referred to now as the 'gold standard' – is one of the strictest ever seen. It expressly bans the construction of uranium enrichment units, to produce fuel, and facilities for reprocessing spent fuel. Twenty-two 123 agreements have so far been signed, but most of them date from the time when US technology and industry monopolized the market. These days prospective purchasers can choose from various suppliers. They can place an order with Rosatom, Areva or Mitsubishi without having to wait while a lengthy agreement is hammered out with the US authorities. With the rising threat in the 2000s from Iran and North Korea, Washington tightened up its policy on export controls. A bill[23] sponsored by a two-party committee of the House of Representatives aims to make it virtually compulsory[24] for purchasing states to undertake never to develop enrichment or reprocessing facilities. But an amendment of this nature could be completely counterproductive, ultimately increasing the risk of proliferation. If Washington sets even stricter rules it will drive potential buyers away from US firms. In other words, if US firms, hampered by excessive anti-proliferation legislation, no longer export their goods, the leverage exerted through export controls will be lost, depriving US policy-makers of the key component in their policy for combating proliferation.

The advocates of a tougher line are adamant that this risk is entirely theoretical. The House of Representatives Foreign Affairs Committee 'believes that a serious effort to convince potential recipients of US nuclear exports to adopt some form of the UAE example would have significant proliferation benefits without sacrificing legitimate commerce'.[25] In their view, there is no evidence to justify concerns that higher requirements in Section 123 agreements would have a negative impact on the competitive position of US industry.[26] According to the hard-liners, many prospective buyers, such as Taiwan or the UAE, are prepared to accept more stringent rules because they are concerned about the quality of their relations with the US. Its seal of approval is still sought after. Furthermore, other exporting countries, yielding to Washington's friendly pressure, will follow its example and set higher, non-proliferation standards.

Opponents of the bill, led by US nuclear companies, claim that none of these arguments hold water. Turkey, which signed a 123 agreement in 2008, would probably not have accepted it if it had been obliged to rule out subsequent development of certain parts of the nuclear cycle. Though an ally of the US, Turkey thinks it is entitled to develop its own fuel enrichment capability, this being a basic right enshrined in the Non-Proliferation Treaty. Any attempt by Washington to deprive it of this right would have been interpreted as a hypocritical, discriminatory measure.[27] Turkey's leaders have not forgotten the favourable terms India obtained from Washington. This country, which is not a party to the Non-Proliferation Treaty, was allowed to reprocess its spent fuel. In addition, it is most unlikely that other exporting countries will toe the line on tougher rules. France, for instance, has in the past displayed much less concern about the risk of proliferation entailed by nuclear trade.[28] The authorities attach great importance to the nation's nuclear industry. They are more inclined to assist exports than to toughen up legislation on export controls, and have actively canvassed many countries in the Middle East and North Africa promoting French nuclear know-how. In the past ten years, Paris has signed cooperation agreements with Saudi Arabia, the UAE, Algeria, Libya, Jordan and Tunisia. Finally, opponents of tougher controls maintain that illicit trafficking is the real problem, not above-board sales of technology. With respect to enrichment and reprocessing, trade has only ever concerned countries which were already equipped,[29] for instance between Australia and France, or France and the US. Up to now, not a single previously unequipped country has built an enrichment or reprocessing unit without involving illicit networks. The best known is the network headed by Abdul Qadeer Khan, the father of Pakistan's atom bomb. In addition to plans for producing nuclear weapons he supplied designs for an enrichment unit to Libya.[30] The same network was also behind the transfer of gas centrifuge technology to Iran and supply of parts to North Korea in order to build centrifuges.[31]

The criticism of stricter export controls voiced by the US nuclear industry is well founded and should convince Congress not to adopt the draft amendment – unless the senators and representatives consider its effect on industry will be negligible. They may be convinced that their country's nuclear industry is doomed, due to the lack of domestic outlets. The exploitation of unconventional gas has lastingly undermined its competitive position, not export controls. So it makes no difference whether they are tightened up or not. With increasingly negligible economic stakes at home, US foreign policy to combat proliferation on security grounds could become even stricter.

so we'll set lower standards.' In keeping with this rationale, export controls would be kept to an absolute minimum, a stance reminiscent of the attitude, outlined above, to collective goods. Why should people act for the common good if it is contrary to their interests? Why should people contribute to funding a common good if they can consume it free of charge? The reader will recall that if everyone takes to free-riding, the good will not be produced at all. Here it is much the same, except that we are dealing with a collective ill. Self-interest means nothing is done to reduce it. So too many ills are produced. For lack of cooperation between parties the battle against proliferation is doomed to failure.

We shall now turn our attention to collective action on export controls, the main player in this field being the Nuclear Suppliers Group. This multilateral organization was formed in 1975 by the seven countries which pioneered nuclear power: the US, the UK, France, the Federal Republic of Germany, Canada, Japan and the Soviet Union. It now represents almost fifty states with varying profiles – emerging economies such as China, states with no real nuclear industry such as Switzerland, or even no equipment whatsoever, as in the case of Austria. One of the main rules established by the NSG is the obligation to publish any refusal to allow restricted material or information to be exported to a buyer country. In this way the state publishing the information has an assurance that other NSG members will behave likewise, strengthening its resolution because no one else will take advantage of its refusal.

The NSG came into existence to act on proliferation at source, in contrast to the IAEA, which devotes most of its energy to monitoring nuclear installations after the fact in the countries where they have been deployed. The NSG thus supplements supervision of compliance with the safeguards imposed by the Non-Proliferation Treaty on countries developing nuclear power. Many cases – Iran and Iraq immediately spring to mind – have highlighted the inability of IAEA inspections to detect civilian nuclear investments being diverted for military purposes. The NSG also stops the gaps left by countries which are not a party to the Treaty and are consequently beyond the Agency's remit. For these countries action at source, through export controls, is the only way of halting proliferation. Indeed, the Group was instigated with precisely this in mind, following India's first nuclear test. A non-party to the Treaty, India used imports of equipment from the US and Canada to develop its bomb. The last aspect of the complementary relationship between the NSG and the IAEA is the obligation imposed by supplier states on their customers to sign up to the Treaty and consequently to accept its constraints, in particular inspection.

Thanks to this two-pronged action, the NSG is a prime instrument for combating proliferation, and certainly a great deal more effective than stacks of national policy on export controls. We have already cited the theoretical mechanism of the collective ill which, in the absence of coordination, reduces national policies to the lowest common denominator. At a practical level, the NSG has succeeded in gradually implementing increasingly ambitious, strict policy on controls. In its early days supplier states concentrated on nuclear goods properly speaking. They drew up a list of equipment for reactors and enrichment facilities, and collectively established guidelines setting conditions for the export of such goods. For example, products on the list could only be sold to countries where the nuclear installations fully comply with IAEA safety rules. In the 1990s the Group extended controls to include 'dual-use' goods and technologies such as certain lasers or machine tools, the purchase of which could contribute indirectly to manufacturing arms. The two lists are updated at regular intervals, with slight delays and, inevitably, wording that is sometimes open to interpretation. Given these imperfections NSG countries have committed themselves not to sell equipment – even if it is not mentioned on either list – to countries developing nuclear weapons. To conclude, we should note the rule adopted in 2011 which makes exports related to enrichment and reprocessing conditional on beneficiaries being a party to the IAEA additional protocol, which establishes stricter, more extensive obligations for inspections.

In addition to stricter safeguards, the NSG has gained in effectiveness as growing numbers of countries have introduced export controls. To qualify for membership states must sign into national law and then deploy controls reflecting NSG guidelines. Forty other states have now joined the Group's seven founder members, extending the impact of their action. Of course they are not all leading supplier countries and some, like Cyprus, produce nothing vaguely resembling exportable nuclear goods. But their participation is nevertheless useful, because illicit trafficking no longer goes from A to B – for instance from North Korea to Iran – but passes through a host of transit countries. Policies on export controls adopted by countries such as Cyprus limit the number of platforms through which contraband can transit.

The effectiveness of the NSG may also be measured with respect to the cooperation permitted by the Non-Proliferation Treaty. We suggested above that without the NSG there would be no more than the sum of uncoordinated national policies. A few years before the Group was established an IAEA committee was convened to review the wording of an article in the Treaty imposing safeguards on exports.[32] But the committee soon ran into two obstacles. Firstly, the conditions and lists drawn up by this body could only apply to importing countries party to the Treaty. It obviously had no control over other countries. Secondly, the Treaty already contained an article which tended to encourage exports. This article stipulates that parties have an 'inalienable right' to develop the production of nuclear energy for peaceful purposes and that they undertake to facilitate the 'fullest possible exchange of equipment, materials and scientific and technological information'.[33] The committee still exists, but in a marginal capacity. It has fewer members than the NSG and simply adopts the latter's lists each time they are updated.

Citing their inalienable right, many countries have accused the NSG of constituting a cartel which holds back technology transfers and prevents developing countries from obtaining nuclear power. In their view, the spirit in which the IAEA was set up – access to civilian technology in exchange for giving up military goals – has been totally disregarded. The notion of fair exchange has vanished. Over and above this political and ideological criticism voiced by non-aligned countries for many years, the comparison to a cartel is relevant. But it is a 'good' cartel, in so far as it is a way of reducing a collective ill. Of course, one must subscribe to the idea that combating nuclear proliferation in general and more specifically its application to export controls contributes to greater global security; that it is not simply the expression of the hegemonic position of a small number of nuclear-weapon states, determined to prevent others from obtaining these weapons. I am convinced by this idea, but in defending it we would stray too far from the field of economics. What matters is that the NSG displays the characteristics of a cartel of states.

Firstly, it restricts supply and competition. The volume of nuclear material, equipment and technology exported is lower than it would be in the absence of multilateral controls. Prices are also higher – in the short term due to a certain scarcity, a mechanical effect of the law of supply and demand; in the long term, too, because the cartel bars the way to newcomers, with enrichment and reprocessing remaining in the hands of the same states and companies.

Secondly, as a cartel, the NSG has difficulty making its members uphold their commitments. Establishing a cartel does not necessarily solve the problem of free-riders. Measures must be taken to ensure that each member abides by their commitments, despite the fact that self-interest dictates that they do not comply or at least only pretend to do so. By cheating, an NSG member could advantage its national industry while reaping the collective benefit of less global proliferation. Take, for instance, Chinese exports to Pakistan.[34] The People's Republic of China joined the NSG in 2004. In so doing it undertook only to engage in trade if the recipient state had enforced an agreement with the IAEA applying safeguards to all its installations. China had helped Pakistan develop its civilian nuclear programme in the 1970s. It wanted to continue along these lines, as did Pakistan, but the latter was against extensive inspection of its nuclear installations, which included weapon stockpiles. China claimed a right of precedence on joining the NSG, arguing that its agreement with Pakistan predated its joining the Group and that it was consequently entitled to continue supplying fuel and various services to the nuclear power plant at Chasma in Pakistan. At the end of the 2000s, when it emerged that Beijing planned to supply two new reactors, it was more difficult to persuade other parties that the deal had again been 'grandfathered' by the original understanding. Washington thought it was a trick, China having made no mention of such plans when it joined the NSG. The members of the Group remain divided on the issue, but also on how to respond to Beijing's opportunistic behaviour. Either way the NSG, as an organization operating on a purely voluntary basis, only has limited margin for manoeuvre on sanctions. There is no treaty binding member states and consequently no scope for litigation against members which fail to fulfil their obligations. NSG commitments are not binding. The only sanction available to its members – at least those with sufficiently persuasive arguments at their disposal, such as the US[35] – is political pressure. Lastly, the NSG has only limited means of checking that its members are keeping their commitments. It is easy enough to check that they have transposed into national law the export safeguards it advocates, but, in the absence of an appropriate administrative body, it is much more difficult to ensure that safeguards are strictly enforced. The NSG is a lightweight organization. It has neither a headquarters nor a secretariat, the latter service being provided by the Japanese delegation to the IAEA. The lack of any means of control is particularly bothersome when monitoring members' obligation to declare exports. The US has complained several times that Russia has failed to provide full details of trade with Iran.[36]

Thirdly, the NSG is prone to instability and paralysis. One way of taking advantage of a cartel's action without paying its price is either not to join, or to leave: witness the Organization of Petroleum Exporting Countries. Countries which are not Opec-members, such as Norway or Russia, sell their oil at a higher price thanks to the organization's work. Former members, such as Gabon or Ecuador, have left; Iraq has threatened on several occasions to do so. Oddly enough, the NSG's stability is less affected by the risk of members leaving, more by the possibility that newcomers might join. Group membership is very appealing because decisions are taken by consensus. Newcomers must bring their export policy into line with NSG guidelines, but in exchange they gain influence over the Group's future decisions, enabling them to block proceedings. Moreover, NSG membership boosts a country's credibility in the eyes of potential buyers. There is no danger of orders being cancelled or partnership agreements scrapped because the international community has outlawed the supplier. Lastly, membership brings knowledge and information which can help a newcomer bolster its market position.

At present, having almost fifty members is in fact a weakness. The interests the NSG represents are too disparate, slowing down or completely stopping new initiatives. For example, it took seven years to make it mandatory for countries importing parts and equipment related to enrichment or reprocessing to sign up to the IAEA additional protocol. There is a great deal of internal tension over how to deal with nuclear-weapon states other than those designated by the Non-Proliferation Treaty. The NSG almost fell apart over the decision to authorize exports to India, but in the end the US, backed by France and Russia, succeeded in overcoming opposition. In 2008 the NSG granted a waiver for the supply of nuclear materials to this country, despite its refusing to allow IAEA inspectors into all its installations. Some members, notably the US, maintained this was an exception, whereas others, led by China, countered that Pakistan should be treated in the same way. The current controversy hinges on whether a country which is not a party to the Non-Proliferation Treaty can join the Group. India has not filed an official application, but it has expressed the wish to do so.[37] Here again the US, France and Russia are thought to support Indian membership, for reasons related to bilateral trade agreements. But its powerful neighbour China is against the idea – unless, of course, it opens the way for Pakistan, another non-designated nuclear-weapon country, to join too. It is a tricky situation, particularly because if India gains membership it will promptly block Pakistan's bid to join. Moreover, a solution based on new members also signing up to the Non-Proliferation Treaty is out of the question, because for that to work both India and Pakistan would have to scrap their nuclear weapons.

Many observers believe the NSG has reached a crossroads.[38] It is time to choose between continuing its political role as a part of efforts to combat nuclear proliferation or changing to become an open club for countries capable of exporting nuclear goods and above all concerned about their collective economic interest: not encouraging proliferation, because the diversion of exports by importing countries for military ends can only strengthen public opposition to the growth of nuclear power. In the first case the NSG would continue to serve as a lever for stiffer upstream controls. For example, it succeeded in forcing recipient countries to adopt the additional protocol of the Non-Proliferation Treaty, an addition which had only been signed by less than a quarter of countries party to the Treaty. In the second case the NSG would cast off the safeguards imposed by the IAEA and start treating nuclear-weapon countries other than the original big five as importers and potential members.

International trade in nuclear goods is thus subject to a delicate balance between contrary forces, torn between promoting and restricting exports. At a national level, there is a political will to encourage exports by an industrial sector often plagued by sluggish domestic demand. Foreign contracts help keep it afloat, perhaps even creating jobs, and boost the political credit and prestige of heads of state. The latter are consequently eager to support their national team and quick to offer sweeteners, particularly if the potential buyer is an ally – or future ally – in the international arena. But the same governments must make allowance for security imperatives, ensuring that exports of nuclear material, equipment and technology do not fuel proliferation.

The extent to which security concerns counterbalance industrial and commercial ambition varies. Security is a more pressing issue in the US than in France, for example. But whether it features to some extent or not at all at home, this concern is imported from abroad via international governance of non-proliferation. We have seen how this governance is organized: the Non-Proliferation Treaty, which bans nuclear weapons; the IAEA, which controls installations downstream; and the NSG, which intervenes upstream. But this governance is also subject to the imperatives of promotion. In pursuit of their mission to develop atomic energy, particularly scientific and technological cooperation, the Treaty and Agency encourage nuclear trade.

International governance thus reproduces the same balance of contrary forces observed at a national level. However, there is an essential difference in the way the balance is achieved. At a national level the legislative and the executive both have a say in reconciling promotion and nuclear controls, in other words the same people who are in charge of economic, diplomatic and defence policy. At the multilateral level, on the other hand, the contradictory forces are balanced by a specialized administrative agency with no head. The focus of IAEA's efforts and the allocation of its budgets, between

294 • Part IV National policies and international governance

promotion and non-proliferation, varies mainly according to contingent events: the personality of its Director-General; the ideological stance of its respective Board members; even the centres of interest of its administrative staff. The only constant, combating proliferation, is reduced to after-the-fact control, due to the need to continue promoting nuclear power. This severely limits the effectiveness of its action, mercifully remedied by the NSG. This situation strongly suggests that the two missions of the IAEA should be separated. All the supervisory work should be entrusted to a single body, whereas promotion should be hived off. The only problem with what might at first sight appear to be simple common sense is that this reform would spell the end of the deal set forth by Eisenhower – access to nuclear power in exchange for giving up nuclear weapons – the deal on which nuclear governance has been founded for over fifty years. Reform of this sort would be difficult.

As we explained in the introduction to this fourth and final part of the book, politics steps in to take decisions held up by uncertainty about the cost, risk and regulation of nuclear power. Policy-makers decide whether or not to adopt nuclear power, prolong its use or phase it out. Such choices, which are the prerogative of sovereign states, have repercussions on safety and security well beyond national borders. They necessitate multilateral coordination, the only approach which can create global collective goods and eliminate global collective ills. Over and above the diversity of multilateral arrangements and responses to uncertainty, some recurrent trends emerge. Firstly, the motives for adopting nuclear power now and in the past are largely similar: prestige, energy independence, growth of science and technology. The only novelty is that sometimes these goals are coupled with the determination to combat global warming. Secondly, decisions to reduce the share of nuclear power in the energy mix more quickly or phase it out altogether are based on approximation, with little real consideration for economic factors. The choice of goals and the timetable for shutting down nuclear power plants are dictated by assumptions about shifts in voter preference and the balance between and within political parties, not by forecasts of the economic costs and benefits for society. Thirdly, little progress has been made towards reducing nuclear power's transboundary impact on safety and security. The multilateral model embodied by the European Union, despite having gone furthest down this path with some notable successes, highlights the handicaps which inevitably plague international governance, due to the diversity and number of parties. Opposition by EU Member States to the continued exploitation or immediate shutdown of atomic energy drastically reduces scope for joint action. In the struggle to limit the deployment of nuclear weapons, the divergent interests of parties to the Non-Proliferation Treaty and members of the Nuclear Suppliers Group are also a major hindrance for effective collective action.

Conclusion

Let us summarize the main points in this book.

With respect to costs, we have seen why the idea of a single, universally valid cost for nuclear power is misleading. Not because figures can be manipulated or assessments influenced by specific interests, but because there is no such thing as the *true* cost. Nuclear costs depend on the options available to economic decision-makers, public or private, and on a range of factors subject to considerable future uncertainty. So it does not cost the same amount to build a new plant in Finland, China or the United States.

The curse of rising costs has dogged nuclear technology from the outset, particularly in the US. Far from falling as more plants have been built, costs have soared, making new nuclear even more expensive. If there is no change in the immediate future, particularly if the price of carbon stays low, the competitiveness of nuclear power compared with other electricity-generating technologies will vanish. The outcome of any decision by a generating company to invest in the construction of a new nuclear power plant, or by a government advocating such a project, remains uncertain.

Regarding risk, we have noted and explained the divergence between expert calculations of the probability of a nuclear accident and the public perception of such a disaster. Nuclear technology is increasingly safe, thanks to the knowledge accumulated on operating reactors and the probabilistic safety assessments developed by scientists and engineers over the past thirty-five years. But this progress makes no impression on public opinion, petrified by pictures of Fukushima Daiichi. At a subjective level, people tend to overestimate risk when it relates to rare, terrifying events. Our understanding of what drives such perception is improving, thanks to the work of experimental psychology, which is gradually shedding the light of reason on irrational behaviour. We have also learnt that we constantly update our prior appraisals of probability, drawing on new, objective data and knowledge. It is time to rise above the pointless opposition between experts and the general public, each accusing the other of rank stupidity. The former are purportedly out of touch, locked up in their laboratories and theories, while the latter are supposedly far too sensitive to disasters and incapable of probabilistic reasoning. We must reconcile subjective and objective probability.

On the matter of regulation, we have presented the economic theory of safety regulation and compared the approaches adopted in the US, Japan and France. There are incentives for nuclear power plant operators to prevent failures and compensate for damage under an unlimited-liability regime. But the resulting safety efforts and investments are limited. Intervention by a regulatory authority is necessary to define an appropriate safety level, prescribe standards and monitor their application.

Regulation is inevitably imperfect – the regulator is not omniscient – but to a varying extent. Among the cases which are known and well documented, nuclear safety regulation as practised in Japan is an example to be avoided. The safety authority has allowed itself to be captured by the nuclear operators it was supposed to supervise and lacks the necessary independence with regard to government, itself under the influence of industry. The immediate cause of the Fukushima Daiichi disaster was natural, an earthquake followed by a very large tidal wave. But its underlying cause was the lack of transparent, independent, competent safety regulation. In contrast, safety regulation in the US and France, though strikingly

different and not without fault (with, respectively, too many standards or vague safety targets), offers valuable examples.

With regard to policy-makers, we have shown how they fill the
vacuum created by uncertainty about costs, risk and regulation, and
how they may agree to provide global collective goods, or to reduce
equally pervasive ills. National policies on nuclear power are widely
divergent. Various countries decided to develop nuclear power several decades ago, some are taking that step now, while others are
opting to retire their nuclear capacity. The will to power, the need
to achieve energy independence, the growth of science and technology and more recently the desire to combat climate change have
all played a part in such decisions. To this we must add efforts to
acquire nuclear weapons, although this only concerns a few cases:
the vast majority of countries operating nuclear power plants have
not taken this route. The Treaty on the Non-Proliferation of Nuclear
Weapons contributed to this state of affairs, reducing the collective
ill of proliferation threatening the planet. But in some cases it made
it worse, by promoting scientific and technological cooperation on
nuclear power: access to this technology by a growing number of
countries increases the risk of proliferation.

Multilateral cooperation has also attempted to improve nuclear
safety. The European Union has gone furthest towards achieving
this collective good. Underpinned by the Treaty on the European
Atomic Energy Community and specific legislation, European safety
governance has proved an undeniable success, notably shutting down
hazardous reactors on its borders. Much as with other forms of safety
cooperation, its effectiveness is hampered by the number of its members and their divergent interests, some in favour of nuclear power,
others against.

Let us now recapitulate the key determinants of the future of
nuclear power worldwide, as analysed in the preceding pages.

The first challenge is to lift the curse of rising costs. Standardization and innovation may be the answer. France has in the past

benefited slightly from large-scale production and learning effects. China could in the future achieve even greater standardization in its reactors. So far, innovation has above all involved building larger, more complex systems. Other routes must be explored, for instance giving priority to modular plants and small reactors.

Secondly, it is essential to pool our understanding of risk. All too often perceived and calculated risk have been at odds, leaving us no option but to side with the experts or the general public. When such opposition is sustained and exploited by leaders of industry and policy-makers, we may fear the worst possible economic outcome. Billions of euros are wasted when nuclear projects, founded on calculated risk and blind to public fears, are shelved at the last moment. Similar amounts are squandered when a government impervious to all but perceived probability orders the premature shutdown of reactors. Experts need to be made aware of how risk perception may be distorted, and the general public educated to recognize this bias and understand probabilistic reasoning.

Thirdly, it is imperative that safety authorities should be powerful and competent, independent and transparent. Giving the regulator extensive powers and a mandate to sanction non-compliance; securing and consolidating its skills with adequate resources; guaranteeing its independence with regard to government and industry; requiring complete transparency in its actions: these are the essential pillars to make regulation as near perfect as possible. Safety can also be much improved by changing the legal framework and balance of power. Many countries need to make progress on safety regulation. Unlike building multiple physical barriers, the financial cost of such gains is almost negligible.

The future of nuclear power is also conditional on the adoption of measures to separate promotion of this form of energy from global governance of security and safety. A throwback to a world divided into three parts – Communist, developed and non-aligned countries – the same international bodies and laws still have a three-pronged mission: to disseminate electronuclear technology; to establish safety principles and standards; and to combat the proliferation of nuclear weapons. This confusion, present even at the heart of the International Atomic Energy Agency, undermines the effectiveness of its work to improve safety, monitor exports and inspect installations.

Lastly, the nuclear industry and corresponding trade must become international. Individual states currently play a key role, by protecting their home market – giving priority to national firms and 'home-grown' technology – and by the active involvement of political leaders in negotiating export contracts. There are few openings for foreign capital, and foreign markets only see competition between national teams. To sustain the growth of both trade and industry, international regrouping is needed, organized along lines closer to oil and gas supply and service than to defence procurement.

Let us end with an inevitable question: for or against nuclear power.

The reader will have gathered that nuclear power is durably established all over the world. Every year new nuclear power plants are commissioned and built, though some will quibble over whether there are too many or too few. The priority is therefore to ensure that the system operates properly.

It should be clear by now that a polemical approach to new nuclear makes no sense. As for existing plants, nothing can do more harm to the general economic interest than the early retirement of reactors which are still perfectly serviceable and have been licensed to operate by the safety operator.

It should also be apparent that the author is in favour of new nuclear and its growth, on condition that costs are contained, risks controlled and safety regulation properly implemented, and that international governance on safety and security is stronger and more effective. On the other hand, the author opposes further growth if costs continue to soar, if some plants go on being operated in an irresponsible manner, if regulation is non-existent in practice and the state omnipresent.

The above observation is not an attempt to dodge the issue. To refuse to take a stand for or against nuclear power is simply to acknowledge the many uncertainties relating to costs, risk, regulation and governance which surround this technology. Economic appraisal can only give categorical answers when the most probable hypotheses have been singled out. Too much uncertainty still besets nuclear power for the general economic interest to serve as a basis for decisions for or against.

Notes

Part I   Introduction

1 For a full, accurate account of the various items of cost, see W. D. D'Haeseleer, Synthesis on the Economics of Nuclear Energy, Study for the European Commission (DG Energy, 2013), available at: ec.europa.eu/ energy/nuclear/forum/doc/final_report_dhaeseleer/synthesis_economics_ nuclear_20131127-0.pdf.

1   Adding up costs

1 Loi *no.* 2010–1448 du 7 Décembre 2010 portant organisation du marché de l'électricité.

2 Cour des Comptes, *Les Coûts de la Filière Nucléaire* (La Documentation Française, Paris, 2012).

3 Centre d'Analyse Stratégique, *La Valeur Tutélaire du Carbone*. Report by the committee chaired by Alain Quinet (La Documentation Française, 2009).

4 Cour des Comptes, *Les Coûts de la Filière Nucléaire*, p. 150.

5 'Is it worth it?', *The Economist* (5 December 2009).

6 F. P. Ramsey, A mathematical theory of saving, *Economic Journal*, 38 (1928), pp. 543–59.

7 The Stern Review of the Economics of Climate Change (2006), available online: http://webarchive.nationalarchives.gov.uk/+/http://www.hm-treasury.gov.uk/sternreview_index.htm.

8 W. Nordhaus, Global warming economics, *Science*, 294:5545 (2001), pp. 1283–4.

9 P. Dasgupta, Comments on the Stern Review's Economics of Climate Change, *National Institute Economics Review*, 199 (2006), pp. 4–7.

10 C. Gollier, Discounting an uncertain future, *Journal of Public Economics*, 85 (2002), pp. 149–66.

11 Oxera Consulting Ltd, A *Social Time Preference Rate for Use in Long-Term Discounting* (2002).

12 Report by the group of experts led by D. Lebègue, *Révision du Taux d'Actualisation des Investissements Publics* (Commissariat Général du Plan, 2005).

13 The intuitive, commonsense solution of a declining, variable discount rate now has a solid base in economic theory: see C. Gollier, *Pricing the Planet's Future: The Economics of Discounting in an Uncertain World* (Princeton University Press, 2013).

14 Cour des Comptes, *Les Coûts de la Filière Nucléaire*, p. 282.

15 US Department of Energy, *Civilian Radioactive Waste Management Fee Adequacy Assessment Report* (2008), RW-0593.

16 Massachusetts Institute of Technology, *Update of the MIT 2003 Future of Nuclear Power* (2009).

17 Economic losses estimated at $148 billion for Ukraine and $235 billion for Belarus. Figures cited by Z. Jaworowski, *The Chernobyl Disaster and How it has been Understood* (2010), available online: www.world-nuclear.org/uploadedFiles/org/info/Safety_and_Security/Safety_of_Plants/jaworowski_chernobyl.pdf.

18 A fleet of fifty-eight reactors with a forty-year service life, or an expected number of accidents of $2,320 \times 10^{-5} = 0.0232$ and damages of $0.023 \times$ €1,000 billion, in other words €23.2 billion.

19 Data compiled from fourteen countries, of which three non-OECD, but not the US: see p. 59 of the joint OECD-IEA report, *Projected Costs of Generating Electricity* (2010).

20 E. Bertel and G. Naudet, *L'Economie du Nucléaire* (EDP Sciences, Paris, 2004).

21 A small part of the difference results from the discounting rates: 5% for South Korea and 10% for Switzerland.

22 Y. Du and J. Parsons, *Update on the Cost of Nuclear Power* (Center for Energy and Environmental Policy Research (CEEPR) 09-004, 2009).

23 Massachusetts Institute of Technology, *The Future of Nuclear Power: An Interdisciplinary MIT Study* (2003).

2   The curse of rising costs

1 A. Lindman and P. Söderholm, Wind power learning rates: a conceptual review and meta-analysis, *Energy Economics*, 34 (2012), pp. 754–61.

2 N. E. Hultman and J. Koomey, A reactor-level analysis of busbar costs for US nuclear power plants 1970–2005, *Energy Policy*, 35 (2007), pp. 5630–42.

3 The overnight construction cost for the French fleet, cited in Cour des Comptes, *Les Coûts de la Filière Nucléaire* (La Documentation Française, Paris, 2012), amounted to about €83 billion$_{2010}$. The report also published the construction cost of each pair of reactors, but these detailed figures do not correspond to the overnight cost, strictly speaking, as they omit engineering expenses and pre-operating costs.

4 Averages based on figures in the Cour des Comptes, *Les Coûts de la Filière Nucléaire*. The difference between Chooz 1 and 2 (€1,635 per kW), and Civaux (€1,250 per kW) vanishes. The high figure for Chooz is due to the fact that these were the first units of the N4 series, a new reactor model.

5 I. C. Bupp, J.-C. Derian, M. P. Donsimoni and R. Treitel, The economics of nuclear power, *Technology Review* 77:4 (1975), pp. 14–25, quoted by Hultman and Koomey, A reactor-level analysis of busbar costs.

6 G. S. Rothwell, Steam-electric scale economies and construction lead times, *Social Science Working Paper*, 627 (California Institute of Technology, 1986).

7 R. Cantor and J. Hewlett, The economics of nuclear power: further evidence on learning, economies of scale and regulatory effects, *Resources and Energy*, 10:4 (December 1988), pp. 315–35.

8 M. B. Zimmerman, Learning effects and the commercialization of new technologies: the case of nuclear power, *The Bell Journal of Economics*, 13 (1988), pp. 297–310.

9 L. W. Davis, Prospects for nuclear power, *Journal of Economic Perspectives*, 26:1 (2012), pp. 49–66.

10 S. Paik and W. R. Schriver, The effects of increased regulation on capital costs and manual labor requirements of nuclear power plants, *The Engineering Economist*, 26 (1979), pp. 223–44.

11 M. Cooper, *Policy Challenges of Nuclear Reactor Construction: Cost Escalation and Crowding Out Alternatives* (Institute for Energy and the Environment, Vermont Law School, 2010).

12 A. Grubler, The costs of the French nuclear scale-up: a case of negative learning by doing, *Energy Policy*, 38 (2010), pp. 5174–88.

13 E. Bertel and G. Naudet, *L'Economie du Nucléaire* (EDP Sciences, Paris, 2004); G. Moynet, Evaluation du coût de l'électricité nucléaire en France au cours des dix dernières années, *Revue Générale Nucléaire*, 2 (1984), pp. 141–52.

14 Grubler, The costs of the French nuclear scale-up.

15 Massachusetts Institute of Technology, *Update of the MIT 2003 Future of Nuclear Power* (2009).

16 Expressed in $\$_{2007}$; the levelized cost increases by 25%.

17 The lower end of the overnight cost for the 2004 study was $1,413$_{2010}$ to $2,120$_{2010}$ with a mean value of $1,765$_{2010}$, hence the increase by a factor of 2.3. Focusing just on the AP1000, the 2004 range was $1,554$_{2010}$ to $2,331$_{2010}$ with a mid-point at $1,943$_{2010}$. So the study used $2,000 per kW and compared this to $4,210 per kW, an increase by a factor of 2.1.

18 Hultman and Koomey, A reactor-level analysis of busbar costs.

19 With a 6% discount rate, the levelized cost in the MIT study is $42 per MWh.

20 Hultman and Koomey, A reactor-level analysis of busbar costs.

21 J.-M. Glachant, Generation technology mix in competitive electricity markets, in F. Lévêque (ed.), *Electricity Reform in Europe: Towards a Single Energy Market* (Edward Elgar Publishing, London, 2009).

22 B. Dupraz and L. Joudon, Le développement de l'EPR dans le marché électrique européen, *Revue Générale Nucléaire*, 6 (2004); P. C. Zaleski and S. Méritet, Point de vue sur l'EPR, *Contrôle*, 164 (2005), pp. 51–6.

23 According to French MP Marc Goua, tasked with reviewing the accounts of Areva and EDF: www.enerzine.com/2/12796+lepr-finlandais-couterait-au-final-6–6-mds-deuros+.html (2011).

24 *Le Monde*, www.lemonde.fr/planete/article/2011/11/10/sur-le-chantier-de-l-epr-a-flamanville-edf-est-a-la-moitie-du-chemin_1602181_3244.html.

25 EDF communiqué, cited in the Cour des Comptes, *Les Coûts de la Filière Nucléaire*.

26 See the EDF Energy press release dated 21 October 2013, 'Agreement reached on commercial terms for the planned Hinkley Point C nuclear power plant'. The figure of €17.2 billion – or €8.6 billion per reactor – can be directly compared with the cost of building the EPR at Flamanville, France. The sum of €19.7 billion includes additional expenditure such as purchase of the land and building a facility for storing fuel. Such expenditure is not included in the cost of Flamanville 3.

27 See second study by the University of Chicago: R. Rosner and S. Goldberg, *Analysis of GW-scale Overnight Cost*, Technical Report (University of Chicago, 2011).

28 For example, in its updated study the MIT revalues the overnight cost per kW of a gas plant, resulting in a 70% increase, and a 130% increase for a coal-fired thermal plant.

29 The levelized cost for the base case was $67 per MWh for nuclear, $43 per MWh for coal and $41 per MWh for gas. With the same financial conditions the cost of nuclear power drops to $51 per MWh. See Table 1, Yangbo Due and J. E. Parsons, *Update on the Cost of Nuclear Power* (Massachusetts Institute of Technology, 2009).

30 The 2004 University of Chicago study suggests that first-of-a-kind costs may amount to as much as 35% of the overnight cost. Dupraz and Joudon, Le développement de l'EPR, estimate that such costs add 20% to the levelized cost of the first in a series, for a series of ten units (€41$_{2004}$ per MWh, rather than €33$_{2004}$ per MWh).

31 Areva défend son EPR, *Energies Actu* (2012), available online at: www.energiesactu.fr/production/areva-defend-son-epr.

32 Organisation for Economic Cooperation and Development, *Reduction of Capital Costs of Nuclear Power Plants* (2000).

33 G. F. Nemet, Demand-pull energy technology policies, diffusion and improvements in California wind power, in T. Foxon, J. Koehler and C. Oughton (eds.), *Innovations for a Low Carbon Economy: Economic, Institutional and Management Approaches* (Edward Elgar Publishing, Cheltenham, 2007).

3 Nuclear power and its alternatives

1 L. Pouret and W. J. Nuttall, Is nuclear power inflexible?, *Nuclear Future*, 5:6 (2009), pp. 333–41.

2 N. Z. Muller, R. Mendelsohn and W. Nordhaus, Environmental accounting for pollution in the United States economy, *American Economic Review*, 1001:5 (2011), pp. 1649–75. Value reported as $28.3 per MWh.

3 P. Epstein et al., Full cost accounting for the life cycle of coal, *Annals of the New York Academy of Sciences*, 1219 (2011), pp. 73–98. Here the value was $269 per MWh, of which $44 per MWh corresponds to the impact on public health.

4 European Commission, Directorate General XII, Externalities of Energy, (2009). The ExternE study estimates the external costs of electricity generated using natural gas (excluding carbon emissions) at between 13.4_{2010}$ and 53.8_{2010}$ per MWh, as against 27_{2010}$ to 202_{2010}$ for coal. The latter figures were reported by S. Grausz, The Social Cost of Coal, *Climate Advisers* (2011). Natural gas produces half as much carbon emissions as coal.

5 Organisation for Economic Cooperation and Development, Nuclear Energy Agency, *The Financing of Nuclear Power Plants* (2009).

6 F. Roques, D. M. Newbery and W. J. Nuttall, Fuel mix diversification incentives in liberalized electricity markets: a mean-variance portfolio theory approach, *Energy Economics*, 30 (2008).

7 Cour des Comptes, *Les Coûts de la Filière Nucléaire* (La Documentation Française, Paris, 2012), p. 51.

8 P. L. Joskow, Comparing the costs of intermittent and dispatchable electricity generating technologies, *American Economic Review*, 101:3 (2011), pp. 238–41.

9 D. M. Newbery, Reforming competitive electricity markets to meet environmental targets, *Economics of Energy and Environmental Policy*, 1:1 (2012), pp. 69–82.

10 Quoted by S. Ambec and C. Crampes, *Electricity Production with Intermittent Source of Energy*, Lerna Working Paper, University of Toulouse 10.07.313 (2010).

11 E. Lantz, R. Wiser and M. Hand, *IEA Wind Task 26: The Past and Future Cost of Wind Energy*, Work Package 2 (National Renewable Energy Laboratory, 2012).

12 In a meta-study carried out for the International Panel on Climate Change, bearing on eighteen estimates, R. Wiser et al., Wind Energy, in *IPCC Special Report on Renewable Energy Sources and Climate Change* (Cambridge University Press, 2011) suggest a 4% to 32% range. But the gap narrows to a 9% to 19% range, if only post-2004 estimates are considered.

13 W. D. D'Haeseleer, Synthesis on the economics of nuclear energy: Study for the European Commission (DG Energy, 2013), available at: ec.europa. eu/energy/nuclear/forum/doc/final_report_dhaeseleer/synthesis_economics_ nuclear_20131127-0.pdf.

Part II Introduction

1 The severity of an event increases tenfold, at each level: accordingly level two is ten times worse than level one, level three ten times worse than level two, and so on.

2 The term 'major accident' used in this part is more general than its usage in the terminology established by the INES scale. In this ranking only level-seven accidents rate as 'major'; a level-five core-melt counts as an 'accident with wider consequences', whereas its level-six counterpart counts as a 'serious accident'.

3 SER (1959), Enrico Fermi 1 (1961), Chapelcross 2 (1967), Saint-Laurent A1 (1969) and A2 (1980), Three Mile Island 2 (1979), Chernobyl 4 (1986), Greifswald 5 (1989). List taken from T. B. Cochran, Fukushima Nuclear Disaster and Implications for US Nuclear Power Reactors (2011), at www.nrdc.org/nuclear/tcochran_110412.asp. This figure only includes grid-connected reactors. It does not include accidents on research reactors such as the SL-1 meltdown in Idaho, USA, in 1961. Note that this list includes cases of very limited core damage. For these cases, the term 'major accident' could be viewed by specialists as an overstatement.

4 Calculating risk

1 Other risk dimensions such as the duration and reversibility of damage are sometimes taken into account too.
2 R. A. Posner, *Catastrophe: Risk and Response* (Oxford University Press, 2004), estimates it at $600 trillion ($6.10^{14}$).
3 The Sievert is an International System (SI) unit used to measure the biological effects of the absorption of ionizing radiation.
4 These methods are open to dispute and actively debated. Readers wishing to pursue the matter may refer to Chapter 4 of W. K. Viscusi, *Rational Risk Policy* (Oxford University Press, 1998).
5 Some recent estimates have also sought to estimate direct and indirect macroeconomic consequences, as well as the impact on society as a whole and on private individuals, through the emotional and psychological disturbance caused by an accident. See L. Pascucci-Cahen and P. Momal, *Les Rejets Radiologiques Massifs Different Profondément des Rejets Contrôlés* (Institut de Radioprotection et de Sûreté Nucléaire, 2012).
6 Versicherungsforen Leipzig, *Calculating a Risk-Appropriate Insurance Premium to Cover Third-Party Liability Risks that Result from Operation of Nuclear Power Plants*, commissioned by the German Renewable Energy Federation (2011).
7 Versicherungsforen Leipzig, *Calculating a Risk-Appropriate Insurance Premium*.
8 Reactors, Residents and Risk, *Nature News* (2011), doi: 10.1038/472400a.
9 The Chernobyl Forum, *Chernobyl's Legacy: Health, Environmental and Socio-Economic Impacts*, second revised version (2005). The estimate is based on the linear no-threshold model.
10 Lisbeth Gronlund, How many cancers did Chernobyl really cause? *Monthly Review Magazine*, available at: http://mrzine.monthlyreview.org/2011/gronlund070411.html.
11 Estimated, for example, at $3.4 billion by B. Sovacool, The costs of failure: a preliminary assessment of major energy accidents, *Energy Policy* (2008), pp. 1802–20, of which $1 billion just for the cost of cleaning up. The remainder is an estimate of the cost of loss of property.
12 Belarus, for instance, has estimated its losses over thirty years at $235 billion: Chernobyl Forum, *Chernobyl's Legacy*, p. 33, n. 6.
13 This figure is taken from the very first studies carried out by EDF in the late 1980s on its 900 MW nuclear reactors. In its subsequent, more detailed studies, the figure was ten times lower, at about 5×10^{-6}. But in both cases the relevant studies made no allowance for external initiating factors such as earthquakes or floods.
14 If there are only two options – such as drawing a red ball or a black ball from an urn only containing balls of these two colours – then once you

know the probability of one option, the other can be deduced, the sum of the two being equal to one. So if the probability of drawing a red ball is one-in-three, the probability of not drawing a red ball is two-in-three; as all the non-red balls are black, the probability of drawing a black ball is two-in-three.

15 US National Regulatory Commission, *Reactor Safety Study: An Assessment of Accident Risks in US Commercial Nuclear Power Plants* (NUREG-75/014) (1975).

16 See in particular the criticism voiced by the Union of Concerned Scientists, published in its report: H. W. Kendall, R. B. Hubbard and C. M. Gregory (eds.), *Risks of Nuclear Power Reactors: a Review of the NRC Reactor Safety Study* (1977).

17 Health and Safety Executive, Nuclear Directorate, *Generic Design Assessment – New Civil Reactors Build* (Step 3, Probabilistic Safety Analysis of the EDF and Areva UK EPR, Division 6, Assessment report no. AR 09/027-P) (2011).

18 Electric Power Research Institute, *Safety and Operational Benefits of Risk-Informed Initiatives* (White paper, 2008).

19 Cochran, Fukushima Nuclear Disaster.

20 EDF studied the risk of falling aircraft for the Flamanville 3 reactor. The probability of an attack on one of its safety functions is 6.6×10^{-8} per reactor-year. See EDF Probabilistic Safety Analysis, available at: www.edf.com/html/epr/rps/chap18/chap18.pdf.

21 Nor is it possible to assign probabilities to the share of known events in an incomplete whole. The sum of all probabilities must be one, but as the probability associated with the subset of disregarded events is not known, it cannot be subtracted from one to obtain the probability assigned to known events.

22 In an even more comprehensive definition of uncertainty, this term also encompasses incompleteness. The term 'radical uncertainty' may be used to distinguish this form of uncertainty from non-specific uncertainty.

23 The intuition underpinning this hypothesis is that all the distributions of black and white balls (one white, fifty-nine black; two white, fifty-eight black; . . . ; thirty white, thirty black; . . . fifty-nine white, one black) are possible, and that there is nothing to suggest that one is more probable than another. It is no more likely that the distribution contains more black than white balls, than the opposite.

24 J. M. Keynes, *A Treatise on Probability* (Macmillan, London, 1921).

25 Quoted by S. Morini, Bernard de Finetti: l'origine de son subjectivisme, *Journal Electronique d'Histoire des Probabilités et de la Statistique*, 3:2 (2007), pp. 1–16.

26 W. Epstein, *A PRA Practitioner Looks at the Great East Japan Earthquake and Tsunami* (Ninokata Laboratory White Paper, 2011).

27 The estimated frequencies for the other nuclear power plants on the same coastline do not display such a large difference. At Fukushima Daini the estimated frequency is ten times lower than the historic frequency; at Onagawa the two frequencies converge. The differences are due to the choice of too fine a mesh to differentiate seismic risks in the Sanriku area. See R. J. Geller, Shake-up time for Japanese seismology, *Nature*, 472 (2011), pp. 407–9.

28 Epstein, *A PRA Practitioner*, p. 52.

29 Japan Society of Civil Engineers, Nuclear Civil Engineering Committee, Tsunami Evaluation Subcommittee, *Tsunami Assessment Method for Nuclear Power Plants in Japan* (2002 guidelines): 'We have assessed and confirmed the safety of the nuclear plants [at Daiichi] based on the JSCE method published in 2002' (Tsunami Study for Fukushima 1 and 2, p. 14); written statement by Tepco submitted to the regulator, cited by Epstein, *A PRA Practitioner*, p. 24.

30 Epstein, *A PRA Practitioner*, p. 23.

31 On Japan's Shindo scale of seismic intensity. Seismic scales not being strictly speaking comparable with one another, seismic intensity six on the Shindo scale is roughly equivalent to between magnitude six and seven on the Richter scale.

32 It is of little concern here whether this was done knowingly or not. This point is addressed in Chapter 8.

5   Perceived probabilities and aversion to disaster

1 I. Gilboa, *Theory of Decision under Uncertainty* (Cambridge University Press, 2009). This work presents the classical and recent axiomatic theories, and discusses their conceptual and philosophical aspects.

2 Imagine the following game in a casino: a coin is tossed a number of times, with an initial kitty of $1, which doubles each time the coin comes up tails. The game stops and the player pockets the kitty when the coin lands heads up. At the first toss, the winner pockets $1 if the coin lands heads up; if it is tails, the game continues, with a second toss. If the coin then lands heads up, the player pockets $2, otherwise it is tossed a third time and so on. The expectation of gain equals $1 \times 1/2 + 2 \times 1/4 + 4 \times 1/8 + 8 \times 1/16 + \cdots$ or $1/2 + 1/2 + 1/2 + 1/2 + \cdots$, making an infinite amount provided the casino has unlimited resources.

3 Equal to $(1/101)(100/100 + 99/100 + \cdots + 1/100 + 0/100)$.

4 Tversky and Kahneman co-authored a great many academic papers, in particular those awarded the economics prize by Sweden's central bank. But Tversky died at the age of 59 and was consequently not awarded the Nobel prize for economics alongside Kahneman.

5 D. Kahneman and A. Tversky, Prospect Theory: An Analysis of
  Decision under Risk, *Econometrica*, 47 (1979), pp. 263–91; and D.
  Kahneman and A. Tversky, Advances in prospect theory: cumulative
  representation of uncertainty, *Journal of Risk and Uncertainty*, 5:4 (1992),
  pp. 297–323.

6 This type of experiment, simplified here, is presented in detail in D.
  Kahneman, J. L. Knetsch and R. H. Thaler, Anomalies: the endowment
  effect, loss aversion, and status quo bias, *Journal of Economic Perspectives*,
  5:1 (1991), pp. 193–206.

7 D. Kahneman, *Thinking, Fast and Slow* (Farrar, Straus and Giroux, New
  York, 2011).

8 Kahneman submitted this problem to his students at Princeton.

9 P. Slovic, B. Fischhoff and S. Lichenstein, Facts and fears: societal
  perception of risk, *Advances in Consumer Research*, 8 (Association for
  Consumer Research, 1981), pp. 497–502.

10 W. K. Viscusi, *Rational Risk Policy* (Oxford University Press,
  1998).

11 Moreover it is not strictly speaking a biased perception of probability.
  Rather the utility function is distorted, depending on whether there is a
  loss or gain.

12 A. A. Siddik and P. Slovic, A psychological study of the inverse
  relationship between perceived risk and perceived benefit, *Risk Analysis*,
  14:6 (1994), pp. 1085–96.

13 Organisation for Economic Cooperation and Development, Nuclear
  Energy Agency, *Comparing Nuclear Accident Risks with Those from Other
  Energy Sources* (OECD, 2010).

14 In all, 80,250 people lost their lives in 1,870 accidents. Which accident
  caused the largest number of fatalities? The Chernobyl disaster? No! The
  failure of the Banquiao and Shimantan dams in China in 1975. This
  accident, disregarded by all but the local population, claimed 30,000
  lives. As we saw in Chapter 4, the number of fatalities at Chernobyl
  did not exceed 60 and 20,000 was an upper-range estimate of subsequent
  early deaths. Even if the OECD study had considered these deaths,
  serious accidents in the coal industry during this period caused more
  deaths. Moreover, in all fairness, the early deaths caused by coal
  should also be taken into account in any comparison with nuclear
  power.

15 G. Gigerenzer, Dread Risks, September 11 and fatal traffic accidents,
  Psychological Science, 15:4 (2004), pp. 286–7.

16 In addition many observers maintain that they have not been very
  effective. See, for instance, K. Harley, Why airport security is broken, *The
  Wall Street Journal* (15 April 2012).

6 The magic of Bayesian analysis

1 p(cancer|positive) = [p(cancer) × p(positive|cancer)]/[p(positive|
cancer)p(no cancer) + p(positive|no cancer)p(no cancer)] = [0.01 × 0.8]/
[0.01 × 0.8 + 0.99 × 0.1] = 0.075.

2 This is not a matter of innumeracy, a shortcoming similar to illiteracy but
for numbers. The experiments described above involved educated
participants, students or graduates.

3 D. Kahneman and A. Tversky, Subjective probability: a judgment of
representativeness, in D. Kahneman, P. Slovic and A. Tversky (eds.),
Judgements under Uncertainty: Heuristics and Biases (Cambridge University
Press, 1982), p. 46.

4 S. Dehaene, Le cerveau statisticien: la révolution Bayésienne en sciences
cognitives (a course of lectures at Collège de France, Paris, 2011–12); C.
Kemp and J. B. Tenenbaum, Structural statistical models of inductive
reasoning, *Psychological Review*, 116 (2009), pp. 20–58.

5 Figure taken from E. Grenier, Introduction à la démarche Bayésienne sans
formule mathématique, *Modulab*, 43 (2010–11).

6 If n equals zero, k equals zero; zero divided by zero is indeterminate.

7 'Thus we find that an event having occurred successively any number of
times, the probability that it will happen again the next time is equal to
this number increased by unity divided by the same number, increased by
two units. Placing the most ancient epoch of history at 5,000 years ago, or
at 1,826,213 days, and the sun having risen constantly in the interval at
each revolution of 24 hours, it is a bet of 1,826,214 to 1 that it will rise
again tomorrow.' – *Essai Philosophique sur les Probabilités* (1825), p. 23.

8 If s is very high, the denominator n is negligible compared to s, while the
numerator k becomes negligible compared to st, and so the ratio is close to
t, the initial expectation of probability.

9 The general formula is obtained by choosing a beta distribution with
parameters $[st, s(1 - t)]$ for the prior function, and a binomial distribution
for the likelihood function. In this case a beta distribution with parameters
$[st + k, s(1 - t) + n - k]$ is used for the posterior function.

10 W. K. Viscusi, *Rational Risk Policy* (Oxford University Press, 1998).

11 See B. Dessus and B. Laponche, Accident nucléaire: une certitude
statistique, *Libération*, 5 June 2011; and the correction made to their
calculations by E. Ghys, Accident nucléaire: une certitude statistique,
Images des Mathématiques (Centre National de Recherche Scientifique,
Paris, 2011).

12 To simplify matters, we have assumed here that the number of accidents
follows a binomial distribution. The probability of there not being a major
accident in Europe over the next thirty years is 1–0.0003 per reactor-year,

or $(1-0.0003)^{30\times143}$, or about 0.28. The probability of there being a major accident in Europe over the next thirty years is therefore 0.72. The choice of a thirty-year period is largely arbitrary; the calculation can be reduced to the probability of an accident in Europe next year, for which we find 0.042, or nearly a one-in-twenty-three chance.

13 The eight core-melt accidents previous to Fukushima Daiichi (see introduction of Part II), plus the meltdown of reactors 1, 2 and 3 at this nuclear power plant.

14 This value is derived from an American study encompassing seventy-five probabilistic risk assessments: US Nuclear Regulatory Commission, *Individual Plant Examination Program: Perspectives on Reactor Safety and Plant Performance (NUREG-1560)*, Vol. 1–3 (1997). This study indicates a mean core-melt frequency of 6.5×10^{-5}. It also gives the 95% confidence interval from which s could be derived. For more details, see F. Lévêque and L. Escobar, How to predict the probability of a major nuclear accident after Fukushima Daiichi, Communication at the International Days of the Chair Modeling for Sustainable Development 2012 (MINES ParisTech, Sophia-Antipolis, 2012), available at: www.modelisation-prospective.org/Days-Chair_2012.html.

15 See also the changes in US probabilistic safety studies highlighted by the Electric Power Research Institute.

16 At least with respect to their location and type. Improvements to safety through changes to equipment and operating procedures mean that a reactor is not quite the same over time.

17 L. Escobar-Rangel and F. Lévêque, How Fukushima Daiichi core meltdown changed the probability of nuclear accidents, *Safety Science*, 64 (2014), pp. 90–98.

Part III   Introduction

1 At least when an economic study is based, as is the case here, on publicly available documents (articles in scientific journals, parliamentary reports, information published by companies or administrative bodies, and so on), rather than detailed interviews with nuclear-safety professionals and practitioners the world over. Field investigations of regulation reveal the distance between stated principles and written rules, on the one hand, and their practical application, on the other.

7   Does nuclear safety need to be regulated?

1 F. Lévêque, *Economie de la Réglementation* (Collection Repères, Editions La Découverte, Paris, 2004).

2 Cour des Comptes, *Les Coûts de la Filière Nucléaire* (La Documentation Française, Paris, 2012), pp. 62–70.

3 J. V. Rees, *Hostages of Each Other: The Transformation of the Nuclear Industry Since 1980* (University of Chicago Press, 1985); N. Gunningham and J. Rees, Industry self-regulation, *Law and Policy*, 4:19 (1997), pp. 363–414.

4 See the detailed work of debate and analysis done by K. Fiore, Industrie nucléaire et gestion du risque d'accident en Europe, PhD thesis in economic science (Aix-Marseille 3 University, 2007), pp. 85–8.

5 For full analysis of the pros and cons of the strict, exclusive liability enshrined in the nuclear civil liability regime, see R. A. Winter and M. Trebilcock, The economics of nuclear accident law, *International Review of Law and Economics*, 17 (1997), pp. 225–43.

6 T. Vanden Borre, Shifts in governance in compensation for nuclear damage, 20 years after Chernobyl, in M. Faure and A. Verheij (eds.), *Shifts in Compensation for Environmental Damage* (Tort and Insurance Law, Vol. 21, Springer, 2007).

7 D. Koplow, Nuclear power: still not viable without subsidies (Union of Concerned Scientists, 2011); R. Bell, The biggest nuclear subsidy: pathetically inadequate insurance for a colossal liability (www. planetworkshops.org, 2012).

8 The first study dates from 1990 and was done by J. A. Dubin and G. S. Rothwell, Subsidy to nuclear power through the Price-Anderson liability limit, *Contemporary Policy Issues* (1990), pp. 73–8. It yielded an estimate of $21.7 million per reactor-year, compared with the then cap of $7 billion. This study contained a mistake which was corrected by A. G. Heyes and C. Liston-Heyes, Subsidy to nuclear power through the Price-Anderson liability limit: comment, *Contemporary Economic Policy*, 16 (1998), pp. 122–4. The estimate was cut to $2.32 million per reactor-year.

9 Congressional Budget Office, *Nuclear Power's Role in Generating Electricity*, (2008), pp. 28–9.

10 M. G. Faure and K. Fiore, An economic analysis of the nuclear liability subsidy, *Pace Environmental Law Review*, 26 (2009), pp. 419–47.

11 The 2008 Congressional Budget Office report adopted a levelized cost of $72 per MWh for its baseline scenario for an advanced generation of nuclear reactors.

12 Faure and Fiore, An economic analysis of the nuclear liability subsidy, took €0.457 per MWh as the value of the highest risk. They compared this amount to a levelized cost for nuclear power of €30 per MWh, which is not very realistic. We have adopted a levelized cost twice as high, at €60 per MWh.

13 Versicherungsforen Leipzig, *Calculating a Risk-Appropriate Insurance Premium to Cover Third-Party Liability Risks that Result from Operation of Nuclear Power Plants*, commissioned by the German Renewable Energy Federation (2011).

14 Also of note is the study by B. A. Leurs and R. C. N. Wit, *Environmentally Harmful Support Measures in EU Member States* (CE Delft, January 2003), for the Environment Directorate General of the European Commission, on energy subsidies and how they harm the environment. In the part on nuclear power, the subsidy through limited liability is estimated, at its upper limit, at €50 per MWh, in other words with a baseline production cost for nuclear electricity of €25, the final cost would be tripled.

15 For example the risk coverage provided by pension funds or cover funds, in the form of bonds. See M. Radetzki and M. Radetzki, Private arrangements to cover large-scale liabilities caused by nuclear and other industrial catastrophes, *The Geneva Papers on Risks and Insurance*, 25 (2000), pp. 180–95.

8 The basic rules of regulation

1 For a detailed account of changes in the conceptions of safety in the US and France, see the PhD thesis by C. Foasso, Histoire de la sûreté de l'énergie nucléaire en France (1945–2000) (Université Lumière-Lyon II, 2003).

2 We have chosen regulation in Japan as an example to avoid because its shortcomings have been largely documented. This does not mean it comes last in any global ranking. Safety regulation in the Russian Federation or Pakistan may be even more defective, but these countries do not publish the information needed to assess their authorities.

3 S. Huet, *Nucléaire: Quel Scénario pour le Futur?* (Collection 360, Editions La Ville Brûle, Montreuil, 2012), p. 132.

4 J. Kingston, Power politics: Japan's resilient nuclear village, *The Asia-Pacific Journal*, 10 (2012), available at: www.japanfocus.org/-Jeff-Kingston/3847.

5 A. Gundersen, The echo chamber: regulatory capture and the Fukushima Daiichi disaster, in *Lessons from Fukushima* (Greenpeace, 2012), pp. 41–9.

6 Citizens Information Center, Revelation of endless N-damage cover-ups, *Nuke Info Tokyo*, 92 (2002).

7 *Japan Times*, 4 May 2011.

8 Culture of Complicity Tied to Stricken Nuclear Plant, *New York Times*, 26 April 2011.

9 *Asahi Shimbun*, 3 May 2011.

10 Final report, Investigation Committee on the Accident at the Fukushima Nuclear Power Stations of Tokyo Electric Power Company (2012).

11 Official Report of the Fukushima Nuclear Accident Independent Investigation Commission, National Diet of Japan (2012).

12 Final report, Investigation Committee on the Accident at the Fukushima Nuclear Power Stations, pp. 414–15.

13 Official Report of the Fukushima NAICC (2012), Executive Summary, p. 73.

14 Official Report of the Fukushima NAICC (2012), Section 5, p. 12.

15 For a definition of its mission, see the Official Report of the Fukushima NAICC (2012), Chapter 5, p. 52.

16 J. M. Ramseyer and E. B. Rasmusen, Why are Japanese judges so conservative in politically charged cases?, *American Political Science*, 95:2 (2001), pp. 331–44.

17 Japanese officials ignored or concealed dangers, *New York Times*, 16 May 2011.

18 G. J. Stigler, The theory of economic regulation, *Bell Journal of Economic and Management Science*, 2:1 (1971), pp. 3–21.

19 'The incestuous relationships that existed between regulators and business entities must not be allowed to develop again.' Official Report of the Fukushima NAICC (2012), Executive Summary, p. 44.

20 Japan ignored nuclear risks, official says, *New York Times*, 15 February 2012.

21 F. Lévêque, *Economie de la Réglementation* (Collection Repères, Editions La Découverte, Paris, 2004), p. 14.

22 Commissions locales d'information (local information committees): see ASN website, www.asn.fr/L-ASN/Les-autres-acteurs-du-controle/CLI.

9   What goal should be set for safety and how is it to be attained?

1 S. Paik and W. R. Schriver, The effect of increased regulation on capital costs and manual labor requirements of nuclear power plants, *The Engineering Economist*, 1 (1980), pp. 223–44.

2 M. W. Golay, Improved nuclear power plant operations and safety through performance-based safety regulation, *Journal of Hazardous Materials*, 1–3:71 (2000), pp. 219–37.

3 Regulatory Guide 1.174, *An Approach for Using Probabilistic Risk Assessment in Risk-Informed Decisions on Plant-Specific Changes to the Licensing Basis* (Nuclear Regulatory Commission, 2002).

4 R. A. Meserve, The evolution of safety goals and their connections to safety culture, *NRC News*, S-01–013 (2001).

5 Author's emphasis.

6 G. E. Apostolakis, How useful is quantitative risk assessment?, *Risk Analysis*, 24:3 (2004), pp. 515–20.

7 A. C. Kadak and T. Matsuo, The nuclear industry's transition to risk-informed regulation and operation in the United States, *Reliability Engineering and System Safety*, 92 (2007), pp. 609–18.

8 Lettre d'orientation (guideline) SIN 1076/77 (1977), on the main safety options for plants operating one or more pressurized water reactors, sent by the minister in charge of industry to EDF's general manager.

9 Nuclear Regulatory Commission Policy Statement, 4 August 1986.

10 Nuclear Regulatory Commission Strategic Plan, fiscal years 2008–13, p. 5. For an older reference on the NRC mandate issued by Congress to *protect the environment* (author's emphasis), see Atomic Energy Act (1954), p. 149.

11 Regulatory Information Conference, 13 March 2012, Rockville, Maryland.

12 Workshops on Frameworks for Developing a Safety Goal, Palo Alto (NUREG/CP-0018) (1981).

13 Nuclear Regulatory Commission, Staff Requirements Memorandum on SECY-89-102, Implementation of the Safety Goals (1990).

14 UK Health and Safety Executive, Office of Nuclear Regulation, *Numerical Targets and Legal Limits in Safety Assessment Principles for Nuclear Facilities* (2006).

15 Whereas most nuclear nations were quick to legislate on the procedures for monitoring nuclear installations, France added a few, very general provisions to an act on atmospheric pollution and odours, passed in 1961, adding more specific rules in a brief ministerial order in 1963. Prior to that, nuclear power plants were subject to a 1917 act on hazardous, inconvenient and insalubrious facilities. See the PhD thesis by A.-S. Vallet, quoted by G. Rolina, in *Sûreté Nucléaire et Facteurs Humains, La Fabrique Française de l'Expertise* (Presse des Mines, Paris, 2009), p. 37. Until 2006 a substantial part of the administration's work monitoring nuclear safety was based on a pragmatic approach that was not legally binding.

16 Law *no.* 2006–686, on the transparency and safety of nuclear facilities, commonly known as the 'Loi TSN'.

17 Article 29, author's emphasis.

18 Groupe Permanent d'Experts pour les Réacteurs Nucléaires, *Directives Techniques pour la Conception et la Construction de la Nouvelle Génération de Réacteurs Nucléaires à Eau Sous Pression* (2000).

19 In 2012 the wording became more precise: Article 3.9 of the ministerial order dated 7 February 2012 establishing General rules relative to basic nuclear installations stipulates that: 'The demonstration of nuclear safety must prove that accidents that could lead to large releases of hazardous substances or to hazardous effects off the site that develop too rapidly to allow timely deployment of the necessary population protection measures

are physically impossible or, if physical impossibility cannot be demonstrated, that the measures taken on or for the installation render such accidents extremely improbable with a high level of confidence.'

20 Lettre d'orientation SIN 1076/77 (see n. 8).

21 Lettre d'orientation SIN 576/78 (1978).

22 C. Foasso, Histoire de la sûreté de l'énergie nucléaire en France (1945–2000), PhD thesis (Université Lumière-Lyon II, 2003), p. 379.

23 A forerunner of ASN, the Central Department for Nuclear Plant Safety (SCSIN) was set up in 1973.

24 The 2006 Act does not mention the principle of continuous progress, but it does appear in the previously cited ministerial order (February 2012), with a whole chapter under this title.

25 A list of basic rules and safety guides can be found at: www.asn.fr/ Reglementer/Regles-fondamentales-de-surete-et-guides-ASN.

26 Foasso, PhD thesis, p. 655.

27 F. Farmer, Siting criteria, a new approach, in *Containment and Siting of Nuclear Power Plants* (International Atomic Energy Agency, Vienna, 1967), pp. 303–29.

28 Giving rise to serious dispute, in particular between CEA and EDF: see G. Hecht, *Le Rayonnement de la France* (Collection Textes à l'appui, Editions La Découverte, Paris, 2004).

29 P. Simonnot, *Les Nucléocrates* (Collection Capitalisme et Survie, Presses Universitaires de Grenoble, 1978).

30 See A. Beltran, J.-F. Picard and M. Bungener, *Histoire(s) de l'EDF, comment se sont prises les decisions de 1946 à nos jours* (Editions Dunod, Paris, 1985) and Pierre Guillaumat, *La Passion des Grands Projets Industriels* (Editions Rive Droite, Paris, 1995).

31 S. Topçu, L'agir contestataire à l'épreuve de l'atome. Critique et gouvernement de la critique dans l'histoire de l'énergie en France (1968–2008), PhD thesis (Ecole des Hautes Etudes en Sciences Sociales, Paris, 2010).

32 G. M. Grossman and E. Helpman, *Special Interest Politics* (Massachusetts Institute of Technology Press, Cambridge, MA, 2001).

33 P. W. MacAvoy and J. W. Rosenthal, *Corporate Profit and Nuclear Safety: Strategy at Northeast Utilities in the 1990s* (Princeton University Press, Princeton, NJ, 2005).

34 *Mainichi Shinbun*, 7 March 2012.

35 T. R. La Porte and C. W. Thomas, Regulatory compliance and the ethos of quality enhancement: surprises in nuclear power plant operations, *Journal of Public and Administration Research and Theory*, 5:1 (1995), pp. 109–37.

36 E. Löfstedt and D. Vogel, The changing of regulations: a comparison of Europe and the United States, *Risk Analysis*, 21:3 (2001), pp. 399–405.

37 However, the reappraisal of the basic rules on nuclear installations that
started in 2006 has led to a significant increase in general regulations,
affecting all plants, and individual prescriptions specific to each case.
38 The report on the Integrated Regulatory Review Service Mission to the
US notes for example that 'licensees have not been as proactive in making
voluntary measures to upgrade systems, structures, and components with
improved technology as many foreign countries have done to enhance
safety'.
39 Article 182 of the US Atomic Energy Act of 1954.
40 With the obvious risk that political decisions may be based on perceived
risk rather than calculations by experts: see Chapter 11.
41 R. Meserve, *International Atomic Energy Agency Bulletin*, 49/1 (2007).

10   Adopting nuclear power

1 Canada is not such a clear-cut example, because its policy on nuclear
weapons has varied over time. As a member of Nato, much like Germany,
it allowed US nuclear warheads to be stationed on Canadian soil for some
time.
2 North Korea has also tried to develop a civilian and military nuclear
programme. However, unlike Pakistan and Iran it has not yet succeeded in
producing nuclear power.
3 Some authors have also presented the UK as the first country to have built
a nuclear reactor and connected it to the grid.
4 M-H. Labbé, *Le Nucléaire à la Croisée des Chemins* (La Documentation
française, Paris, 1999), ch. 6, discusses in detail the studies, reports and
debate preceding Eisenhower's speech.
5 The reference to the Apocalypse highlights the religious side to the speech
to the UN General Assembly. Humankind must be saved, while
redeeming the scientists and engineers who laboured to build the bomb.
Civilian nuclear power would earn them absolution and wash away the
original sin of the atom bomb. The longest analysis (162 pages) devoted to
the Atoms for Peace speech was produced by a little known specialist in
religious studies at the University of Colorado at Boulder: Ira Chernus,
Eisenhower's Atoms for Peace (Texas A&M University Press, 2002).
6 Between 1955 and 1970 Pakistan signed thirteen bilateral agreements on
nuclear power with the countries mentioned in addition to France,
Belgium, Denmark, the USSR, Spain and the Federal Republic of
Germany.
7 S. D. Thomas, *The Realities of Nuclear Power: International Economic and
Regulatory Experience* (Cambridge University Press, 1998). Chapter 7 is a
monograph devoted to Canada.

8 Israel is the only exception. This country has nuclear weapons but not a single grid-connected nuclear power plant. This unusual choice is no doubt due to the secrecy surrounding its nuclear armament, now and in the past. Israel has not signed the non-proliferation treaty and has never officially acknowledged possessing nuclear weapons. Moreover, the limited size of its power grid and the target which a nuclear power plant would constitute for enemy attacks make it most unlikely that such a plant will ever be built.

9 It should, however, be noted that during this time a significant part of CEA research, and therefore expenditure, targeted technology and applications with no direct or indirect connection to the demands of the nuclear fleet.

10 The UK also adopted graphite-moderated, gas-cooled technology, but unlike France it went on to use it for its own fleet of reactors.

11 For discussion of this decision, in its technical and institutional context, see D. Finon and C. Staropoli, Institutional and technological co-evolution in the French electronuclear industry, *Industry and Innovation*, 8 (2001), pp. 179–99.

12 According to Robert Schuman, had De Gaulle stayed on as president, the gas-cooled graphite-moderated programme would have continued. Quoted by G. Hecht, *Le Rayonnement de la France* (Collection Textes à l'Appui, Editions La Découverte, Paris, 2004), p. 261.

13 Quoted by Hecht, *Le Rayonnement de la France*, p. 269.

14 Christian Bataille and Robert Galley, *Rapport sur l'aval du cycle nucléaire*, volume 2: *Les coûts de production de l'électricité*, ch. 1, sect. II (Rapport de l'office parlementaire d'évaluation des choix scientifiques et technologiques, 1999), available at: http://www.assemblee-nationale.fr/ rap-oecst/nucleaire/r1359.asp.

15 Hecht, *Le Rayonnement de la France*, in particular ch. 7, La guerre des filières.

16 China has already exported equipment to Pakistan, but now hopes to take part in international tenders, rather than just making do with mutual agreements governed exclusively by strategic considerations.

17 J. Goldemberg, Nuclear energy in developing countries, *Daedalus* (2009), pp. 71–80.

18 OECD countries still feature largely in this selective list, but this is misleading, because not many of them now want to extend their nuclear-power capacity; their preponderance is due to the filter used to eliminate doubtful applicants. Turkey, Chile and Poland are the only OECD members out of a total of fifty, but all three are on the short list. Disregarding their real potential and chances of remaining solvent over the next twenty years, developing countries account for most applications to adopt nuclear power.

19 So far only Mexico and Iran have gained a foothold in nuclear power.

20 Poland is not strictly speaking a newcomer to nuclear power. In the 1980s work started at Zarnowiec to build four Russian reactors, but the project was shelved in 1991.

21 This is the nuclear industry's first build, own and operate contract. It goes much further than the sale of a turnkey plant, for the foreign investor is not only taking a risk as the main shareholder, but also as the operator of the plant. The only source of revenue is future sales of electricity, the price of which is fixed in advance. A transaction of this sort, by which an installation is supplied in exchange for the purchase of electricity shows that competition between vendors is very stiff, playing into the hands of buyers. All other things being equal, this situation is an incentive for aspiring countries to take the plunge.

11 Nuclear exit

1 The Swedish Parliament banned construction of additional reactors in 1980, but overturned the decision thirty years later.

2 The deal was negotiated in 2000 with Germany's four nuclear operators (Eon, RWE, Vattenfall and EnBW).

3 The CDU returned to power in 2005, but as the senior partner in a broad coalition with the SPD and CSU. So Angela Merkel could not go back on the 2000 agreement between the Federal Government and the utilities.

4 J. H. Keppler, The economic costs of the nuclear phase-out in Germany, *NEA News*, 30 (2012), pp. 8–14.

5 This amount corresponds to the cost of building and operating alternative capacity. The author has, however, allowed for the fact that part of the 20.5 GW capacity which was retired early did not need to be replaced. In anticipation of nuclear exit, investment shifted to other generating technologies from 2000 onwards, mainly coal-fired and to a lesser extent gas-fired plants. This outlay should consequently not be treated as an additional cost.

6 Or by electricity not consumed, given the expenditure on boosting energy efficiency, or the costs due to network outages.

7 A study by various research institutes for the German Economy and Technology Ministry put the cost of early exit at €48 billion (Energiezenarien 2011, Projekt 12/10, available at: www.prognos.com/fileadmin/pdf/publikationsdatenbank/11_08_12_Energieszenarien_2011.pdf); another study, by the Institute for Energy Economics at Stuttgart University, put the cost at €42 billion.

8 'The nuclear power plant at Fessenheim, which is the oldest in our fleet, will be closed at the end of 2016', speech by President Hollande at the opening of the Environmental Conference.

9 In the course of a television debate, prior to the second round of the presidential election, between François Hollande and the incumbent Nicolas Sarkozy, the former said: 'People ask: "Why [close] Fessenheim?" [I answer] it is the oldest one in France. It is in a seismically active area, beside the Canal d'Alsace. There is considerable pressure, from all sides, to have it closed.' – Full transcript of the debate, *Le Monde*, 3 May 2012.

10 M. Berthélémy and F. Lévêque, Don't close nuclear power plants merely because they are old!, energypolicyblog.com (March 2011).

11 Roughly speaking and making a few assumptions, nuclear electricity will account for half of France's energy mix in 2025, with all the reactors aged over 40 having been shut down. But age is not a relevant technical or economic criterion when deciding to retire a plant. The 40-year age limit corresponds to a rule governing the period of depreciation used in EDF accounts.

12 The lack of anything other than political and communication considerations in the choice of a 25% cut by 2025 is also apparent in the possibility of this slogan making the wrong impression on advocates of nuclear exit. With sustained growth in domestic demand, no change in foreign trade and a mediocre load factor, retiring reactors before the age of 40 would make it necessary to build several new EPRs in order to attain the requisite 50%. See 50% d'électricité nucléaire implique la construction d'au moins 13 EPR, rebellyon.info/50-d-electricite-nucleaire-en-2025.html.

13 In a radio interview just a few days after the speech by Mr Hollande at the Environmental Conference, the Minister of the Economy and Finances said, 'We are putting figures on the table with which I'm not familiar, regarding a decision announced by the President the day before yesterday' – Arrêt de Fessenheim: le paiement de lourdes indemnités en question, *Le Nouvel Observateur* (16 September 2012).

14 *Le Journal du Dimanche* predicted €2 billion costs on 16 September 2012; eight months later it led with the headline, 'Five to eight billion [euros] to close Fessenheim' (5 May 2013).

15 French MP Hervé Mariton, Rapport Législatif 251, Annexe 13 (2013), estimates the loss entailed by shutdown in 2016 rather than 2022 at €2.4 billion. To justify this figure, he suggests a net profit on the Fessenheim plant of €400 million multiplied by the number of operating years lost. According to an anonymous blogger, Olivier68, Quel impact économique si on arrêtait Fessenheim? (AgoraVox.fr, 2013), the loss due to early shutdown would amount to about €10 billion. He tested several assumptions for additional operating life (ten or twenty years), average cost of replacement electricity (€110 or €130 per MWh) and discount rate (4% and 8%).

12 Supranational governance

1 In France the head of the Central Department for Protection against Ionizing Radiation (SCPRI), Pierre Pellerin, was accused of minimizing the effects of Chernobyl on French territory and concealing information. A journalist credited him with the apocryphal claim that 'The cloud from Ukraine stopped at our border.' On the legal front, the handling of the crisis and the impact of the disaster in France gave rise to much litigation. This ended in 2012 when the Cour de Cassation (final court of appeal) dismissed charges that Pellerin had endangered people who subsequently suffered cancers due to radiation. The court acknowledged that 'with the current state of scientific knowledge it is impossible to establish a certain relation of cause and effect between observed pathologies and the fallout from the radioactive cloud from Chernobyl'.

2 Except for islands such as Cyprus and Malta, and the Baltic states. The electrical isolation of the latter from the rest of the EU should end before 2020, thanks to an undersea connection between Estonia and Finland and a land connection between Lithuania and Poland.

3 Unless, of course, one opts for one of Europe's many islands, most of which are not on the grid.

4 Europeans and Nuclear Safety (2010), http://ec.europa.eu/energy/nuclear/safety/doc/2010_eurobarometer_safety.pdf, p. 42.

5 For a detailed examination of the conflict between the Czech Republic and Austria, and the part played by the EU, see R. S. Axelrod, Nuclear power and EU enlargement: the case of Temelin, *Environmental Politics*, 13 (2004), pp. 153–72.

6 World Nuclear Association, Early soviet reactors and EU accession, www.world-nuclear.org/info/Safety-and-Security/Safety-of-Plants/Appendices/Early-Soviet-Reactors-and-EU-Accession/.

7 R. S. Axelrod, The European Commission and Member States: conflict over nuclear safety, *Perspectives*, 13 (2004), pp. 153–72.

8 L. Scheinman, *Euratom: Nuclear Integration in Europe* (Carnegie Endowment for International Peace, New York, 1967).

9 Often anticipating the European Commission, national governments also asked their own nuclear safety authorities to carry out stress tests.

10 Désaccord européen sur les stress tests nucléaires, *Le Monde* (12 May 2011).

11 Les relations se tendent entre Bruxelles et l'Autorité de sûreté du nucléaire, Euractiv.fr (2012).

12 Communication from the Commission to the Council and the European Parliament on the comprehensive risk and safety assessments ('stress tests') of nuclear power plants in the Union and related activities (Brussels, 2012).

13 ASN has reservations about the communication of the European Commission (press release, Paris, 5 October 2012).

14 French nuclear regulator slams EC, Oettinger over EU stress tests, www.platts.com (2012).

15 J. Delors, Pour une Communauté européenne de l'énergie, in S. Andoura, L. Hancher, and M. Van Der Woude, *Vers une Communauté européenne de l'énergie: un projet politique* (Notre Europe, Etudes et Recherches 76, 2010); J. Delors et al., L'Europe de l'énergie c'est maintenant, *Le Monde* (25 May 2013).

16 Z. Laiidi and R. Montes Torralba, *Les Conditions de Mise en Oeuvre de la Solidarité Energétique Européenne* (funded by Conseil Français de l'Energie, Centre d'études européennes de Sciences Po, Paris, 2012).

13   International governance to combat proliferation

1 S. E. Miller and S. D. Sagan, Nuclear power without nuclear proliferation? *Daedalus: Journal of the American Academy of Arts and Sciences*, 138:4 (2009), pp. 7–18, based on measurements by the World Bank of state performance on good governance, and terrorism data from the US Counterterrorism Center.

2 For more details on the connection between the NPT and the IAEA, see La Commission des affaires étrangères, Les Enjeux Géostratégiques des Proliférations (Assemblée Nationale, Paris, 2009), available at: www.assemblee-nationale.fr/13/rap-info/i2085.asp.

3 These safeguards apply to all parties to the NPT, except a few African countries (Guinea Bissau, Eritrea) and small island states (Micronesia, East Timor, Sao Tome and Principe).

4 Quoted by Professor Ole Danbololt Mjos during the award ceremony of the 2005 Nobel Peace Prize to the IAEA and its Director General Mohamed El-Baradei.

5 North Korea signed the NPT in 1985, then left in 2003. The Treaty allows parties to resign membership after nine months. So a country can start by signing up to benefit from the science and technology cooperation on nuclear power provided by the IAEA then, having gained its expertise, withdraw and use it for military purposes in complete impunity.

6 M. Kroenig, E. Gartzke and R. Rauchhaus (eds.), *Causes and Consequences of Nuclear Proliferation* (Routledge Global Security Studies, Routledge, Abingdon, UK, 2011).

7 B. L. Cohen, *The Nuclear Energy Option* (Plenum Press, New York, 1990), ch. 13.

8 Anne Lauvergeon, former Areva CEO and well known for being plain-spoken, cited the pods invented by Nestlé in 2008: 'Our model is

Nespresso, we sell coffee machines and the coffee to go with them. And coffee is very profitable.' – *Le Point* (10 December 2010): www.lepoint.fr/economie/areva-un-geant-de-l-atome-de-la-mine-d-uranium-au-traitement-des-dechets-10-12-2010-1273598_28.php.

9 K. Piram, Stratégies gouvernementales pour le développement de l'énergie nucléaire civile: pratiques françaises et américaines sur le marché des centrales nucléaires, *Cahier Thucydide*, 8 (2009).

10 US Government Accountability Office, Nuclear Commerce (GAO-11–36, 2010).

11 US Government Accountability Office, Nuclear Commerce.

12 For a review of the French export offering, see D. Finon, *La Recomposition de l'Industrie Nucléaire Française est-elle Nécessaire?* (Document de travail du CIRED, Paris, 2011).

13 Hitachi holds an 80% share of GE-Hitachi Nuclear Energy, a company resulting from the merger of the two companies' nuclear interests; Toshiba acquired Westinghouse in 2006, and has enjoyed full control over it since 2012.

14 Half the AP1000s and EPRs ordered by China will be fitted with pressure vessels manufactured by Chinese firms.

15 South Korean elite forces arrive in UAE, *The National* (13 January 2011): www.thenational.ae/news/uae-news/south-korean-elite-forces-arrive-in-uae.

16 F. Chevalier and K. Park, The winning strategy of the late-comer: how Korea was awarded the UAE nuclear power contract, *International Review of Business Research Papers*, 6 (2010), pp. 221–38.

17 In 2012 State-owned Rosatom received an initial payment of $750 million. This sum was taken out of the national budget, as a share in the assets of the company specially created to build, own and operate the nuclear power plant at Akkuyu.

18 M. Berthélémy and F. Lévêque, Korea nuclear exports: Why did the Koreans win the UAE tender? Will Korea achieve its goal of exporting 80 nuclear reactors by 2030? (Cerna Working Papers Series, 4, 2011).

19 Before the tender, former NRC Director-General William Travers was the Executive Director of the Emirati authority. He contributed to framing Abu Dhabi's nuclear strategy. David F. Scott is on the board of the Emirates Nuclear Energy Corporation, which will be operating the plants.

20 The French state owns a 36.7% stake in GDF-Suez but in this capacity has no say in the firm's international development policy, unlike EDF in which it holds an 84.5% share.

21 The Korean case is unusual in that the long-standing publicly owned monopoly was split into various units, including KHNP, which operates

hydraulic and nuclear power plants. It was due to be privatized, but a change of government derailed this plan and all the subsidiaries, including numerous firms involved in nuclear power, are still wholly owned by Kepco, in which the state holds a majority stake.

22 J. A. Glasgow, E. Teplinsky and S. L. Markus, *Nuclear Export Control: A Comparative Analysis of National Regimes for the Control of Nuclear Materials, Components and Technology* (Pillsbury Winthrop Shaw Pittman LLP, Washington DC, 2012). This study compares export controls imposed by the US, Japan, France and Russia.

23 House of Representatives bill 1280: 'To amend the Atomic Energy Act of 1954 to require congressional approval of agreements for peaceful nuclear cooperation with foreign countries, and for other purposes', 31 March 2011.

24 Congress has ninety days to oppose a draft 123 agreement submitted by the US President. To do so, a majority of both chambers must approve a motion rejecting the agreement. In which case the President would very probably use his veto, which would mean that Congress would have to vote down the agreement by a two-thirds majority. To get round this almost insurmountable obstacle, the bill provides that Congress should approve, before it comes into force, any agreement which does not include a permanent ban on a potential customer ever acquiring enrichment and spent-fuel reprocessing facilities. The lack of a majority in favour of the agreement in one or other chamber would be sufficient to block the project.

25 Report to amend the Atomic Energy Act of 1954 to require congressional approval of agreements for peaceful nuclear cooperation with foreign countries, and other purposes (House of Representatives, Washington DC, 2012).

26 There is no evidence to support the concern 'that a wider application of the "gold standard" might have a potentially negative impact on commercial sales by the US nuclear industry, which asserted that efforts to secure commitments from countries not to engage in ENR activities would place US companies at a competitive disadvantage vis-a-vis their foreign competitors' (Report to amend the Atomic Energy Act of 1954).

27 J. C. Varnum, US nuclear cooperation as nonproliferation: reforms, or the devil you know?, *The Nuclear Threat Initiative* (2012): www.nti.org/ analysis/articles/us-nuclear-cooperation-nonproliferation-reforms-or-devil-you-know/.

28 La Commission des affaires étrangères, Les Enjeux Géostratégiques.

29 Only the US, France, Russia and, as part of a joint venture, the Netherlands, the UK and Germany, possess large-scale enrichment capacity. Similarly, only France, Japan, Russia and the UK have industrial reprocessing units.

30 D. Albright, Holding Khan accountable, an Isis statement accompanying Release of Libya: a Major Sale at Last, *Institute for Science and International Security* (2010).

31 A. Rose, interview with M. Hibbs, How North Korea built its nuclear program, *The Atlantic* (10 April 2013).

32 Treaty on the Non-Proliferation of Nuclear Weapons, Article III, section 2.

33 Article IV of the Treaty states that 'Nothing in this Treaty shall be interpreted as affecting the inalienable right of all the Parties to the Treaty to develop research, production and use of nuclear energy for peaceful purposes without discrimination and in conformity with Articles I and II of this Treaty' and that 'All the Parties to the Treaty undertake to facilitate, and have the right to participate in the fullest possible exchange of equipment, materials and scientific and technological information for the peaceful uses of nuclear energy.'

34 M. Hibbs, *The future of the Nuclear Suppliers Group* (Carnegie Endowment for International Peace, 2011).

35 The same process also worked in the opposite direction, when the US had to persuade other NSG members to agree to the waiver granted to India.

36 F. McGoldrick, *Limiting Transfers of Enrichment and Reprocessing Technology: Issues, Constraints, Options* (Belfer Center, Harvard Kennedy School, 2011).

37 Oliver Thränert and Matthias Bieri, *The Nuclear Suppliers Group at the Crossroads* (CSS Analysis, 127, Center for Security Studies, 2013).

38 M. Hibbs, I. Anthony, C. Ahlström and V. Fedchenko, *Reforming Nuclear Export Controls: The Future of the Nuclear Suppliers Group* (SIPRI Research Report 22, Oxford University Press, 2007).

Index

Lightning Source UK Ltd.
Milton Keynes UK
UKHW020741050722
405332UK00019B/445

9 781107 455498